MH370

THE SECRET FILES

**AT LAST... THE TRUTH BEHIND THE GREATEST
AVIATION MYSTERY OF ALL TIME**

NIGEL CAWTHORNE

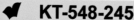

KT-548-245

JB

JOHN BLAKE

Published by John Blake Publishing Ltd,
3 Bramber Court, 2 Bramber Road,
London W14 9PB, England

www.johnblakebooks.com

www.facebook.com/Johnblakepub ▪
twitter.com/johnblakepub ▪

First published, as *Flight MH370: The Mystery*, in paperback in 2014
This revised, updated and expanded edition first published in paperback in 2016

ISBN: 978-1-78418-989-1

British Library Cataloguing-in-Publication Data:

A catalogue record for this book is available from the British Library.

Design by www.envydesign.co.uk

Printed in Great Britain by CPI Group (UK) Ltd

3 5 7 9 10 8 6 4 2

Papers used by John Blake Publishing are natural, recyclable products made
from wood grown in sustainable forests. The manufacturing processes conform
to the environmental regulations of the country of origin.

Every attempt has been made to contact the relevant copyright-holders,
but some were unobtainable. We would be grateful if the appropriate
people could contact us.

CONTENTS

INTRODUCTION

On 8 March 2014 Malaysia Airlines Flight 370 disappeared. The mystery of the missing plane quickly seized the world's imagination. Almost immediately I realized that there was a book in it and got in touch the publisher John Blake. By 25 March, I had a contract, giving me three weeks to write the book, which was to be called *Flight 370: The Mystery*. I delivered the manuscript on 15 April and the book was published on 15 May.

I mention this because when I appeared on Nine Network's *Today* programme in Australia, I was accused, among other things, of rushing out a book in indecent haste. But my book was not the first, though it was the first in print. The others had come out as ebooks to be downloaded to Kindles and other electronic devices. And, by the time my book came out, the world had endured nearly ten weeks of newspaper and television coverage.

Then a curious thing happened. *The Sydney Morning Herald* reported my book "to some extent supports the theory that the aircraft may have been accidentally shot down during a joint Thai-US military exercise in the South China Sea". This was picked up by newspapers around the world that were soon saying that the book "reportedly claims that the plane may have been shot down accidentally during joint United States–Thai military exercises in the South China Sea" and that "searchers were sent the wrong way as part of a cover-up". The book was freely available, but apparently none of the journalists had bothered to read it.

The shoot-down theory was one of the numerous conspiracy theories that were circulating on the internet which I examined and discounted. In the book, I say: "I am not saying that is what happened."

I have even written for some of the newspapers who reported that I said MH370 was shot down, but no one bothered to ring me up and check. Even when I appeared on the BBC World News channel the interviewer began by saying that I had said that the Americans had shot the plane down. Patiently, I explained that that was not what I had said at all – indeed, it could not have been the case. Although it is possible to make a plausible case that the plane was shot down by accident in a live-fire exercise in the South China Sea, and that the world's media were then thrown off the scent by bogus reports of signals leading them to believe that the plane was at the south of the Indian Ocean (one of the remotest regions of the world where it was unlikely that anyone will ever find it), to pull off such a cover-up you would need the collusion of the US, Chinese and Vietnamese governments. That was never going to happen.

Needless to say, when I was researching this book, I went on the BBC website to find: "Author Nigel Cawthorne believes the plane was shot down by US/Thai fighters during a military exercise."

I asked for this to be taken down, but nothing has happened.

Now, I am not complaining. I suppose, all publicity is good publicity and this must have helped book sales. However, we do depend on the media – especially august institutions such as the BBC – to check their facts at least. We depend on them for our picture of the world. Sure, the world is screwed up, but whatever faults the US may have, it does not accidentally shoot down civilian planes and shut up about it.

When the USS *Vincennes* accidently shot down Iran Air Flight 655 on 3 July 1988, *The New York Times* carried the story the next day, quoting the Chairman of the Joint Chiefs of Staff, Admiral William J. Crowe Jr and President Ronald Reagan. By 17 July, they were offering to pay between $100,000 and $250,000 to each of the families of the victims.

It was *The Sydney Morning Herald*'s piece that got me invited onto Australia's *Today* programme to be grilled by Karl Stefanovic, who I have since learned is a notorious "Rottweiler". I had not heard of him at the time. His researchers assured me that, as this was a breakfast show, the interview would be light and there would be no tough questions. I am sure that was his intention.

I was being interviewed down the line from a studio on the South Bank in London where I was led into a darkened room. A camera was focused on my face and an earpiece stuck in my ear. I could not see my interrogator, though I imagine that he could see me. Again I was accused of rushing out this book with indecent haste – though the *Today* programme had been running the story for over two months.

The families were understandably upset and I was also accused of making money out of other people's misery. I pointed out that Mr Stefanovic was being paid for the interview, I was not. His defence was that he was a journalist and that was his job. I pointed out that I was an author and that was my job.

It seems to me that newspaper and television coverage is ephemeral. A story surfaces in the news one day; the next it is forgotten. A book is a more permanent thing and those missing on Flight MH370 and their families need to be remembered.

Since then, little has been done to assuage the loved-ones' grief. Soon enough MH370 disappeared from the headlines. Then one small piece of wreckage washed up thousands of miles from where the plane went missing, keeping the hope alive that we might, one day, discover what had happened to it. The search continues, but again the coverage flagged. With no solution readily to hand, the world's attention turned to other, more pressing problems.

One cannot help but feel the pain of the families. Most of us have travelled on aeroplanes and can imagine the myriad ghastly fates that can befall them. Most of us have been to the airport to await a family member, friend or lover, coming off a plane so it is not hard to step into their shoes. The loved ones of those missing on MH370 have suffered the most excruciating of fates. The time of any sensible hope is long gone, but they still have no idea of what happened to those they have lost.

One of the problems the families have is that there really has been a cloud of secrecy. From the beginning, the Malaysian government has been taciturn and disingenuous. Since its independence in 1963, the country has been governed by one party, the United Malays National Organisation. It is riven by internal strife and allegations of corruption. Nevertheless it is forceful in suppressing the political opposition and controlling the media. Its present leaders spring from a Malay aristocracy that thinks itself a superior class.

After Flight MH370 went missing, a western diplomat said: "They just didn't know what to do. They were overwhelmed and their instinct was to keep everything secret."

INTRODUCTION

The US sent teams from the National Transportation Safety Board, the FBI and the CIA. Britain's MI6 worked with Malaysian Special Branch to help screen the passengers and crew for anyone suspected of a connection to terrorism. The Australians, who had six nationals on board, also sent a team of officials, while France sent experts from the Bureau d'Enquêtes et d'Analyses, its air crash investigation agency. This organisation was acknowledged as a world leader in the field after co-ordinating the recovery of Air France Flight 447 after it crashed into the Atlantic in 2009.

All of them were frustrated by Malaysia's reticence. The authorities were reluctant to hand over such things as cargo manifests, crew records, maintenance data, radar tracks and radio recordings.

"Getting anything out of them was like getting blood from a stone," said an Australian defence official. The French went home after a short stay.

It has to be said that the Chinese government is not famously forthcoming either, and without international co-operation the search for MH370 would prove fruitless. Two years on, we are no nearer knowing the truth.

Meanwhile the internet has filled up with ever more bizarre theories. As various security services around the world have been involved, the authors of these theories claim to have access to these secret files. So it is time to look into what they say.

Nigel Cawthorne
Bloomsbury, February 2016

CHAPTER ONE

BEACHED

On Wednesday 29 July 2015, beach-cleaner Johnny Bègue was leading an eight-man team tidying up a popular tourist trail along the beach near the town of Saint-André. It is on the east coast of the small French island of La Réunion, east of Madagascar in the Indian Ocean. During his mid-morning break, Bègue wandered off to find a pebble to crush chillies, a key ingredient in the local cuisine.

"It was then that I saw a weird thing on the shore," said Bègue. "It was half in the sand and half in the water... I knew immediately it was part of an aircraft, but I didn't realize how important it was, that it could help to solve the mystery of what happened to the Malaysian jet."

The crew belonged to an agency called E3, charged with looking after the coastline, and had set off at seven that morning.

"At around 8.45 am, I was walking the shoreline looking for a *kalou* – a stone which can be used as a pestle for grinding spices," he said. "That was when I saw some debris washed up on the pebbles. I immediately thought it was plane debris – the length and curve of it, there were screws on it that hadn't gone rusty."

He called his colleagues over to examine the six-foot rounded chunk of metal.

"I immediately saw that it was a piece of a plane," said fellow beach-cleaner Cedric Gobalsoumy.

"As it was windy I called over my colleagues to come and help me pick up the piece and place it higher up the shore," said Bègue.

It was clear the wreckage had been washed up and the team dragged it off the beach onto more solid ground so that it would not be at risk of being swept out to sea again, or crushed against the volcanic rocks that made up most of the beach. At first they intended just to leave it there and move on, then they had second thoughts.

"A piece of a plane in the sea is not normal," said Gobalsoumy. "We told ourselves that people could have died in this aircraft and that their families would want to know."

Bègue had thought of turning it into some sort of memorial set on a lawn.

"To begin with we thought about taking it to use as a decoration but then we thought of the families … families we don't know," said Bègue. "But afterwards we said we would place flowers around it to make it look pretty. And then we thought we shouldn't sit on it because if there was a crash or something like that there are dead families, so we should respect them. So we said we'll put the flowers there to make it pretty."

One of the men went online with his cellphone and googled plane disasters. He found the story of the missing Malaysian plane, Flight MH370. They decided to alert the local radio station, who in turn got in touch with the gendarmerie.

"Afterwards we called the local radio station, Radio Freedom," said Bègue. "They called the police, everyone, straight away."

Within hours, the world's media was onto the find. Bègue became an instant celebrity on the island, giving interviews to visiting journalists.

Although the best guess about the fate of the plane was that it had crashed into the sea 3,500 miles from Réunion, this piece of wreckage might be the first tangible clue to what had happened to it.

Examining the photographs that were soon circulating, experts identified debris as a "flaperon" – one of the hinged control surfaces along the trailing edge of an aircraft wing that sits between the inner wing flap and the aileron. Pictures then emerged showing the serial number 657-BB. This was the part number of the flaperon on a Boeing 777. Every part of such a plane had inventory markings of some sort on it and could be cross-referenced in the company's records.

The flaperon also had barnacles on it. The species, *Lepas anatifera*, grows at a rate of between one and two centimetres a year. Their size indicated that the wreckage had been in the water for over a year. Malaysian Prime Minister Najib Razak said it was "very likely" the part came from MH370. It was almost inconceivable that it could have come from any other 777. Only four other 777s have been written off due to accidents since the aircraft entered service in 1994. None of those were lost over the sea and all had been accounted for.

"There is no other recorded case of a flaperon being lost on a 777," said the Australian Transport Safety Bureau's (ATSB) chief commissioner, Martin Dolan, who was leading the search.

The gendarmes took the flaperon away. It was to be sent to the Bureau d'Enquêtes et d'Analyses, France's air-crash investigators in Toulouse.

The next day, eight feet from where the flaperon had been, Bègue found a chestnut-coloured suitcase whose rusty zips indicated that it had been in the sea for some time.

"Perhaps it was a suitcase of passengers," said Bègue. "I don't know. Now for me what I'm proud of is that I was maybe of service to the Malaysian people. I don't know and if so they may be able to grieve in peace, if this piece of the wing is from the MH370 aeroplane."

The suitcase was in tatters. There were no identifying marks on it and Bègue had not taken much notice of it when he had first see the flaperon.

"It gives me the shivers," he said. "The piece of luggage was here since yesterday but nobody really paid attention."

Soon the hunt was on for other debris. If ocean currents had brought the flaperon to the island of La Réunion, maybe smaller items from the plane, particularly luggage, seat cushions and airline blankets may have arrived too, though if so they had been dismissed as worthless pieces of flotsam. Teams of local people were brought together to search the coastline and dozens of policemen were combing the black sands, while planes and ships from France, Australia, Malaysia and China were deployed to join in the hunt for floating debris. Soon it was reported that bottles of Chinese water and Indonesian cleaning fluid had been found that might help solve the riddle of Flight MH370.

Wreckage washing up on La Réunion fitted with the theory that the missing plane had been seen flying over the Maldives at the southern tip of India, some two thousand miles to the east and roughly halfway from its last known position, around eight hours after it went missing. It was travelling in the direction of La Réunion. However, a chart drawn up by the oceanographers from the University of Western Australia showed that, in the seventeen months since it disappeared, debris from the computed search site in the southern Indian Ocean could have washed up on the island.

"It makes sense based on some of the modelling we did twelve months ago, that some time within eighteen to twenty-four months this could be the area the debris would have ended up in," said UWA oceanographer Professor Charitha Pattiaratchi. Indeed, Prof Pattiaratchi insisted that the wreckage could only have come from the current search zone of the west coast of Australia.

"It's likely that more will wash ashore in the coming weeks," he said.

The South Equatorial Current would have carried debris from the putative crash site westwards at around five miles a day. A huge counter-clockwise gyre runs east along the Southern Ocean near Antarctica, up the west coast of Australia, then westwards below the equator towards Réunion and Madagascar, before turning south again.

The Australian-led search operation had already scoured more than 19,000 square miles of the sea floor, about 60 per cent of a search zone in the Indian Ocean that was determined via expert analysis of signals from MH370, detected by a satellite the day it went missing. But the four search vessels towing 10-kilometre cables fitted with sophisticated sonar systems that scan the seabed had turned up little except shipping containers and a previously uncharted shipwreck.

Rough weather, the pitch-black extreme depths of up to 4,000 metres, and the rugged nature of the previously unmapped sea floor have made for a slow, frustrating search. Investigations on land into the cause of the crash have proved similarly fruitless. A 584-page report by a nineteen-member independent investigation group went into minute details about the crew's lives, including their medical and financial records and training.

It also detailed the aircraft's service record, as well as the weather, communications systems and other aspects of the flight. Nothing unusual was discovered. However, it did reveal that the battery of the locator beacon for the plane's flight data recorder had expired more than a year before the jet vanished. The battery powering the locator beacon of the cockpit voice recorder was working at the time it went missing, though, by the time the flaperon washed, it would have long expired.

Investigators still hoped that if they could locate the two recorders they could get to the bottom of what has become one of aviation's biggest mysteries. Nevertheless, if the flaperon proved to be from MH370, it may have provided vital clues to where they should be looking.

ATSB Chief Commissioner Martin Dolan, who was leading the seabed search, said the discovery of a part of a Boeing 777 in La Réunion would not alter his search plans. If the find proved to be part of the missing aircraft, it would be consistent with the theory that the plane missing crashed within the 120,000 square kilometres (46,000 square mile) search area 1,800 kilometres (1,100 miles) south-west of Australia. Up to that point the search had cost $150 million.

"It doesn't rule out our current search area if this were associated with MH370," he said. "It is entirely possible that something could have drifted from our current search area to that island."

But Dolan said search resources would be better spent continuing the seabed search rather than reviving a surface search for debris, if the find proved to be from Flight MH370.

However, he added: "Confirmation that the wing part was the first trace of Flight 370 ever found would finally disprove theories that the airliner might have disappeared in the northern hemisphere."

Although that theory had long fallen out of favour, there were some who clung to the idea that the plane had been hijacked, flown northwards and landed on a secure airfield in central Asia.

Even though confirmation that the flaperon had come from MH370 had yet to materialize, Australia's transport minister, Warren Truss, added: "It establishes, really beyond any doubt, that the aircraft is resting in the Indian Ocean and not secretly parked in some hidden place on the land in another part of the world."

More optimistically, the *Daily Telegraph* announced: "Debris promises to solve MH370 mystery." Malaysian officials shared the newspaper's confidence, saying they were "close to solving the mystery" of flight MH370.

But experts had their doubts. Although the wreckage would be swabbed for any evidence of explosives, lengthy exposure to saltwater was likely to have washed off any traces. Nevertheless, forensic examination might give investigators at least some clues as to what happened to the aircraft. For example it could help them understand whether the plane broke up in mid-air or had hit the water intact. Experts might also be able to determine the angle the aircraft entered the water from wreckage and also to ascertain whether the plane was still under the pilots' control.

"Depending on the nature of the damage to that part, they will be able to tell how it separated from the rest of the plane," said Jason Middleton, head of the aviation school at the University of New South Wales in Sydney. "The twisted structure and the technical aspect of how it separated will give a reasonable indication of how violent the impact was."

French aviation safety expert Xavier Tytelman said: "With a microscope you can learn from the torn metal. You can tell whether a crash was more horizontal or vertical. You can extrapolate a lot."

It was thought that this should ultimately help to resolve the question as to whether the plane broke up on impact with the ocean after a deep dive initiated by a possibly suicidal pilot, or else glided into the water after running out of fuel.

"One of the things I guess is a little surprising is how intact the flaperon is," said William Waldock, a former US Coast Guard officer and a professor at Embry-Riddle Aeronautical University in Arizona. "It argues that it wasn't a very violent impact, which goes along with some of theories that it just ran out of gas and glided down."

Other experts claimed to detect signs of scarring on the flaperon from the photographs, and could not rule out theories that the plane went into a nosedive.

"One assumption is that when the aircraft ran out of fuel it made an almost straight spiral down," said David Soucie, a former accident investigator for the Federal Aviation Administration and the author of *Why Planes Crash*. "That creates incredible turbulence, so much that it could cause fluttering, as evidenced by the back of the flaperon that is so torn up, while the front has very little damage."

Equally intriguing were the barnacles on the debris that marine biologists believed could help them trace the path that the wreckage took across the ocean. It was thought that this could lead them back to where the rest of the aircraft might be found.

David Gallo, an oceanographer who led the search for Air France Flight 447 that ditched in the Atlantic in 2009, said investigators would begin a process known as "retro-drift modelling".

"Because it's been 400 and some days, the ocean currents are not such a reliable guide, but the organisms that attached themselves to that bit of plane will tell us a lot," he said. "These live in different batches of water with different temperatures and salinity; because of that the biochemists will get a lot of information."

The flaperon had floated because it was hollow and had air trapped inside it. Even if the plane had broken up, most of the parts would have been solid or quickly become waterlogged, sinking to the bottom where it came down. But that did not mean finding it was impossible.

"We know they are going to be pretty big parts, they are going to be intact because the engines are a solid build. Regardless of how bad the impact is, they'll stay large," was the opinion of Australian air-crash investigator Peter Foley. And for Foley, the search had become personal after meeting the relatives of some of those who had been on board. The fact that the aircraft had disappeared without a trace had spawned many conspiracy theories, adding to the pain suffered by family members of those on board.

"I sound like a bit of a wuss now, but I invariably shed a tear when I speak to the families of the people who were on the aircraft, because they are really hurting," he said.

Operating in depths that exceed three miles in one of the world's least-explored undersea zones, the scale and complexity of the search could not be foreseen.

"We knew from the start this was going to be a long operation," he continued. "The only thing that guarantees success is to search a big enough area, given the fact that we have such scant information."

More was known about the surface of Mars than the bottom of the sea in the search area when the hunt began. Investigators have encountered towering undersea volcanoes, plummeting chasms and fields of rock that could easily hide a plane – even one as big as a Boeing 777.

At the very least, the flaperon might prove that the missing plane came down somewhere in the Indian Ocean. An American aviation safety expert, John Goglia, was convinced from the pictures alone that the wing part came from Flight MH370.

"It confirms that the airplane is in the water and hasn't been hijacked to some remote place waiting to be used for some other purpose," he told the Associated Press.

However, this would hardly bring closure.

Jiang Hui, whose father was travelling on the flight, said: "Even if we find out that this piece of debris belongs to MH370, there is no way to prove that our people were with that plane."

Ghyslain Wattrelos, a French businessman whose wife and two children were on MH370, said discovery of the debris had been "extremely painful". The families' anguish was only increasing.

"This doesn't give hope," he explained. "This is a moment I have been fearing. As long as there wasn't any evidence of a crash, of wounded, of dead or whatever, there was a little glimmer of hope for us."

Steve Wang, of Beijing, whose fifty-seven-year-old mother was on the flight, said: "I think it's still too early to talk about the next step. I hope this debris can provide more clues for investigation."

Danica Weeks, of Perth, who lost her husband, Paul, stated: "There's been so many red herrings: the pings, the oil, the debris on the west coast of Australia … I'm not willing to speak about it until we know for sure that is actually from the plane."

There had been false alarms before. In April 2014, a month after MH370 had gone missing, a sheet of metal with rivets in it was found on Australia's south-west coast, six miles from the town of Augusta. It was quickly discounted. Then in July 2014, a Malaysia Airlines paper towelette was found on Crevantes beach,

125 miles north of Perth, but there was no way to tell whether it had come from the missing plane.

Jennifer Chong, who lost her husband Chong Ling Tan on Flight MH370, said she was terrified that this could be the development she has been waiting for.

"My initial response was that 'this cannot be it' since we had so many false leads before," she said. "Yet I cannot stop myself searching and scavenging for more information over the internet."

"Sometimes I hope that this is it and at times, I hope that this isn't the plane," Elaine Chew, wife of the missing steward Tan Size Hiang, told *The Straits Times*: "I would fall asleep, then wake up again. I just kept thinking of the plane and Size Hiang. It's starting all over again."

Zhang Qihuai, a lawyer representing some of the families, said that around thirty relatives had agreed they would proceed with a lawsuit against the airline if the debris was confirmed to be from MH370. Six months earlier, Malaysia Airlines had already declared the plane's disappearance an accident, clearing the way for a settlement.

"Regardless of whether our loved ones return or not, I will definitely sue Malaysia Airlines," said Li Zhen, whose husband was on board. "They have put us through so much pain and suffering, they must be held responsible."

Relatives of many of the 153 Chinese passengers of MH370 said they wanted authorities to be completely certain the part was from the missing plane. A statement said: "We want them to be a hundred per cent positive. We care more about where our families are rather than where the plane's wreckage is."

The search even suffered a setback when the French authorities concluded that the remnants of a suitcase Bègue had found came from a different source. Investigators had long been puzzled as to why nothing of that sort had been found. When the Air France A330 Airbus on Flight AF447 from Rio to Paris came down in the Atlantic on 1 June 2009, lifejackets and personal possessions floating to surface were the first evidence of disaster. This had led experts to believe the 777 was deliberately flown into the sea in such a way as to minimize the break-up of the plane. That would explain why the flaperon had become detached. This theory was consistent with the possibility that, during ditching, one or more wing flaps became detached. As well as assisting in turns, the flaperon extends from the wing for reduced-speed flying. If the plane had been ditched deliberately, it would have been lowered and extended, and easily ripped off when it hit the water. The flaperon was built with airtight compartments. If undamaged, it would hold enough air to keep it at, or close to, the surface of the ocean as it made its way on its westward path.

CHAPTER TWO

THE FLAPERON

The flaperon found on the beach at La Réunion was loaded onto an Air France Boeing 777 to be flown to Paris on the night of 31 July, after an unexplained delay. On 30 July, the day after the wreckage had been found, there had been five flights from Réunion to Paris and one each to Lyon and Marseilles. It could have been transported on any one of those.

When it arrived in Paris, it was transported by road to Toulouse, home of Boeing's rival Airbus. Experts from France's air-accident investigation bureau, the BEA, would examine the wreckage at a military laboratory in the Toulouse suburb of Balma. The bureau has already provided advice on the undersea search, using experience garnered during the two-year search for the wreckage of the Air France Rio-Paris flight, AF447, in the Atlantic.

Back on La Réunion a church service was held in memory of the 239 people on board the missing plane at Cambuston church in Saint-André, just a few minutes from the beach where the wreckage had been found. More than four-hundred people attended and the service concluded with each member of the congregation lighting a candle for the victims.

Parishioner Christine Robert-Kirbidy said: "Since the debris was found close by, we thought it appropriate to pay homage to the victims and the families."

Nadia Tipaka, representative of the mayor of Saint-André, said that the Pope had called up Gilbert Aubrey, the island's bishop, asking for a service to be held.

"The ceremony was a fitting tribute for the families affected. We will do all we can to help them commemorate their families," Tipaka stated.

Meanwhile a further search of the island's coastline was being carried out by helicopter in an effort to spot more debris, but nothing was found. However, local man Nicolas Ferrier claimed that a seat that could have been from a plane had been washed up earlier. As he did not watch television or listen to the radio, he had had no idea of their significance.

"I found a couple of suitcases, too, around the same time, full of things," he said. "I burnt them. That's my job. I collect rubbish, and burn it. I could have found many things that belonged to the plane, and burnt them, without realizing."

He said that hundreds of items could have been washing up on La Réunion over the past few months, but no one was paying attention.

"For me, it was something totally normal – I see it all the time," he said. "I can't really say if it was the first time or the last time I saw bits like that, because I never pay attention. From now on I will look more closely."

He was asked if he had found any other interesting or unusual objects.

"Maybe," he said. "But I wouldn't know. I just throw them on the fire."

Ferrier also claimed to have seen the flaperon on the beach some time earlier, but was unaware of its significance. Like other islanders he was shocked to suddenly find himself in the global spotlight. For them, flotsam and jetsam were just part of everyday life on the inhospitable volcanic beaches of Le Réunion. Nobody dared to venture though the pounding surf into shark-infested waters, and journalists were left to examine a pile of ashes.

Another local told an incredulous journalist that two bottles had been found.

"And they were definitely from the plane," said the finder, "because they were special drinking water given to pilots to keep them awake during long flights."

The two local police standing nearby smiled and rolled their eyes.

Local news website *Zinfos974.com* quoted one woman who claimed she had seen another part drifting inshore almost three months earlier.

"It was the beginning of the holidays – around May 10," she reported.

The French authorities and Boeing quickly confirmed that the piece of wreckage that had arrived in Toulouse was part of a 777. As MH370 was the only 777 to have been lost in the southern hemisphere, this strongly suggested that it came from the missing plane. The news prompted the coastguards on Mauritius, Madagascar, the Comoros Islands, the Seychelles and the Maldives to step up their searches.

On Réunion, a small piece of twisted metal with Chinese characters etched onto it was handed over to police. It turned out to be part of a domestic stepladder, though other sources claimed it was the handle of a kettle. However, there were no doubts that the flaperon, at least, was genuine.

"Today, 515 days since the plane disappeared, it is with a very heavy heart that I must tell you that an international team of experts have conclusively confirmed that the aircraft debris found on Réunion Island is indeed MH370," said Malaysian Prime Minister Najib Razak. "We now have physical evidence that flight MH370 ended in the southern Indian Ocean. The burden and uncertainty faced by the families during this time has been unspeakable. It is my hope that this confirmation, however tragic and painful, will at least bring certainty to the families and loved ones of the 239 people on board MH370. They have our deepest sympathy and prayers."

Malaysia Airlines added: "Malaysia Airlines would like to sincerely convey our deepest sorrow to the families and friends of the passengers on board Flight MH370 on the news that the flaperon found on Réunion Island on 29 July was indeed from Flight MH370."

However, the families were used to the Malaysians jumping to conclusions prematurely, and the French warned that the mystery of the missing Malaysian plane was far from solved. They had yet to determine whether the plane exploded in mid-air and plunged downwards, or hit the sea at a shallow angle, indicating a controlled descent.

"Was it in a violent impact with the sea or not?" asked BEA director Jean-Paul Troadec. "This piece looks like it is in good condition, it doesn't look like the part of a plane that fell vertically into the water at 900 kilometres an hour."

This rekindled frustration among the group of Chinese families who had protested regularly outside the Malaysian embassy in Beijing since the first flight disappeared.

THE FLAPERON

"We're very curious as to why Malaysia is in such a hurry again to come to a conclusion over the whole incident," said Steven Wong, whose mother was on board Flight MH370. "As a matter of fact, even if the debris comes from MH370, that is still only a beginning as so many things remain unknown to us. For example why the plane flew there, what exactly happened, who should take responsibility for the accident, including what punishment the people should face who failed to take action when the plane turned around and left Malaysian airspace. There has been no conclusion to any of that."

The situation was far from clear.

"Why the hell do you have one confirm and one not?" asked Christchurch, New Zealand, resident Sara Weeks, whose brother Paul Weeks was aboard the flight.

"Why not wait and get everybody on the same page so the families don't need to go through this turmoil?" she went on. "After seventeen months, we need definite answers. We need to progress, get answers, move toward further answers, and get some closure along the line."

Speaking from her home in Beijing, Xu Jinghong, whose sixty-seven-year-old mother is missing, said: "I am very angry – so angry that my hands and feet are cold. The announcement was made without experts from France present. I don't understand how the procedure can be like this."

Malaysia Airlines representatives met with some of the Chinese families who arrived outside their offices in Beijing that morning carrying photos and placards.

"Why are they trying to fool us?" asked Zhang Meiling, whose daughter was on board. "To make us take the compensation money?"

Many of the relatives asked to be taken to Réunion, after

Malaysia said that more wreckage, believed to be window parts and seat cushions, had been recovered. But French officials again cast doubt, saying said they "have not as yet received new plane debris" as they promised to bump up their search off Réunion.

Liow Tiong, the Malaysian transport minister, said: "We appreciate the French team and their support and respect their decision to continue with the verification."

Further muddying the waters, Mr Liow claimed that a Malaysian team had found more debris on the island. This included a window and some aluminium foil.

"I can only ascertain that it's plane debris," he said. "I cannot confirm that it's from MH370."

French officials involved with the investigation in both Paris and Réunion were baffled by this announcement. Mr Liow also insisted that a maintenance seal and the colour of the paint on the flaperon matched the airline's records, but an Australian government official said that the paint is not a unique identifier for Flight 370.

"Rather, it comes from a batch that Boeing used on all its planes when the missing plane was manufactured," the official added.

Protesters threw themselves on the ground outside the Malaysian embassy in Beijing. They hammered on the glass doors of Malaysia Airlines. They held up banners that read "We want the truth!"

An elderly woman turned to a camera crew and said: "For more than five-hundred days we have eaten only bitterness."

The families' protests have been tolerated to an extent by the Chinese government, who also expressed their concern.

"We request that the Malaysian side diligently fulfil their promises, continue to investigate the cause of the plane crash, make utmost efforts to deal with the aftermath and guarantee the lawful rights and interests of the families," said a spokesman for the Chinese foreign ministry.

"They never trusted the Malaysians again," commented a Chinese reporter who is close to foreign ministry officials.

Two-thirds of the passengers on the flight from Kuala Lumpur to Beijing were Chinese, and the Chinese families' protests kept up the pressure to find the aircraft in a search that had cost millions of dollars by that time.

"We are not living in denial ... but we owe it to our loved ones not to declare them lost without 100 per cent certainty!" a family member posted on their online chatroom.

Hu Xuifang, who lost her son, daughter-in-law and grandson, insisted: "It might be a fake." And Dai Shuqin, who had five relations on board including her sister, said: "The Malaysians are telling lies but we'll follow the truth."

A contributor to a local website stated: "Why is Malaysia seemingly in a hurry to sweep the incident under the carpet?" Another gave the opinion: "Najib is an absolute disgrace. He and his team have cocked up the MH370 issue from the beginning."

Jackqita Gomes, wife of crew member Patrick Gomes, was more sanguine. She remarked: "Now that they have confirmed it as MH370, I know my husband is no longer of this world but they just can't leave it with this one flaperon. We urge them to continue searching until they find the plane and bring it back. It's not over yet."

Outside the lab, the Independent Group (IG) of fifteen scientists, engineers and aviators from around the world who were monitoring efforts to locate the missing aircraft reported their analysis of photographs of damage to the wing part. They said it had plainly been ripped off the body of the plane before it crashed because of the speed at which it was travelling. This lent weight to theories that the pilots were not in control of the aircraft when it crashed and posed a setback to those who have argued that the cause of the crash was pilot suicide or a deliberate, controlled ocean ditching.

The photographs showed that the rear of the flaperon had suffered severe damage but the front of it was almost unaffected. The IG report argued that the flaperon probably lost its rear edge because the aircraft was travelling too fast as it spiralled down towards the ocean, running out of fuel. The group reckoned that the port engine ran out of fuel first. With the starboard engine still running, the plane would turn to port. Then as the starboard engine also began to falter, the plane would spiral downwards. As it accelerated, increasing stress would be put on the airframe, causing the trailing edge of the flaperon to break up. Then, just before the jet hit the ocean, the whole flaperon was torn away from the wing, leaving minimal damage to the leading edge.

However, the report also outlined an alternative scenario of a deliberate, pilot-controlled ditching in which the flaperon was damaged because a pilot had set it to the "down" position. But it concluded that a deliberate, controlled ditching scenario was unlikely, because, if the flaperon had still been attached to the aircraft when it hit the water, there would have been compression damage to the front of it.

"There is virtually no apparent compression damage," said the report which was written on behalf of the group by Michael Exner, a US engineer and atmospherics expert.

The group's findings support the official theories that something had happened that incapacitated the pilots. Under this hypothesis, the jet flew south over the Indian Ocean on autopilot for about six hours until it ran out of fuel.

All this conjecture cut little ice with Irene Burrows, mother of missing Australian passenger Rod Burrows, who was lost with his wife Mary. She said that she did not expect the mystery of Flight MH370's disappearance to be solved in her lifetime. However, when the plane first went missing, she pointed out: "All I just want is a bit of the plane. It's all I want to know – where they are."

That small wish, it seemed, had come true.

"We're quite pleased that it's been found," she commented from her home in Queensland.

However, that small piece of the aircraft began to cause problems when German scientists from the Geomar Helmholtz Centre for Ocean Research in Kiel said that the barnacles on it indicated that the Australians were looking in the wrong place. They said that the species attached to it lived well to the north of the search area.

Further raining on the parade of those who were certain was *New York Magazine*'s online *Daily Intelligencer*. A month after the flaperon had been found, it was reporting that the serial numbers on the flaperon should have allowed it to be definitively linked to the missing plane within twenty-four hours. When that deadline passed, news outlets had then told their readers that the ID should be nailed down within a few days, then by the following week.

What was holding things up, it turned out, was that the ID plate that should have been attached to the inboard edge of the flaperon was missing. And that was not the only problem. According to *The New York Times*, Boeing and the National Transportation Safety Board found that modifications to the flaperon did not match those in Malaysia Airlines' maintenance records.

Then, on 21 August, the French regional news chain *La Dépêche* ran a report citing sources within the investigation who said that the technical examination of the flaperon had ended without finding conclusive proof that it had come from the missing plane. A few days later, *Le Monde* ran a report that echoed *The New York Times*'s earlier reporting: "Maintenance work that Malaysia Airlines has indicated it carried out on the flaperon does not exactly match that observed on the discovered piece."

"Airplane parts are engineered precisely and any changes made to them are logged meticulously by maintenance personnel," stated science writer Jeff Wise. "If a part has four holes instead of five, it doesn't just 'not match exactly' – it does not match."

Soon the internet was abuzz with speculation that the flaperon might have been a replacement part not yet put into service, or a spare part pulled off a scrapped airframe. There was further speculation about how it turned up on the beach in La Réunion.

"According to a Toulouse aeronautics expert who requested anonymity," *La Dépêche* reoprted, "the element of the wing would not have floated for several months at the water's surface but would have drifted underwater a few meters deep."

The photographs clearly showed that the flaperon found on La Réunion was encrusted on every edge with goose barnacles. These crustaceans attach themselves to a floating object while young and spend their entire adult life affixed to the same spot. Since they can only survive underwater, their distribution around the object suggested that it must have spent several months submerged.

The *Daily Intelligencer* explained: "Therein lies the mystery. While it's easy to imagine a submarine or a scuba diver hovering peacefully ten or twenty feet under the surface of the water, this is not something that inanimate objects are capable of doing on their own: Either they are more buoyant than water, in which case they float, or they are less buoyant, in which case they sink."

At least one expert concurred.

THE FLAPERON

"My experience is that things will go up or down – they will never stay statically neutral," observed ocean-drift expert Curtis Ebbesmeyer, professor emeritus of oceanography at the University of Washington.

"So, how could a six-foot-long chunk of airplane remain suspended beneath the ocean surface for a long period of time?" *New York Magazine* asked.

It was only on 2 September that the Paris prosecutor's office formally announced that: "it is possible to state with certainty that the flaperon discovered on Réunion July 29, 2015 corresponds to that of Flight MH370".

Cheng Liping, whose husband was on the plane, stated: "We have been anxiously waiting for such a long time and the confirmation of just one piece of debris can hardly tell us what happened to the plane." She also added that she still needed to see her husband's body and wanted the plane's black boxes to be found.

So the discovery of the flaperon had not proved as conclusive as everyone had hoped. Even if it was from the missing Malaysian plane, it begged the question: why had only one small piece of the plane been washed up onshore?

Two months after the flaperon had been found, reports surfaced that a woman hunting birds has stumbled upon a fuselage full of skeletons – even the remains of a pilot strapped in his seat – and a Malaysian flag in the thick jungle of the remote island of Sugbai in the Philippines. The reports were quickly discounted. The news media, it seemed, were clutching at straws.

CHAPTER THREE

VANISHED

Everything started ordinarily enough as Malaysia Airlines MH370 taxied toward the runway at Kuala Lumpur International Airport (KLIA). The 227 passengers had gone through the usual stringent checks as they entered the departure lounge. They had been made to empty their pockets and remove their belts before walking through the metal detectors. Their shoes had been removed and inspected. Bottles of water and other fluids had been confiscated, and laptops opened and switched on to check that they were what they purported to be. After that the passengers were let loose in the airport shopping mall to buy some duty-free luxury, a last-minute gift or perhaps even a book or a newspaper, or have a bite to eat or something to drink while awaiting the final call. According to industry polls the facilities in Kuala Lumpur International make it the traveller's third favourite airport in the world.

The two pilots were going through the pre-flight checks as the

10 cabin staff helped passengers board; the plane was a Boeing 777-200ER. Malaysia Airlines had 15 of the wide-bodied planes in a fleet of 88 aircraft. The list price is US$261.5 million (£156 million) and over 1,000 of them were in service around the world. In 20 years of flying, 777s had only ever been involved in nine accidents leading to the deaths of just three passengers. It was an enviable safety record. Malaysia Airlines had only had two crashes that resulted in fatalities in over 40 years of flying – one of which had been a hijacking. In 2013, it was voted Asia's leading airline at the World Travel Awards, beating 11 other big name full service carriers.

MH370 was bound from Kuala Lumpur to Beijing, a distance of some 2,700 miles (4,345km or 2,346 nautical miles). This was well within its maximum range of 8,885 miles (14,300km or 7,720 nautical miles). Its route would take it almost due north, over the Malay Peninsula, out over the South China Sea, then across Vietnam, Cambodia, Thailand and Laos, until it crossed into Chinese airspace.

Among the passengers was a young man who made a last-minute call, telling his sister he was on board; he said he would see her at the airport in Beijing. Also on board was a Malaysian couple taking a longed-for holiday after the anguish of a miscarriage. A Chinese father had changed his flight at the last minute and was coming home a day early to take his child to the dentist. Then there were 24 artists and their families, returning from an exchange calligraphy exhibition in Kuala Lumpur, and a group of Buddhists who had flown to Kuala Lumpur to participate in a religious ceremony earlier that week.

The plane took off from Kuala Lumpur International Airport at 00.41 am local time on Saturday, 8 March 2014 – 16.41 pm GMT – on Friday the seventh. It was expected to land in Beijing at 6.30 am local time. And it was not full: two of the passengers were infants so at least 89 of the seats would have been empty.

After takeoff, it took 20 minutes to climb to its assigned cruising altitude of 35,000ft (10,668m) and was travelling at 471 knots (542 mph or 872 km/h). Six minutes later the crew confirmed that they were at 35,000ft.

Since the 1980s, planes have been fitted with ACARS – the Aircraft Communications Addressing and Reporting System. This is an automatic datalink that transmits vital information about the aircraft at regular intervals. The last ACARS transmission from MH370 was sent at 1.07 am.

At around 1.19 am Malaysian air traffic control told MH370: "Please contact Ho Chi Minh City, good night."

The first officer on board MH370 is said to have responded calmly, saying famously: "All right, good night." This was not the standard sign-off procedure and there was speculation that it might have been a signal that all was not well on the flight deck. True, his communication was somewhat casual but it gave no indication of what was about to happen.

This was the last anyone would hear from the plane. Around a minute later, the transponder that identifies the aircraft to air traffic control via ground radar was switched off. It was last seen on radar at 1.30 am (17.30 GMT) 140 miles (225km) northeast of Kota Bharu, at the northern tip of Malaysia, around the point where the South China Sea meets the Gulf of Thailand. Then MH370 lost contact with Subang air traffic control one minute before it entered airspace controlled by Vietnam. But MH370 had not contacted air traffic control in Ho Chi Minh City to announce its presence.

At around the same time, Vietnamese air traffic control asked another plane en route to Tokyo to attempt to contact MH370.

The captain said that he was able to establish radio contact via an emergency channel, but all he could hear was mumbling and static.

"We managed to establish contact with MH370 just after 1.30 am and asked them if they had transferred into Vietnamese airspace," the captain explained. "There was a lot of interference, static, but I heard mumbling from the other end. If the plane was in trouble, we'd have heard the pilot making the Mayday distress call."

He added that he believed the voice belonged to the co-pilot, Fariq Abdul Hamid. Then he lost contact.

Another airline pilot who flew within 100 nautical miles (115 miles or 185km) of the route 12 hours before the Malaysia Airline flight disappeared said there were large thunderstorms in the area, with some turbulence. But the skies that night were clear and the weather did not appear to pose serious problems for commercial flights.

At 01.37 am MH370 missed its regular ACARS transmission, but there is no automatic alert if it is switched off as ACARS is not mandatory for all planes and is not always set up in a standard way. The plane had another automated system that communicated with Inmarsat. This is a satellite communications system originally set up by the UN's International Maritime Organization in 1979 to enable ships to stay in constant touch with the shore or to summon help in an emergency. The firm was privatized in 1999 and became the world's biggest provider of satellite communications services. It has 10 satellites permanently orbiting the earth, which can be "spoken to" by devices ranging from handheld satellite phones to radio equipment fitted to ships and aircraft.

The 777 made regular calls via Inmarsat, sending data back to

Boeing and engine-makers Rolls-Royce so that any faults could be detected. If the ground station does not hear from an aircraft for an hour it will transmit a "heartbeat" signal via satellite, asking whether it is still logged on. The aircraft automatically returns a short message if it is (this exchange is called a "handshake"). At 02.11 am, Inmarsat made a handshake with MH370.

Though MH370 was no longer on the radar screen of any air traffic controller, at 02.15 am Malaysian military radar tracked the plane flying over the heavily populated island of Penang, far to the west of its scheduled course. They lost contact 200 miles (322km) to the northwest, just south of Phuket Island, 25 minutes later. However, the military were unaware of the significance of this sighting. The transponder was switched off so they could not identify the plane and did not inform the airline.

At 06.30 am, MH370 missed its scheduled landing at Beijing and relatives and friends waiting in the arrivals hall were told it had been delayed. Airline officials and air traffic controllers were beginning to fear the worst, though. No distress call had been heard and, prior to its disappearance, the pilots had reported no problem with the aircraft, but somehow, despite all the modern means of monitoring and communication, MH370 had simply vanished.

At 07.24 am Malaysia Airlines announced that the plane was missing, initially with a statement on its Facebook page. It seemed the plane had vanished from the real world and travelled into cyberspace.

Unbeknown to the airline, Inmarsat made another handshake with MH370 at 08.11 am. Eight minutes later, in another mystery yet to be explained, there was another unscheduled partial handshake with the plane. Media reports on the missing flight began to appear at 08.30 am. The next scheduled ping by Inmarsat went unanswered; MH370 had now well and truly disappeared.

Search-and-rescue teams were alerted and the next of kin of the aircrew were contacted. Malaysia had dispatched 15 planes and 9 ships to the area; more came from Singapore, China, Vietnam and the Philippines. The US also offered to join the search.

In Terminal 3 of Beijing Airport, concerns grew among waiting friends and relatives. One told reporters that when she had first asked about the non-arrival of the flight, an airline employee told her it had never taken off. Rumours circulated that it had been cancelled.

After an hour, the terrible news began to emerge: MH370 was missing and a search-and-rescue operation had begun. In the arrivals hall, pandemonium broke out as waiting relatives began to fear a dreadful fate might have befallen their loved ones. Frantic for news, they mobbed the information desk, but the two female attendants, dressed in bright red uniforms, could only smile and shrug their shoulders. One woman burst into tears in the middle of the concourse and was quickly surrounded by photographers and a television camera crew. Police began ushering relatives into a staff area at the side of the hall.

By mid-morning, a taciturn official had scrawled a notice on a whiteboard, telling relatives and friends of passengers that transport was provided to take them to the Metropark Lido Hotel, half an hour's drive from downtown Beijing, to await further information. Already fearing the worst, one woman on board the bus wept, while saying into a cellphone: "They want us to go to the hotel. It cannot be good!"

At the hotel they were taken into a closed area and reporters were kept away. But little was done to allay their fears and a man in a grey hooded sweatshirt stormed out, complaining about a lack of information. In the modern world of satellite surveillance, someone must know something. Surely there was information that the authorities had that they were holding back?

This was China, where dissension was not encouraged. The man refused to give his name, but said he was a Beijing resident. His mother was on board the flight, accompanying a group of 10 tourists.

"We have been waiting for hours and there is still no verification," he said. This was to be the beginning of a long ordeal which, for some, would never end.

Late on Saturday, Vietnamese air force jets spotted two large oil slicks and a column of smoke, close to where MH370 had gone missing. The slicks were spotted off the southern tip of Vietnam and were each between 6 miles (10km) and 9 miles (14km) long. While it was not claimed that the slicks were related to the missing plane, a statement issued by the Vietnamese government said they were consistent with the kind that would be produced by the two fuel tanks of a crashed jetliner.

By the time the oil slicks were spotted, it was getting dark and the search was suspended for the night. Meanwhile, the airline began contacting the next of kin. Of those aboard, 152 passengers were from China, 50 from Malaysia, seven from Indonesia, six from Australia, five from India, three from the US, and others were from Indonesia, France, New Zealand, Canada, Ukraine, Russia, Taiwan and the Netherlands – 14 nations in all. Their fate was to become one of the enduring mysteries of modern aviation.

CHAPTER FOUR

AIR SAFETY

Flying is one of the safest ways to travel and it's getting safer. But planes do crash. Each year some 500 people die due to air accidents where the aircraft is damaged beyond repair. But then more than three million people take to the air every day, so over a billion fly every year. Current losses are only around a quarter of those at the peak of fatalities in the 1970s and 80s, though fewer planes flew back then.

If you board a plane you have over an 8 million-to-one chance of surviving the flight. But when planes crash the results can be catastrophic. In the 9/11 attacks, 2,996 people died, including the terrorists. On 27 March 1977, 583 people were on board when a KLM Boeing 747 ran into a Pan Am 747 on the island of Tenerife. Only 61 survived.

Japan Airlines Flight 123 crashed into a mountainside on 12 August 1985, killing 520. The Boeing 747 suffered an explosive decompression when a poorly repaired aft pressure bulkhead blew out. This ruptured all four hydraulic systems and blew off the vertical tail plane. The plane could only be controlled by varying the thrust of the engines. It flew on for another 32 minutes before hitting Mount Takamagahara 60 miles (96.5km) from Tokyo. By the time rescuers reached the plane only four survivors were still alive; it was the most fatal single-plane accident.

The world's deadliest mid-air collision happened on 12 November 1996 when Saudia Flight SVA763 and Air Kazakhstan Flight KZA1907 met over Haryana, India. All 349 on board the two planes died. An eyewitness saw "a large cloud lit up with an orange glow". The tail of the Kazakh Ilyushin Il-76 cut through the left wing of the Saudi 747. It broke up before hitting the ground at 705 mph (1,135 km/h), followed by the Ilyushin, which hit a field, structurally intact. Two passengers from the Saudi flight survived the crash, still strapped to their seats, only to die soon after of internal injuries.

American Airlines Flight 587 bound for Santo Domingo in the Dominican Republic killed all 260 on board, plus five on the ground, when it crashed into the Belle Harbor neighbourhood of Queens, New York, shortly after the Airbus A300 had taken off from John F. Kennedy International Airport on 12 November 2001... And the list goes on.

Until 8 March, the Boeing 777 was considered one of the safest planes in the skies. The twin-engine inter-continental jet had been in service since 1994. Malaysia Airlines received their first in 1997 and their latest in 2004.

The 777 is capable of flying non-stop 7,250 miles (11,668km). Its two Rolls-Royce Trent 875 engines each have 74,600 pounds (33,838 kilos) of thrust, letting it cruise at Mach 0.84, or nearly 640 mph (1,030 km/h). The engines are so big a row of at least five coach seats could fit inside. Having just two engines, the plane burns through less fuel than four-engine jets, like the Boeing 747, which it essentially replaced.

These long-haul planes are popular with airlines. A 777 can fly non-stop from New York to Hong Kong and stay airborne for some 16 hours. They are frequently used on such busy routes as London to New York and San Francisco to Tokyo. But, like all planes, they have their faults. On 17 March 2003, on United Airlines Flight UA842 from Auckland to Los Angeles, a Boeing 777-200ER carrying 255 passengers suffered oil overheating in engine number two, which had to be shut down. It flew on, on one engine, for 192 minutes, to make a safe landing at Kona International Airport (KOA) on Hawaii, setting the record for an emergency diversion. A Boeing 777-200ER – the Extended Range version – was also used on the Flight MH370 that went missing.

There had been other accidents – and three hijackings, though these resulted in no fatalities. On 5 September 2001, British Airways Flight BA2019 landed at Denver International Airport. The Boeing 777-200ER taxied to the gate, the engines were shut down and passengers began to disembark. Meanwhile, the aircraft was being refuelled and made ready for the return flight.

One of the refuelling trucks was stationed under the left wing. Ten passengers and the crew of 16 were still on board when the refuelling hose broke loose. As it flapped around, it sprayed fuel all over the area. In the heat of the afternoon, the kerosene evaporated. The mist ignited and the 24-year-old refueller was engulfed in flames. A fire truck arrived within two minutes and extinguished the flames, but six days later the refueller, who was new to the job, died of his horrific injuries. The plane had suffered some damage, but was repaired and returned to service.

At first, it was thought that a clue to the fate of Flight MH370 might lie in an accident that occurred to another Boeing 777-

200ER on 17 January 2008. British Airways Flight BA38 from Beijing to London was approaching Heathrow Airport when it lost power. Without warning, the aircraft simply shut down. The pilot lost all power and avionics. Suddenly the nose lifted as he tried to glide the plane in to land, just feet above nearby houses. He managed to send out a Mayday just three seconds before the impact and was still wrestling with the controls when the plane hit the deck 1,000ft (305m) short of the runway.

Narrowly missing the perimeter fence, the 777 hit the ground at around 110 mph (177 kph). The pilot had decided to land it on the grass rather than risk skidding out of control on the runway. There was an enormous bang; the undercarriage was ripped off and the wheels bounced away as the plane dug into the grass and skidded to a halt.

One passenger said the plane had come in at a funny angle and belly-flopped onto the grass. Another recalled: "We were coming in to land but the plane felt like it should have been taking off. The engines were roaring and then we landed and it was just banging. Some people started to scream. It was quite terrifying, although people seemed to be quite calm. I think people were quite surprised when they were told to evacuate down the chutes."

Passengers were evacuated in minutes and instructed to sprint for safety as emergency crews raced to the jet, fearing a possible explosion.

"Everything was very well conducted by the crew – we were all out in minutes," said businessman Fernando Prado. "I feel I won the lottery today."

All 136 passengers and 16 crew escaped, though 47 were injured. An eyewitness recounted the pilot had done a magnificent job and "deserves a medal as big as a frying pan".

The Air Accidents Investigation Branch said that the crash-landing was probably caused by a build-up of ice in the fuel system on the plane, restricting the flow to the engines. Damage to the wing roots meant the plane had to be written off and a critical component of the engine that warmed the fuel was redesigned after two other Boeing 777 engines suffered a temporary loss of power.

Another Boeing 777-200ER belonging to EgyptAir was written off after the cockpit caught fire while it was preparing for departure at Cairo Airport. The 307 passengers and 10 crew members were quickly evacuated. The fire had started in the area under the console where the crew's oxygen system runs; the cockpit was extensively damaged. Two holes were burnt through the aircraft's outer skin and throughout the cabin there was smoke damage. The Federal Aviation Administration in Washington and the European Aviation Safety Agency (EASA) ordered oxygen pipes on the 777 fleet to be replaced by an alternative that does not conduct electricity.

It was thought that the loss of another Boeing 777-200ER on 6 July 2013 might provide a clue. Asiana Airlines Flight 214 from Seoul was landing at San Francisco International Airport when it hit a rocky sea wall just short of the runway. The plane lost its tail. Two passengers, both Chinese teenage girls, were killed and dozens of others were injured. The surviving passengers scrambled for safety as the plane caught fire.

A third victim, a 16-year-old girl named Ye Mengyuan who sat toward the rear of Flight 214, survived the crash-landing, but was killed on the ground when she was hit by a fire truck.

Flying the plane was Lee Gang-kuk, a pilot with nearly 10,000 hours' flying experience, but just 35 hours on a Boeing 777. Gang-kuk had recently completed training that qualified him to fly passengers in the 777, and was about halfway through his post-qualification training, needing 60 hours to get his full licence for that type of plane. He was seated in the left-hand cockpit pilot seat. In the co-pilot position was Lee Jeong-Min, an experienced captain who was supervising his training (he had clocked up more than 3,000 hours on Boeing 777s). It was Lee Gang-kuk's first time landing a 777 at San Francisco, although he had landed there some 30 times in other types of aircraft. There was a third pilot in the jump seat who was supposed to monitor the aircraft's controls.

Up until the point the plane crashed, everything about the flight had been normal and the weather over San Francisco had been near perfect: sunny with light winds. As the plane descended to 1,600ft (488m), the autopilot was turned off. At 1,400ft (427m), the plane's airspeed was about 170 knots (196 mph or 314 km/h).

At 11.27 am and 1,000ft (305m), the pilots made contact with the airport tower. When they were cleared to land in 12 seconds, the plane's altitude had dropped to about 600ft (183m). The plane was configured for its approach and the landing gear was down. The airspeed was about 149 knots (171 mph or 276 km/h). A target speed of 137 knots (158 mph or 254 km/h) was set.

At 500ft (152m) there was an audible automated altitude alert. The airspeed was about 134 knots (154 mph or 248 km/h) – they were too low and too slow. Then the pilots realized the plane was not properly lined up with the runway and they tried to make a correction.

At 200ft (61m) another automated altitude alarm sounded. The airspeed had slowed to 118 knots (136 mph or 219 km/h) – well below what it should have been. If the plane is more than 5 knots (6 mph or 9 km/h) below target speed, the pilots should abort the landing, race the engines, raise the nose and go round again. However, at no point in between 500 and 100ft (152 and 30m) did the pilots make any comment about the airspeed, according to the cockpit voice recorder.

However, at 200ft (61m) – 16 seconds before impact – Lee Jeong-Min, the instructor pilot, noticed that the auto-throttles were not maintaining the correct air speed. At 125ft and 112 knots (38.1m and 129 mph or 207 km/h), both throttles started to move forward and more fuel was sent to the engines to increase power to pick up speed. That was eight seconds before impact. At any time, either of the pilots in the two front seats could have reached down and pushed the throttle levers forward manually to increase power.

Then the third pilot in the jump seat realized the plane was travelling too slowly and called for an increase in speed. A second later, the noise of Lee Gang-kuk's stick shaker rattling could be heard on the voice recorder. This shakes the pilot's control yoke, warning him that the plane was about to stall because it was travelling dangerously slowly and had lost lift.

The two front-seat pilots then realized the plane was in trouble. They both reached for the throttles and pushed them forward. There was a loud roar as the engines revved up in a last-minute attempt to abort the landing but it was too late. At three seconds before impact, the plane had slowed to 103 knots (118.5 mph or 191 km/h). At this time, one of the pilots called for the landing to be aborted. Power was increasing and the engines were up to 50 percent thrust.

At one and a half seconds before impact, another of the pilots called for an aborted landing.

At 11.28 am, the airspeed had climbed 3 knots (3½ mph or 5½ km/h), but the increased speed was not enough to keep the plane in the air. The nose pulled up, but the landing gear, then the plane's tail, collided with the sea wall – San Francisco Airport is built out into the bay. The plane veered wildly before slamming down on the tarmac and sliding about 1,000ft (304m).

"What touched the ground was not any type of landing gear, it was all plane," an eyewitness recounted. "I'm not a pilot, but I'm pretty sure that shouldn't happen."

Another said she heard a "horrible thud".

The tail had sheared off the three cabin crew seated at the back of the plane, who fell out and landed among the rocks from the sea wall, and pieces of the mangled landing gear were strewn along the runway. The nose of the plane bounced twice, then the remains of the fuselage spun round and left the runway.

An eyewitness posted on Twitter that she had witnessed the crash and said the "plane came in at a bad angle, flipped, exploded". Another witness watching from a nearby hotel said he saw the plane cartwheel down the runway and the tail and a wing fly off.

"You heard a pop and you immediately saw a large, brief fireball that came out from underneath the aircraft," he recalled. "At that moment, you could see the aircraft was again starting to lift and it began to cartwheel. The wing broke off on the left-hand side. You could see the tail immediately fly off of the aircraft. As the aircraft cartwheeled, it then landed down and the other wing had broken."

A third witness noted the plane looked out of control.

"We heard a boom and saw the plane disappear into a cloud of dust and smoke," he said. "There was then a second explosion."

Many of the 291 passengers and 17 crew of the flight that originated in Shanghai before passing through Seoul escaped, unharmed, before the fuselage was partly gutted by fire.

"I just crash landed at SFO," tweeted one passenger. "Tail ripped off. Most everyone seems fine. I'm ok. Surreal." He added: "Fire and rescue people all over the place. They're evacuating the injured."

Survivors were seen jumping down the inflatable emergency slides. Forty-nine were immediately taken to hospital. Among them were two children, six women and four men. Ten were in a critical condition, many with spinal injuries. Another 132 less seriously injured followed later. Most spoke only Korean. Despite the deaths of two Chinese schoolgirls and the injuries suffered by many of the plane's 291 passengers, safety experts subsequently said that the safety features of the Boeing 777 helped to prevent a far worse disaster. Headline writers called it the "Miracle of Flight 214".

A navigational aid at the airport, which is used to help pilots maintain the optimum glide slope with an angle of three degrees as they approach the runway, was out of operation at the time of the crash. However, Federal Aviation Administration officials said that the navigation aid was not considered necessary in clear conditions and that planes had been cleared for visual landings. Officials played down the possibility that this had been a factor in the crash.

Like the 777, Malaysia Airlines had a good air-safety record, despite several periods running at a loss. There had been deaths and accidents, though.

On 4 December 1977, Flight MH653 was hijacked on a scheduled domestic flight from Penang to Kuala Lumpur's Subang Airport. At 19.54 hours the Boeing 777-200 was at an altitude of 4,000ft (1,219m) and beginning its descent when the crew radioed the tower, saying there was an "unidentified hijacker" on board. Immediately emergency preparations were made at the airport.

A few minutes later, the crew radioed: "We're now proceeding to Singapore. Good night." Flight 653 never arrived there.

At 20.15 hours, all communication with the aircraft were lost. Then, at 20.36 hours, the residents of the small village of Tanjung Kupang in Johor reported hearing explosions and seeing burning wreckage in a swamp. The wreckage was later identified as the missing plane; MH653 had crashed into the ground at a near-vertical angle at a very high speed. There were no survivors and no recognizable body or weapon was found. The remains of the seven crew and 93 passengers were X-rayed, but no bullets were found among them. However, a series of gunshots were heard on the cockpit voice recorder. Investigators concluded both the pilot and co-pilot had been shot and the plane crashed with no one competent at the controls. Was this what had happened on Flight MH370?

On 18 December 1983, a Scandinavian Airlines Airbus A300 on loan to Malaysia Airlines crashed 1.2 miles (2km) short of the runway at Subang Airport. No one on board Flight MH684 from Singapore was killed, but the aircraft was a write-off.

The Fokker 50 of Malaysia Airlines Flight MH2133 crashed into a shanty town near Tawau Airport, Malaysia, in northern Borneo, on 15 September 1995. Of the 49 passengers, 32 were killed, along with two of the four-man crew; nine people on the ground were also injured. Pilot error was said to have been responsible.

Perhaps another clue could have lain in the fate of Malaysia Airlines Flight MH85 from Beijing to Kuala Lumpur. After the Airbus A300 had landed, baggage handlers were unloading 80 canisters weighing 4,400 pounds (2,000kg) when they were hit by strong toxic fumes. Five ground handlers became ill. Airport fire and rescue personnel revealed the canisters contained a chemical called oxalyl chloride. Several canisters had leaked, causing severe damage to the aircraft fuselage. The aircraft was considered damaged beyond repair. Airborne, such a leak could have caused a catastrophe. Flight MH370's cargo manifest would have to be rigorously checked.

Then, on 1 August 2005, another Boeing 777-200ER of Malaysia Airlines on Flight MH124 from Perth, Australia, to Kuala Lumpur was climbing through 38,000ft (11,582m) when the crew heard a low airspeed warning. Then the instruments indicated that the aircraft was simultaneously approaching its over-speed limit and its stall speed limit. The plane pitched up and climbed to approximately 41,000ft (1,250m) and the indicated airspeed decreased from 270 knots (311 mph or 500 km/h) to 158 knots (182 mph or 293 km/h).

The stall warning and stick shaker also activated, indicating the plane was about to stall. Disconnecting the autopilot, the captain lowered the nose of the aircraft. The auto-throttle then tried to increase the thrust, but the captain countered this by manually moving the thrust levers to the idle position. At this the aircraft pitched up again and climbed another 2,000ft (610m).

The captain contacted air traffic control, saying they could not maintain altitude. He requested a descent and radar assistance. Air traffic control were able to verify the aircraft's speed and altitude. The autopilots now caused the aircraft to bank and pitch the nose down, so the captain decided to fly the aircraft manually and turned back toward Perth. As the aircraft approached the runway there, the crew found the wind gusting from the north-west was causing turbulence below 3,000ft (914m). During the approach, the aircraft's warning system indicated a dangerous windshear, but the crew continued the approach and landed the aircraft safely.

On investigation it was discovered that there was a glitch in the Boeing 777's fly-by-wire software, which had incorrectly measured the plane's speed and acceleration. In modern aircraft, the pilot's controls are no longer connected to the control surfaces so they do not have any feel for how the plane is flying. They are totally dependent on the plane's computer to keep the aircraft in the air.

After the loss of control of Flight MH124 had been reported, an airworthiness directive was issued. This is similar to a car recall and instructed all owners to make safety checks and modifications. The same fault was found on another 500 777s and the software quickly updated on planes around the world.

Had a similar fault plagued the 777 on Flight MH370?

CHAPTER FIVE

A WATERY GRAVE

The air crash that the disappearance of MH370 put people in mind of was Air France Flight 447, which crashed into the sea on 1 June 2009. The Airbus A330-203 had been on its way from Rio de Janeiro to Paris when it disappeared over the middle of the Atlantic. Over four years the plane had clocked up 18,870 flying hours, but had recently undergone a major overhaul.

Leaving Rio de Janeiro–Galeão International Airport at 19.19 pm local time (22.29 GMT) on 31 May, it was scheduled to arrive at Paris–Charles de Gaulle Airport at 10.03 am the following day. The last time anyone heard from the aircraft was three hours six minutes after departure, at 1.35 GMT, when the crew reported they had just passed a waypoint 351 miles (565km) off the coast of Brazil. Eleven minutes later it was out of range of Brazilian radar.

While the A330-203 could be flown by two pilots, three pilots were on board as the 13-hour flight exceeded the 10 hours permitted by Air France. With three pilots on board, they could take a rest in rotation in the sleeping cabin situated just behind the cockpit in an A330.

The captain sent one of the co-pilots to take the first break. At 1.55 GMT, he woke the second pilot. After a briefing, the captain started his own rest break at 2.01 GMT. Five minutes later, the pilot warned the cabin crew that they were about to enter an area of turbulence. He then turned the plane slightly to port to avoid it and dropped the speed from Mach 0.82 to Mach 0.8 (this lower speed minimizes stress on the airframe). The engine de-icing was turned on.

The pilot then switched off the autopilot and disengaged the auto-throttles. At this the plane then began to roll to the right. The pilot countered this by pushing his joystick to the left, but he overcompensated and for the next 30 seconds the plane rolled alternately right and left. At the same time, he pulled the nose up. The stall warning sounded and the airspeed seemed to plummet from 274 knots (315 mph or 507 km/h) to 52 knots (60 mph or 96 km/h).

With the nose up, the plane began to climb at nearly 7,000ft per minute (2,134m per minute). It seems there was something wrong with the airspeed indicator. The speed rose rapidly to 215 knots (247 mph or 398 km/h). The plane continued with its nose up to its maximum altitude of 38,000ft (11,582m) but instead of levelling off, the pilot increased the "angle of attack", raising the nose even higher and the engines were revving as if the plane was taking off.

Normally, the Airbus's fly-by-wire computer would have prevented such a high angle of attack to check the plane stalling but the aircraft was being flown manually and, in the thin air at that altitude, the wings lost lift and it stalled.

Realizing something was wrong, the captain returned to the cockpit. By then, the plane was 40 degrees nose-up. It had dropped to 35,000ft (10,668m) and the engines were running at full throttle. With the nose up while the plane was descending rapidly, the on-board computers could make no sense of the data that was being passed to them. The pilot dropped the nose slightly and suddenly the figures made sense and the stall warning sounded. But the plane remained nose-up until it crashed into the water. The whole calamity had taken less than four and a half minutes.

The flight data recordings stopped at 02:14:28 GMT, or three hours 45 minutes after takeoff. At that point, the aircraft's ground speed was 107 knots (123 mph or 198 km/h), and it was descending at 10,912ft (3,326m) per minute, which is roughly the same as its ground speed. The plane was still 16.2 degrees nose-up and had rolled 5.3 degrees to the left. During its descent, the aircraft had turned more than 180 degrees to the right – heading back the way it came. The passengers and crew, taken by surprise, were thrown around during the terrifying descent.

The aircraft remained stalled during its entire three-minute-30-second descent from 38,000ft (11,582m) before it hit the ocean surface at a speed of 151 knots (174 mph or 280 km/h). On impact the aircraft broke up and it is assumed that all 228 people on board died instantaneously.

During its descent, equipment on the plane sent out automated messages to the Aircraft Communication Addressing and Reporting System (ACARS). Six failure reports and 19 warnings were transmitted. One of them indicated that there was a problem with the "pitot-static system" which, among other things, measures the airspeed. Without an accurate measure of airspeed, at high altitude, it is very difficult to prevent a plane from stalling.

Another warning message indicated there was a disagreement

between the three independent data systems on board. This would serve to confuse the pilot. A final warning indicated the plane was descending at high speed.

The plane was due to pass from Brazilian airspace into Senegalese airspace at around 2.20 GMT before moving on into the airspace of Cape Verde at 3.45. By 4.00 neither had heard from AF447, so air traffic control in Senegal tried to raise the plane – with no success. The controller then contacted another Air France flight – AF459 – and asked them to try to raise AF447. They, too, got no response.

A Brazilian air force plane and a French reconnaissance aircraft from Senegal then set out to look for the missing aircraft. They were followed by planes from Spain and the US. Unlike Flight MH370, it was assumed almost immediately that AF447 had been lost. Officials figured that soon after its scheduled arrival time in Paris, if it had not already crashed then it would have run out of kerosene. Experts immediately pointed out that, if it had come down over the sea, the chances of anyone surviving were small.

Like the Boeing 777, the Airbus A330 had a good safety record – the 777 had been introduced as a direct competitor. Since the A330 had taken to the air in 1992, it had not been involved in any fatal accidents involving passengers – until the loss of AF447, that is. However, in June 1994, on a test flight simulating an engine failure on takeoff, one crashed in Toulouse, killing all seven people aboard. And in October 2008, an A330 carrying 303 passengers and 12 crew from Singapore Changi Airport to Perth had to make an emergency landing at Learmonth Airport in Western Australia when the aircraft made uncommanded dives, throwing the crew, passengers and luggage around the cabin. Eleven passengers and one crew member were seriously injured, while 95 passengers and eight crew suffered minor injuries. A fault was found in the software and details of new procedures were issued.

AF447 was carrying 216 passengers and 12 crew. Of the passengers, 126 were men and 82 were women; seven children and a baby were on board. Air France said the pilot had flown 11,000 hours, 1,700 of them on the Airbus A330, making him a highly experienced pilot. Of the two co-pilots, one had 3,000 hours of flying time and the other 6,600 hours.

The day after AF447 went missing, wreckage was found 400 miles (644km) off the northeast coast of Brazil. No survivors were spotted. One debris field was about three miles (5km) long; another lay close by. Both lay near the flight path from Rio to Paris. Later that day, a French freighter arrived on the scene and confirmed that the wreckage came from the missing plane. Among the debris was a slick of jet fuel. This indicated the plane had not been blown up by bomb as, in that case, the fuel would have been burnt.

Four days later, the bodies of two males were found, along with some personal items. Fifty-one bodies were recovered. Most had suffered broken pelvises and fractured femurs, classic signs of such a high-speed impact. They were identified using dental records and DNA testing. The corpses were not wearing their life jackets, so the crash had happened with warning; the pilots had no time to send a Mayday – MH370 had sent no Mayday either.

The French Navy sent a nuclear submarine to the area to look for the "black boxes" – the flight recorder and the cockpit voice recorder. They were lost in waters that were in some places 16,000ft (4,877m) deep. The sea floor there is very rugged. The submarine would use its sonar to listen out for the black boxes' "pingers" which, when immersed in water, emitted an ultrasonic pulse. They can be heard several miles away and will go on giving out a signal for up to a month before the battery runs out. France asked the US to lend them two towed hydrophones to help pick up the pulse from the pingers.

After the month was up, three robot submarines were deployed to search the sea floor. Nine months later a team from the Oceanographic Institution at Woods Hole, Massachusetts found part of the fuselage with bodies still trapped inside, along with other debris from the plane. The wreckage was almost 2.5 miles (4km) below the surface of the Sargasso Sea. The flight recorder and cockpit voice recorder were found nearly two years after the plane had gone down. They were retrieved using autonomous underwater vehicles – unmanned submarines – and were taken to the Bureau d'Enquêtes et d'Analyses (BEA – Bureau of Investigation and Analysis) at Le Bourget, outside Paris. Meanwhile, another 104 bodies were recovered from the wreckage. The search and recovery cost over US$55 million (£32.5 million).

Investigators succeeded in extracting data from the black boxes. Within 24 hours, reports were circulating, suggesting the crash seemed more likely the result of pilot error than a manufacturing flaw by Airbus. Until then it had been assumed that, for some reason, the crew of Flight AF447 had steered the plane directly into a severe storm that eventually caused the speed sensors to ice over, but the flight path recorded by the black box showed the crew had been trying to find the safest possible path through the storm front. They initially appear to have succeeded as the flight data did not contain any evidence of severe turbulence. Indeed 12 other flights shared roughly the same route that Flight AF447 was following at the time of the accident.

The cockpit voice recorder gives a vivid sense of panic and confusion in the minutes before AF447 crashed:

02:13:40 Co-pilot David Robert: "Climb...
climb...
  climb... climb..."
02:13:40 Co-pilot Pierre-Cédric Bonin: "But
I've
  had the stick back the whole time!"
02:13:42 Captain Marc Dubois: "No, no, no...
Don't
  climb... no, no!"
02:13:43 Co-pilot David Robert: "Descend...
Give
  me the controls... Give me the controls!"

Robert takes control and lowers the aircraft's nose. A hazard warning sounds, telling them the surface of the sea is fast approaching.

02:14:23 Co-pilot David Robert: "Damn it, we're
  going to crash... This can't be happening!"
02:14:27 Captain Marc Dubois: "Ten degrees of
  pitch..."

At that point, the recording ends. The French news magazine *Le Point* later revealed that, just before he handed control over to the co-pilots, Captain Dubois remarked: "I didn't sleep enough last night. One hour – it's not enough."

The BEA's final report issued on 5 July 2012 concluded that the narrow pitot tubes used to measure airspeed gave a faulty reading. This caused the autopilot to disengage. Errors made by the crew then compounded the problem, leading to the crash. Various modifications and changes to procedures were recommended.

Some black boxes tell an even more chilling tale. On 31 October 1994, an American Eagle turboprop on Flight 4184 was waiting for clearance to land in Chicago. The cockpit voice recorder included the captain calling the first officer in the cockpit.

> Captain: "Hey, bro!"
> First Officer: "Yeah."
> Captain: "I'm busy with the ladies back here."
> FO: "Oh."
> Flight attendant: (sound of snicker)
> Captain: "Yeah, so if, so if I don't make it up there within the next say, 15 or 20 minutes, you know why."
> FO: "OK."

Minutes later, the plane plunged into a field at 375 knots (431.5 mph or 694.5 km/h), killing all 64 passengers aboard. Icing of the control surfaces was thought to be the cause.

CHAPTER SIX

SORROW AND SUSPICION

So what had gone wrong with Malaysia Airlines MH370? The conditions over the South China Sea in March 2014 were nothing like those over the South Atlantic in June five years earlier. Another pilot who flew through the area at the time said it was "a beautiful clear northeast monsoon night". Radio communications with air traffic control were also good.

Was there something wrong with the plane then? The 11-year-old 777, registration 9M-MRO, had been involved in an incident before. While taxiing at Pudong International Airport outside Shanghai, the wing tip collided with the tail of China Eastern Airlines A340 and a 3ft (0.9m) section had broken off. No one was hurt and the wing was repaired. Otherwise the plane had a clean bill of health and had recently been serviced.

The crew were experienced too. MH370's 53-year-old pilot Zaharie Ahmad Shah had more than 18,000 flying hours and had been with Malaysia Airlines since 1981. For him flying was a passion. Online, he posted on several forums for flight simulation enthusiasts. The first officer, 27-year-old Fariq Hamid, had about 2,800 flying hours and had flown for the airline since 2007. Nevertheless, they came under suspicion.

Only in February, the co-pilot on Ethiopian Airlines Flight 702 from Addis Ababa to Rome hijacked his own plane. He waited until the pilot had gone to the toilet before locking the cockpit door, then radioed Geneva, requesting emergency refuelling. When the pilot tried to open the cockpit door and threatened to smash it down, co-pilot Hailemedehin Abera Tagegn warned he would crash the plane. Flight 702 landed safely in Geneva, where Tagegn sought political asylum. Arrested and charged with hostage taking, Tagegn faces 20 years in jail for needlessly risking the lives of his passengers and the Ethiopian government have requested his extradition.

The fact that MH370 had disappeared at the very moment of moving from Malaysian airspace into Vietnamese airspace seemed suspicious.

"If I was going to steal the aeroplane, that would be the point I would do it," said Stephen Buzdygan, a former British Airways pilot who flew 777s. "There might be a bit of dead space between the air traffic controllers. It was the only time during the flight they would maybe not have been able to be seen from the ground."

BA's former air safety chief John Lindsay agreed. "This would have been the ideal time to take over the aircraft because it would give a period of time when no one was aware of what it was doing," he observed. "It seems to be more than just a strong coincidence that the loss of contact with the aircraft happened at the point of hand-over."

Then it was discovered that two of the passengers were travelling on stolen passports. Both passports had been reported stolen in Thailand. One belonged to Italian citizen Luigi Maraldi. The foreign ministry in Rome confirmed he was not on the plane. He had reported his passport stolen the previous August and called home when he heard reports that an Italian bearing his name was on board the missing plane.

"Mr Maraldi is now in Phuket, but somebody who used his passport died on the flight. It is something we don't understand," said Dr Francesco Pensato, Italy's honorary consul on the Thai island of Phuket, where Maraldi now lives.

The real Luigi Maraldi appeared at a police station in Phuket to clarify that he had lost his passport while renting a motorcycle in Patong, the resort island's tourist centre, the previous year. He said the woman in the shop had told him she had given his passport to another Italian man who "looked similar". Elsewhere it was reported that the interloper "said Mr Maraldi was his husband".

The police visited the Salzburg home of 30-year-old Austrian Christian Kozel, who was also listed on the manifest, and found him safe and well. A foreign ministry spokesman in Vienna said: "Our embassy got the information that there was an Austrian on board. That was the passenger list from Malaysia Airlines. Our system came back with a note that this is a stolen passport." The passport was stolen two years earlier while Kozel was on a flight from Phuket to Bangkok.

It was immediately suspected that these two bogus passengers were terrorists. After all, hijackers had used stolen passports before, but there could be less sinister explanations. In 2010, when an Air India Express flight overshot the runway at Mangalore, killing 160, it emerged that 10 of those on board had fraudulent passports.

An official of the US Department of Homeland Security told

The Los Angeles Times it would be a first if the plane was brought down by two terrorists who boarded the jet carrying stolen passports. "We've never seen that," he insisted.

Nevertheless, speculation that the two passengers carrying stolen passports were terrorists continued to gain momentum. Most of the passengers on the missing plane were Chinese and China was involved in a conflict with Muslim separatists along its western border. Less than a week before MH370 went missing 33 people had been killed and 130 were wounded in a mass stabbing at Kunming train station in China's southwestern Yunnan province. According to Chinese state media, it was a premeditated attack carried out by ethnic Uighur separatists from the volatile western province of Xinjiang – or East Turkestan, as the Turkic-speaking Uighurs call it. A group of people armed with knives entered the train station at about 9 pm local time on Saturday and attacked travellers indiscriminately. The incident became known as "China's 9/11".

"The fight against China is our Islamic responsibility and we have to fulfil it," one of the terrorist group commented afterwards.

Tensions between Uighurs and Han Chinese have been simmering for years. The Chinese have bulldozed great swaths of Kashgar, the historic Uighur capital, and drafted hundreds of thousands of Han Chinese into the sensitive border region. Like the Tibetans, the Uighurs now find themselves a minority in their homeland.

In 2009 riots in the regional capital of Urumqi left more than 100 dead. In October 2013, a vehicle carrying three Uighurs ploughed into pedestrians near Tiananmen Square, killing five people and injuring another 38. A bomb went off in Urumqi's southern railway station and those fleeing were attacked with knives on 30 April 2014, when President Xi Jinping was visiting the area. The Chinese authorities blamed the attack on the East Turkestan Islamic Movement, a militant Uighur group said to have links to the Taliban and Pakistani jihadi networks. There were also specific Uighur grievances that link Malaysia and China. In 2011 and 2012, groups of Uighurs were deported to China from Malaysia after being caught using false passports. Human rights groups said at the time that, by returning them to China, Malaysia was in effect delivering the deportees to a nation that could subject them to torture.

The fact that the passports were stolen in Thailand also invited suspicion. Although Thailand is a mainly Buddhist country, it has a long-running Muslim insurgency and ranks eighth on the global list of terror targets behind Somalia, Afghanistan and Iraq, according to the Global Terrorism Index published by the Institute for Economics and Peace. The GTI lists 173 separate terrorist incidents in Thailand that resulted in 142 deaths.

"Creeping Islamization is changing the nature of this previously low-level conflict," said a report last year.

While there was nothing to tie the two bogus travellers on MH370 to any terrorist group, the possibility remained. Asked whether terrorism was suspected, Malaysian Prime Minister Najib Razak told reporters: "We are looking at all possibilities, but it is too early to make any conclusive remarks."

A US intelligence official told CNN that the authorities were checking on stolen passports, combing passenger manifests and going back through intelligence.

"We are aware of the reporting on the two stolen passports," another senior official told NBC News. "We have not determined a nexus to terrorism yet, although it's still very early, and that's by no means definitive. We're still tracking."

A third senior US intelligence official was quoted by *The New*

York Times as saying: "At this time, we have not identified this as an act of terrorism. While the stolen passports are interesting, they don't necessarily say to us that this was a terrorism act."

The fact that the pilots had not made a distress call could have meant that there was a bomb on board. A complete electrical failure was another possibility. An airline tracking website suggested the jet plunged 650ft (198m) and changed direction before vanishing, possibly indicating that some incident had occurred on the flight deck.

What had happened to the missing plane seemed shrouded in secrecy. Chinese relatives of passengers waiting in the Lido Hotel accused Malaysia Airlines of keeping them in the dark. Tempers began to fray.

"Malaysia Airlines has not told us a single thing," said one relative. "No one from the company has even been in to see us. They cannot keep hundreds of us here for hours without any information."

"There's no one from the company here, we can't find a single person," said another. "They've just shut us in this room and told us to wait. We want someone to show their face. They haven't even given us the passenger list."

"They are treating us worse than dogs," added a third.

During the agonizing wait they were asked to fill in forms, giving personal details. Despite these distractions, one thing was increasingly clear. "They are all gone!" cried a woman waiting for family members.

Meanwhile, the Chinese government called in the ambassadors of Vietnam and Malaysia for urgent talks. The Chinese foreign minister, Wang Yi, told a press conference that the disappearance was "very disturbing".

At the same time users of Twitter were hard at it, cruelly

tweeting that the plane had landed safely at Nanning Wuxu International Airport in southern China, giving those waiting false hope. Others tweeted that the plane had run out of fuel or that it had been downed by a missile, while level-headed air accident investigators looked into the possible failure of both engines – though in such circumstances the plane would have glided long enough for the crew to have broadcast a Mayday. Cruising at 35,000ft (10,668km), there was ample time to report any fault.

"Something happened and the pilots did not tell anyone. Why? It's a good question," said David Learmount, operations and safety editor of the aviation website *Flightglobal*. "It's extraordinary the pilots failed to call because they had plenty of time to. Unless there was a bomb on board but there has been no evidence of that. If the engines were to fail because of some interruption to the fuel flow, they can glide with no problems whatsoever for about forty minutes at that height."

However, he also said that the time when the plane went missing could be significant. "Between midnight and 2 am you're not at a mental or physical performance high – you're at the lowest performance standard in the twenty-four-hour cycle."

Dan Macchiarella, chair of the aeronautical science department at Embry-Riddle Aeronautical University, Daytona Beach, Florida, noted that if a jet at such a high altitude had engine problems it might still be able to glide for up to 100 miles (161km), during which time Mayday calls could be made. Even if all power from the engines was lost, emergency back-up power was still available to the pilots.

"It's pretty baffling," said Macchiarella. "Whatever happened on that flight deck, the pilots did not do what pilots do. They aviate, they navigate and they communicate. If something happens at altitude, the first thing they want to do is squawk emergency."

His colleague, Les Westbrooks, an associate professor of aeronautical science at Embry-Riddle, noted it was possible, though highly unlikely, that the radio systems had failed. He said he suspected catastrophic failure and doubted the aircraft turned around because, if it had time to do so, it would have had time to make – and could have made – a radio call. It was possible something happened but the pilots initially maintained control, "continuing on to try to land in possibly Vietnam or somewhere else… then the situation got worse".

The other puzzle was the transponder, which responds to the air traffic controller's radar beam and identifies the plane. It was highly unusual for the device to fail, but it was possible that the antenna outside the plane was damaged. Another possibility was that the crew had turned the transponder off.

"If the crew knew that they were flying in a non-radar environment, they might very well turn the transponders off," Westbrooks explained. "Not necessarily that that's standard operating procedure – but they're up there, nobody's interrogating this, let's just turn it off."

They might have done that "to save wear and tear on the electronics," he added. The other possibility was that the plane blew up at the last point where its transponder communicated with the radar.

Other possibilities were examined. The cargo manifest was studied for potential hazards and the passenger list also came under detailed scrutiny. The possibility that the jet was deliberately downed – for example, by a hijacker or a bomb – could not be ruled out. Rumours circulated that life jackets had been seen in the South China Sea.

Malaysia Airlines also resorted to Twitter. As the volume of complaints grew, it tweeted: "We understand everyone's concern on MH370 pax & crew. We're accelerating every effort with all relevant authorities to locate the aircraft."

At noon on 8 March 2014, the line at the top of the arrivals board in Beijing saying Malaysia Airlines MH370 was delayed finally blinked off, but the smiling staff behind the travel desk still had no information. A man named Song who clung on at the airport said: "My parents were on board – they were in Kuala Lumpur for an accountancy project for five days. I will wait here until I am told something. No one from Malaysia Airlines has told us anything all day."

In Kuala Lumpur, officials asked relatives to bring their travel documents to the airport, ready to board evening flights to Vietnam. But their hopes were dashed when the news came through of the sighting of the oil slicks off the Cà Mau Peninsula, the southern tip of Vietnam. Officials said these were consistent with the kind that would be produced by the burst fuel tanks from a crashed airliner. All the TV monitors in the airport displayed red signs, reading: "Let us pray for Flight MH370".

Thirty-four-year-old Norliakmar Hamid and husband Razahan Zamani, the daughter and son-in-law of 56-year-old Malaysian policeman Hamid Ramlan, were on the flight, intending to take a holiday in Beijing. Ramlan handed out photographs of the missing couple. "My wife is crying. Everyone is sad," he said. "My house has become a place of mourning. This is Allah's will, we have to accept it. Being a policeman over thirty-three years, this is my worst day."

Norliakmar's 31-year-old brother, Mohd Lokman Hamid, only discovered that his sister was on Flight MH370 when he logged onto Facebook that morning and saw her status update, which she had posted the night before. He also discovered on Facebook that the plane had gone missing after losing contact with Malaysia's Subang air traffic control.

Mohd Lokman Hamid told reporters: "I know they had been planning to go to Beijing for a holiday, especially after she suffered a miscarriage." After hearing that the plane had gone missing, he said: "I immediately called the airline to verify the story, but they said they will call me back for confirmation. I'm terribly worried as too many speculations have been made about the incident. Some even say that the aircraft has issues with its GPS [Global Positioning System]. I just hope that my sister and brother-in-law, as well as other passengers on board the aircraft, are safe."

Norliakmar and Razahan had met at Aeon, a Japanese supermarket chain in Kuala Lumpur where they both worked. The sales assistant and administrative assistant were married in 2012 and were on a long-delayed honeymoon trip to Beijing. A visit to the Malaysian resort of Cameron Highlands was cancelled when Norliakmar fell ill. As the day of the flight grew closer, she posted a photograph on social media of one of her five cats sitting on her suitcase. Flight MH370 was the first time she and Razahan had been on a plane together.

Razahan's father, Zamani Zakaria, also expressed his frustration at the lack of information being provided. "They have not found the aircraft," he said. "We are sad, and we hope and pray that our son is alive and well and the aircraft will be found soon."

Selamat Omar, a Malaysian whose 29-year-old son Mohamad Khairul Amri Selamat was a passenger on the flight, was more sanguine. He had expected a call from his son at 6.30 am when the plane arrived in Beijing. Instead he got a call from the airline to say the plane was missing. "We accept God's will. Whether he is found alive or dead, we surrender to Allah," Selamat said.

Chrisman Siregar carried a portrait of his son, Firman, dressed in his graduation robes, as his family gathered in tearful silence to watch news of the search-and-rescue operation. Others were clutching their passports, ready to be flown to Vietnam.

On 9 March 2014, Vietnam's state-run newspaper, *Thanh Nien*, said Lieutenant-General Vo Van Tuan, deputy chief of the general staff of the Vietnam People's Army, had reported that searchers in a low-flying plane had spotted an object suspected of being a door from the missing jet and possibly part of its tail. They were seen in waters about 56 miles (90km) south of Tho Chu island, in the same area the oil slicks had been spotted the previous day. "From this object, hopefully we will find the missing plane," Tuan said. *Thanh Nien* added that two ships from the maritime police were heading to the site.

Then the confusion began. Malaysia's air force chief Rodzali Daud told a press conference that, like the tracking website, radar indicated that Flight MH370 may have turned back, but would not give any further details on which direction it went or how far it veered off course. However, it would not have been flying on toward Vietnam.

"We are trying to make sense of this," Daud said. "The military radar indicated that the aircraft may have made a turn back, and in some parts this was corroborated by civilian radar."

Malaysia Airlines chief executive Ahmad Jauhari Yahya then told the press conference that pilots are supposed to inform the airline and air traffic control authorities if the plane does a U-turn. "There was no such distress signal or distress call per se, so we are equally puzzled," he said.

Captain Michael Fortune, who had made more than 2,500 flight hours in a Boeing 777, said: "It is beyond baffling. There is voice communication and a data communication in the cockpit –

both extremely good. If it hit bad weather or came down after a freak event the pilots would have had time for a Mayday call."

Meanwhile, a multinational fleet was searching for the missing plane. A total fleet of 40 ships and 34 aircraft from Malaysia, Thailand, Australia, Singapore, Indonesia, China, the United States and Vietnam were converging on the spot where the Vietnamese pilots had reported seeing wreckage.

"We are doing everything in our power to locate the plane. We are doing everything we can to ensure every possible angle has been addressed," Malaysian defence minister and, now, acting transport minister Hishammuddin Hussein told a news conference. "We are looking for accurate information from the Malaysian military. They are waiting for information from the Vietnamese side."

Suspicion again turned to the two passengers travelling on stolen passports.

"I can confirm that we have the visuals of these two people on CCTV," said Hishammuddin Hussein. "We have intelligence agencies, both local and international, on board."

Footage of the suspects as they moved from check-in to departure was being examined, he said, but he declined to give further details, saying it might jeopardize the investigation. The stolen passports were on a database set up by Interpol after 9/11 but, officials lamented, airlines rarely checked them.

An intelligence source said: "It's unusual for one person to board a plane with a stolen passport but very rare for two to do this."

Chris Yates, who heads a consultancy specializing in aviation security, concurred. "It's extremely rare to find two people on the same flight with stolen passports," he said. "I would err on the side of caution as to calling it terrorist related." However, he added the plane's sudden disappearance did "give rise to an element of suspicion that something catastrophic and manmade caused the problems".

Malaysia Airlines had played down the use of two stolen passports, saying that any passengers headed to Beijing would have had to apply for a Chinese visa, so the passports would have been checked. And there was, indeed, a connection between bogus passports and terrorism. A suspected member of the al-Qaeda terror cell responsible for several attacks in Madrid – including the 2004 11-M train bombings, which killed 191 people and injured 1,800 others – was travelling on a false passport. Information from that suspect would lead, several years later, to the arrest in September 2009 of an Iranian-born Briton, Ahboor Rambarak Fath, at Bangkok's Suvarnabhumi Airport. Stopped as he got off a flight from Spain, Fath was carrying a bag of 103 stolen European, Canadian and Israeli passports destined, he confessed, for the veritable forgery factory that police found in the apartment of a 39-year-old Pakistani national named Muhammed Ather "Tony" Butt in the hours after Fath's arrest. In one room of the flat, officers from Thailand's Department of Special Investigation found computers, a high-definition scanner and printer, and more than 1,000 stolen passports, along with photographs and counterfeit data pages for EU, Canadian, Chinese and Israeli passports, plus assorted sets of US and Schengen-group visa stickers and stamps.

Muhammed Butt himself was arrested, together with his Thai girlfriend, Sirikalya Kitbamrung, as they were crossing into Laos from the northeastern Thai province of Nong Khai on 30 November 2010 in a joint Thai-Spanish operation codenamed "Alpha". Later that same day, officers from Thai police arrested a second Pakistani, 27-year-old Zezan Azzan Butt, in the Rat

Burana district of Bangkok. At about the same time, on the other side of the globe, Spanish police were raiding addresses in Barcelona, arresting six Pakistanis and one Nigerian in the process.

According to DSI deputy director-general Narat Savetnant, Muhammed Butt was the kingpin of a major international gang that stole and doctored passports, then sold them on to international criminal groups involved in arms trafficking, human trafficking and terrorism. Along with the Madrid bombers, the gang also supplied passports to the Pakistan-based Lashkar-e-Taiba group, accused of plotting the 2008 Mumbai attacks that left 164 people dead and more than 300 injured, and to Tamil Tiger separatists in Sri Lanka.

In June 2012, when Butt was sentenced to 15 years in jail, the DSI smashed another major counterfeiting syndicate. This one was thought to have issued some 3,000 falsified passports and visas over five years. Two of them went to Iranians convicted of carrying out a series of botched bomb attacks in Bangkok in February 2012, supposedly aimed at Israeli diplomats. The counterfeiting gang's alleged ringleader, 45-year-old Iranian-born Seyed Paknejad, was arrested but jumped bail and fled to Malaysia on a fake Turkish passport. He was rearrested there in 2013, carrying 17 stolen New Zealand passports. Thailand has asked for his extradition.

While it was not known where the passengers who had assumed the identities of Maraldi and Kozel had acquired their passports, it was discovered that they were both booked on onward flights from Beijing. They had reserved seats on the 11.55 KLM flight to Amsterdam on 8 March. Maraldi was then to fly to Copenhagen; Kozel to Frankfurt.

Carrying EU passports meant that they would not have needed visas or to undergo further checks to transit in China. And if they had booked onward flights, it was unlikely that they were planning an act of terrorism on board MH370 – to blow it up or crash it into the sea. It did not make sense.

CHAPTER SEVEN

PREPARE FOR THE WORST

When 30 hours had passed without contact with the plane, relatives were told to prepare for the worst. Pilots writing on the PPRuNe (Professional Pilots Rumour Network) Internet forum concluded Flight MH370 had suffered a sudden, catastrophic event. One believed a "bomb, terrorist attack or structural failure" was to blame. Another said: "Aircraft do not just suddenly fall out of the sky without some huge catastrophic event occurring."

An American government official told *The New York Times* that the Pentagon had reviewed its surveillance system that looks for flashes around the world and saw no evidence of an explosion.

The loss of the plane set off a torrent of speculation on Chinese social media as well as on specialist aviation websites. An Asia-based expert in aero engines said that engine failure would be extremely unlikely while the aircraft was cruising. And if it lost power in one engine, it could continue using only the other.

Guy Gratton, an aviation safety expert at Brunel University, told *The Sunday Times* that there were two obvious starting points for a catastrophic failure. The first was a complete electrical failure on board. However, he said this was extremely unlikely in a 777 that has four radios and numerous electrical back-up systems.

The second, and in his view more likely, possibility was what investigators call a "controlled flight into terrain" accident, where pilots lose situational awareness and unintentionally fly into the ground or sea. In this context, he mentioned the crash of Air France Flight 447, which plunged into the Atlantic after its pilots failed to react effectively to technical problems.

Finally, a passenger list was leaked to a Chinese website with one name mysteriously blurred out. The missing included two French teenagers, 17-year-old Hadrien Wattrelos and his 18-year-old girlfriend Zhao Yan. They had enrolled together at the Lycée Français International de Pékin, which was known in Beijing simply as the French School. A picture of the couple posted on Wattrelos's college page on 29 July 2013 was accompanied by the words: "*Je t'aime* [I love you]".

"*Haaaaaa mon amour, trooooop mignon* [Ha my love, too cute]," Zhao had responded. Both French citizens, the couple gave Paris as their hometown.

On Flight MH370 they were accompanied by Hadrien's 52-year-old mother Laurence, and his sister Ambre, 14; both lived in Beijing. Ambre was also a student at the French School and Laurence was listed as vice-president of the Association des Parents d'Elèves du Lycée Français International de Pékin, a French parent-teacher organization, on the association's website.

Junior minister for French citizens abroad Hélène Conway-Mouret confirmed their identities and said: "I wish to send a message of support and solidarity to the families of those who disappeared on Flight MH370 during this difficult time."

Canadians Muktesh Mukherjee, the 42-year-old vice-president of China operations for mining company Xcoal Energy & Resources, and his 37-year-old Chinese-born wife Xiaomo Bai were also on the flight. They were returning to their family home in Beijing, where they lived after moving from Montreal. The names of their two young sons did not appear on the manifest; the couple had left the children at home while they took a beach holiday in Vietnam. Photographs on their Facebook page show them to have been a happy, smiling family. Xiaomo Bai had also posted pictures of their holiday on social media shortly before boarding the flight. Mukherjee's grandfather, a former Indian government minister, died in a plane crash outside New Delhi in the 1970s. His uncle, Manoj, still had not given up hope and said: "Miracles do happen. We pray it will happen this time."

The airline had not been able to get in touch with their families but had contacted the Canadian High Commission in Malaysia. Stephen Harper, Canada's prime minister, tweeted his condolences, and Canada's Department of Foreign Affairs released a statement, saying: "Our thoughts and deepest sympathies are with those affected by the disappearance of Malaysia Airlines MH370".

The three Americans on board were two children, Leo Meng, two, and Nicole Meng, four, and 50-year-old Philip Wood, an IBM executive and father of two sons from Texas. He was working as a technical storage executive at IBM Malaysia and had been transferred from Beijing to Kuala Lumpur. This was to be his last trip to the Chinese capital, before moving permanently to Malaysia, and he was excited by the new beginning.

His partner, 48-year-old Sarah Bajc from Atlanta, who was

getting ready to move with him to Malaysia, said she continued to hope he would be found. "Until there's proof that Philip is dead, I refuse to believe it," she told NewsOn6 in Oklahoma City. "If there's anybody that could survive something like this, it's him. I mean, he's such a fighter and he has so much to live for."

She added: "He's very level-headed and I think he is the kind of person who would help to calm a really chaotic situation. Of course, I have to prepare for the worst."

His brother James Wood, who lived in Dallas, said: "In a situation like this when a plane just disappears, it leaves you with a lot of questions. There is a shock, a very surreal moment in your life." Waiting for news involved "a lot of pain". Nevertheless, he said, "We are not giving up hope because if there are no answers, there is no finality. So, miracles have happened, and I'm sure you've heard of the man that was floating out on the ocean for a year, and survived."

Their mother, Sandra Wood, was stoical. She told *USA Today*: "Do you want to know how it feels to lose a son at the age of fifty? It's devastating. But I know in my heart that Philip's with God, and I plan to be there with him, because I have a deep faith in my God."

Mrs Wood, from Keller, Texas, said her son had recently been back to the US to visit family and she knew he would be on the flight. "He was a wonderful person and very intelligent," she said. "I could talk forever about him. He's my son, and any mother would be proud of their son."

Philip's own two sons were in their twenties.

"Philip Wood was a wonderful man," his ex-wife Elaine Wood wrote on her Facebook page. "Although we were no longer married, he is still family. His sons and I just want peace and quiet right now."

The provincial government of Sichuan said celebrated

calligraphers 72-year-old Zhang Jinquan and 64-year-old Meng Gaosheng were also on the flight, along with 73-year-old Zhao Zhao Fang, a calligrapher and retired professor who had collected a number of titles for her work.

"I can only pray for a miracle," said Daniel Liau, organizer of the calligraphic and painting exhibition in Malaysia. "I feel very sad," said Mr Liau. "Even though I knew them for a short time, they have become my friends."

Wang Linshi and Xiong Yunming were also aboard the flight as part of a group of Chinese artists touring Malaysia. Their son Wang Zhen heard the announcement on television from another hotel where he had been staying. He said his mind "was a mess" following the bad news.

Twenty-nine-year-old Sanved Kolekar arrived at Beijing Airport on the Sunday morning, expecting to meet his father, 63-year-old Vinod Kolekar, his mother, 59-year-old Chetana Kolekar, and younger brother, 23-year-old Swanand, who were travelling from Mumbai via Kuala Lumpur to attend the convocation ceremony of Sanved, who had recently completed his PhD in astrophysics.

"My parents are on the flight," he said. "They were supposed to come here at 6.30 am. I don't know what happened. They haven't given me any information, it's very difficult because I don't under-stand the local language."

Two Australian couples, 59-year-old Rodney Burrows and his 54-year-old wife Mary, and 54-year-old Catherine Lawton and her 58-year-old husband Robert from Brisbane, had been on the flight together. Robert Lawton's brother David said: "Dad phoned this morning and said 'Bobby's plane's missing'. I couldn't believe it. I still can't believe it. We just want to know where it is, where the plane's come down, if there's anything left."

Neighbours said the Lawtons were kind and doting grandparents who enjoyed travelling. Their neighbour Caroline Daintith recalled: "They mentioned in passing they were going on another big trip and they were really excited."

They had made several trips abroad and were looking forward to their holiday.

"Their kids had moved on. All successful, all happy," said Mandy Watt, another neighbour. "This was their time."

Similar things were said of Mr and Mrs Burrows. "They are lovely people," a friend said. "They were excited about the trip."

Sydney couple Yuan Li and Naijun Gu were also onboard. They left two young daughters.

Two New Zealanders were on Flight MH370: 50-year-old Ximin Wang and 39-year-old mining engineer Paul Weeks, who was on his way to start a dream job in Mongolia. He left behind his wife Danica and sons, Lincoln, three, and Jack, ten months, at their home in Perth, Western Australia.

Danica Weeks told reporters she was praying for a miracle to bring him home. "I can't give up hope," she said. "I would love him to walk through that door, hold him one more time."

On his last day at home with their two sons, Paul had told her that he had left a wedding ring and watch in the house.

"He said: 'If something should happen to me then the wedding ring should go to the first son that gets married and then the watch to the second'," Danica told Australia's Nine News. "I said, don't be stupid, come back, I'll give them to you and you can give them to the children."

The time since the plane had gone missing was telling on her. "It feels like an eternity with no finality to it," she admitted.

Later, she said: "You want an outcome but not the worst one. I really hope he is out there somewhere. I am praying for a good outcome. I pray he is out there."

A former soldier, Paul moved his young family to Perth, Western Australia, in 2011 to make a new start after their home in Christchurch, New Zealand, was devastated by a series of earthquakes. Shortly before he left, Mr Weeks took a series of photographs of his family.

"He took lots of photos because he had his Surface [tablet] which he was taking with him, so we did video 'selfies' of the four of us," his wife explained. She hoped that her husband had looked at the photos on board the aircraft.

"He is the most amazing husband and father," she added. "He spent so much time with his children. Lincoln was like his father's little shadow, and of course he adored Jack." The worst part, she said, was having to explain his absence to their sons. She told Lincoln: "You know Daddy has gone away… and on the way Daddy got lost."

But hope was fading. "It's a rollercoaster ride," she admitted. "One moment I'm fine and the next I'm a wreck. I wish I felt I had some positivity that he was coming back."

US electronics firm Freescale Semiconductor, based in Texas, said 20 of its employees were among the passengers: 12 were from Malaysia and eight from China. The company was organizing round-the-clock support for their families.

Freescale vice-president Mitch Haws said: "These were very important people. It's a big loss for the company."

There were no Britons among the passengers. However, two Chinese students who had been studying in England were among those missing. Originally from Mongolia, 26-year-old Yue Wenchao was studying at Hull University.

Hull University said: "We are deeply concerned to hear that Yue Wenchao, a student in the final stages of his MSc degree with Hull University Business School, may be among the passengers on board the missing Malaysia Airlines flight. Although we are not able to confirm these reports at this time, our thoughts are with the friends and relatives of all those affected."

Next to a picture of his girlfriend, Wenchao posted "See you in Beijing!" on the Chinese micro-blogging site Sina Weibo an hour before he boarded the flight. She was still awaiting his arrival.

Rachel Smith, a fellow student at Hull, said: "We met in the library and he would always come over and say hello and have a little chat. You could tell he was well-loved by his closest friends and was extremely hard-working and dedicated to getting the best grade that he could."

According to his Facebook page, Wenchao was keen on horse-riding and reading.

"He was a very nice person and hard-working," said another student, Chloe Li. "It is shocking to think somebody so close to home was on the missing plane. We have all seen it and it is very sad. But this makes it more awful. We hope Yue is safe."

Another student named Zhang Jiamen said: "Yue was my close friend's room-mate. Yue is a nice man and always studied very hard. Everyone has good things to say about him. We all want him to be found safe and well."

"There is a real element of shock on campus," said student Simon Taylor. "It is bad enough knowing about the missing plane, but when it has affected someone who lived here, it really hits home. It could have been any of us."

French lecturer Eleonore Cossade said: "It's scary to think this horrible event has possibly involved one of our students. We desperately hope everyone is found safe and well."

Also on Flight MH370 was Dr Yuchen Li, who had recently graduated from Cambridge with a doctorate in engineering. The previous month Churchill College had congratulated him on his marriage to partner Mingfei Ma and the university confirmed he had begun a "high-flying" job in Beijing. They said it was "heartbreaking" a member of their alumni was on the missing flight and that their thoughts were with his family.

A Malaysian student who was educated in the UK was also on board. Forty-six-year-old Huan Peen Chan had spent four years studying at Sunderland University and played the organ at his local church during his time as a student. Graduating in engineering, he then returned to his native Malaysia, where he married and had two sons.

John Cropley was pastor of Sunderland Free Church when Chan – known as Jesse – was a member of the church. "It's devastating. He was just one of life's lovely guys," he said. "He was so gentle, he had a lovely smile and he was so willing. He played the organ and piano in church. He was never grumpy, always the same and you could depend on him – just a gentle soul."

Chan had graduated in 1995, but the former pastor said members of the church kept in touch and would regularly visit him and his wife Janet in Malaysia.

"We cannot imagine how Janet and the boys are feeling," Cropley added.

Jun Kun, a 35-year-old Hollywood stuntman who had been making a film in Malaysia, was also on board. He was married with two children.

The oldest person on the flight was 79-year-old Lou Baotang, a Chinese national whose calligraphy has been cited in reference books by many cultural institutions in China, Britain and the US.

Among five small children on the plane – three from China, two from the US – the youngest was Wang Moheng, who was eleven weeks short of his second birthday. The toddler was going back to Beijing after a holiday with his parents and grandparents, and travelling with three family members, aged 40, 64 and 60, all of Chinese nationality. According to China's state-run newspaper, *The People's Daily*, Wang's father worked for Boston Consulting Group, while his mother, 32-year-old Jiao Weiwei, left her job at an Internet company to take care of him.

"She often said that she smells her baby from head to toe," recalled one of Jiao's former colleagues. "People at the company really loved her."

One name on the passenger list drew special attention. It was that of 35-year-old Maimaitijiang Abula. He was a Muslim and ethnic Uighur from the troubled Xinjiang region. However, the Chinese media said he was a member of the delegation of artists and a Communist party member, suggesting he was considered a loyal citizen.

The list also included Memetjan Abra, an ethnic Uighur painter from the northwestern region of Xinjiang.

"He is a good painter, husband and father," his wife Memetjan Abra told Xinhua, China's state newswire. She also said she had spoken to Abra on Friday night, just before he boarded the plane.

Zhao Qiwei, the head of his company's environmental materials department, was taking a holiday with his wife and child, while Wang Rui was taking his wife and three other family members on what he hoped would be a dream trip abroad. There was also a Beijing student who had been travelling abroad for the first time and a young man returning home after being conned into taking a job on a dodgy building site.

Then there was Bian Liangjing. The salary he had received as a junior medic in China was so poor that he ditched it for a £4,000-a-year job as a construction worker in Singapore. Some 18 months earlier, he had kissed his eight-month-old son goodbye and had only ever spoken to him since via Skype. Liangjing had finally saved enough for a visit home to Hebei in northeast China, and the cheapest flight was MH370.

As evening drew on, those waiting at the Lido Hotel grew weary. The hotel made up rooms for them and said costs would be taken care of. Some vowed to wait until they had firm news on the fate of their loved ones but there was little point in waiting up – the rescuers could not search in the dark and the planes were returning to their bases. The only news that Malaysia Airlines could give them was that "at this stage, our search and rescue teams from Malaysia, Singapore and Vietnam have failed to find evidence of any wreckage". It added: "The sea mission will continue while the air mission will recommence at daylight."

CHAPTER EIGHT

TERROR IN THE SKIES

Forty-eight hours after the disappearance of Flight MH370 and the mystery of its fate was no nearer resolution. One baffled Malaysian official said the plane appeared "to have disintegrated at around 35,000 feet". But aviation experts said it was impossible to know whether it had disintegrated until wreckage was found. None had.

Meanwhile, the FBI had moved in when it appeared as many as four other passengers had suspect passports. Transport minister Hishammuddin Hussein explained the authorities "do not want to jump the gun", but had "informed the counter-terrorism units of all relevant countries". It later transpired that the CIA, FBI and MI6 were all on the case.

Chinese state media reported that one of the passport numbers listed on the manifest belonged to a man from Fujian, eastern China, who was safe and well. He told police his passport had not been lost or stolen. The name alongside his passport number was not his; apparently it belonged to another Chinese man. Two other passengers were thought to be travelling on stolen Ukrainian passports.

There was a brisk trade in stolen passports in South East Asia and Interpol had 40 million lost or stolen passports recorded in its database – equivalent to the entire population of Poland. Some 270,000 passports belonging to Britons alone are lost or stolen every year.

Gangs have targeted Thailand mainly because of the very large numbers of Europeans, Americans and Australians who visit each year. An unnamed agent of Thailand's Department of Special Investigations told the *Bangkok Post* that the country was also attractive because it is relatively easy to enter and leave, and "you can negotiate with some law enforcement people". Local officials, it seems, do not see the forgery of foreign, as opposed to Thai, passports as a serious offence.

In the 1980s, Thai criminal gangs employed hotel staff, tour guides and sex workers to steal not just tourists' travellers cheques but also passports (without a passport the travellers cheques could not be cashed). Once credit cards started to replace travellers cheques, the gangs coupled this expertise with sophisticated techniques of document falsification and became bespoke providers of fake documents. They also imported passports, driving licences and ID cards, doctoring and selling them on to anyone prepared to pay. Some hard-up travellers even sold or "rented" their passports to gangs.

The passports were commonly faked by printing a false photo page – with the holder hoping it would never be checked. Other methods included persuading a look-alike to get a legitimate replacement passport, then paying them to allow another person to use it.

By 2012, around 20 Thai gangs were involved in various forms of passport fraud. An undoctored stolen passport sells for between US$1,500 and US$3,000 (£900 and £1,800), depending on its condition, nationality and the number of years it has left to run. Italian, British, Spanish and other European passports fetch about US$1,000, while Israeli passports cost US$1,500–$2,000 (£900–£1,200) and Canadian passports can go for up to US$3,000 (£1,800).

With 12 million visitors a year, Phuket is a hotbed of identity theft, and complaints of lost and stolen passports are rife. According to Italian honorary consul Francesco Pensato: "We have 250,000 Italian tourists a season, so it's normal that some lose a passport."

Pensato confirmed that Luigi Maraldi had had his passport stolen while in Phuket in July 2013, and that the number of the passport used to board Flight MH370 was the same as that of the stolen passport. This ruled out any possibility there was another man named Luigi Maraldi with the same date of birth on board.

"Any flight of that size in Asia would be carrying a couple of people with false passports," explained Clive Williams, who studied counter-terrorism at Australia's Macquarie University. "When you think about the number of passports that have been stolen or [have] gone missing around the world, it could be related, but it is probably not."

However, others insisted if it was a coincidence, it was a remarkable one. "What are the chances that one person boards a Malaysia Airlines plane on a stolen Caucasian passport?" asked one aviation expert who asked not to be named. "Maybe it is one in a thousand. Two? One in a million."

Hugh Dunleavy, an executive vice-president at Malaysia Airlines, said it was not the carrier's responsibility to validate a passport.

"We just need to make sure that if we see a passport, it doesn't look like it has been forged and it has a legitimate visa," he explained. "If it all looks legitimate and everything else about the customer is legitimate, we will load them on the plane."

Another spokesman for the airline added that all passports had been checked and the photographs in them had matched the passengers. However, the Malaysian authorities promised to tighten security at Kuala Lumpur after criticism that it had grown lax in recent years. But they could not duck their share of the responsibility. Interpol Secretary General Ronald Noble said: "Whilst it is too soon to speculate about any connection between these stolen passports and the missing plane, it is clearly of great concern that any passenger was able to board an international flight using a stolen passport listed in Interpol's databases. This is a situation we had hoped never to see. For years Interpol has asked why countries should wait for a tragedy to put prudent security measures in place at borders and boarding gates. Now, we have a real case where the world is speculating whether the stolen-passport holders were terrorists, while Interpol is asking why only a handful of countries worldwide are taking care to make sure that persons possessing stolen passports are not boarding international flights. For the sake of innocent passengers who go through invasive security measures prior to boarding flights in order to get to their destination safely, I sincerely hope that governments and airlines worldwide will learn from the tragedy of missing Flight MH370 and begin to screen all passengers' passports prior to allowing them to board flights."

However, Interpol themselves came under fire. It turned out that only law enforcement agencies could check passports against the database; airlines were not allowed to use it. If border control or immigration failed to carry out the checks, then nobody else would, said security expert Tom Craig.

"Anybody who needs to do a criminal check should be able to do it," he said. "Whether your passport is properly checked depends on where you are."

Interpol then said it had begun a study which would allow banks, airlines and hotels to use the database. Nevertheless Secretary General Ronald Noble warned that basic steps were not being taken, which "could lead to another 11 September, another 7 July [the 2005 London bombings], another 11 March in Madrid". He went on: "If Malaysia Airways and all airlines worldwide were able to check the passport details of prospective passengers against Interpol's database, then we would not have to speculate whether stolen passports were used by terrorists to board MH370."

Why the two men posing as the Italian Luigi Maraldi and the Austrian Christian Kozel were using false documents was still unclear. Terrorism was a possibility, but they may have been asylum seekers. Six Syrians hoping to secure refugee status in Sweden had been detained for over a month at Phuket International Airport after attempting to fly to Stockholm via Beijing on Greek passports. Local media outlet *Phuket Wan* revealed that the group said they had chosen to fly through Phuket and Beijing because other refugees had reached Sweden using the same flight path.

However, the man posing as Maraldi was bound for Copenhagen, while "Kozel" was heading for Frankfurt. The two men had purchased their one-way tickets at the same time from China Southern Airlines, which codeshares with Malaysia Airlines, through a travel agency in the Thai beach town of Pattaya the day before they boarded the ill-fated Flight MH370.

Terrorism expert Rohan Gunaratna from Singapore's Nanyang Technological University added fuel to the fire, saying there were only two categories of traveller using stolen passports: criminals and terrorists.

"To blame Malaysian authorities for this is probably unfair," he said. "They have to get it right all the time and potential hijackers just have to get through once."

Malaysia Airlines' officials addressed the question of terrorism at a press conference. It could have been a reason why the plane appeared to have attempted to turn back. It seemed hijackers could have got on board when it became clear that there had been serious lapses in security at Kuala Lumpur International Airport (KLIA).

A few months earlier, the Malaysian Anti-Corruption Commission and police formed a flying squad to investigate allegations of immigration officers accepting bribes to allow illegal immigrants into the country. At the same time human trafficking gangs were reportedly selling a "Get into Malaysia package" for US$750 (£450). Once the purchaser was smuggled into the country they were given a fake "MyKad", the identity document compulsory for all Malaysian citizens.

Malaysia's deputy Minister of Home Affairs Wan Junaidi Tuanku Jaafar admitted "there may be some black sheep among the staff".

A senior police official said people armed with explosives and carrying false identity papers had in the past tried to fly out of Kuala Lumpur International Airport.

"We have stopped men with stolen passports and carrying explosives, who have tried to get past airport security," he explained.

According to the CCTV footage, the two passengers on Flight

MH370 using the stolen Italian and Austrian passports were of Asian appearance.

"I am still perturbed," said the Malaysian Interior Minister, Ahmad Zahid Hamidi. "Can't these immigration officials think? Italian and Austrian passport holders, but with Asian faces."

However, the question of identification was further muddied by Malaysia's Department of Civil Aviation chief, Azharuddin Abdul Rahman, who said that the two men were of "non-Asian" appearance. When asked by a reporter "roughly" what they looked like, he said: "Do you know of a footballer by the name of Balotelli? He is an Italian. Do you know how he looks like?"

Mario Balotelli played for Manchester City before being sold to Milan and was famous for his Mohican haircut, sometimes bleached blond.

A reporter then asked: "Is he black?"

Azharuddin Abdul Rahman replied: "Yes."

Then he added, enigmatically: "I don't want to dwell on it."

Biometric information and CCTV footage of the men has been shared with Chinese and US intelligence agencies, who were helping the investigation. According to Interpol, more than a billion air journeys were taken over the previous year without the passenger's details being checked with their stolen-passport database. The two passports stolen in Thailand had not been checked by any country against the database, so it was unclear how many times they had been used.

Naturally the investigation was causing tension and China urged Malaysia to "step up its efforts" in the search for the missing plane. Its foreign ministry spokesperson Qin Gang said: "We have a responsibility to demand and urge the Malaysian side provide relevant information to China correctly and in a timely manner."

Global Times, a newspaper close to China's ruling Communist Party, wrote a scathing editorial.

"The Malaysian side cannot shirk its responsibilities," it said. "The initial response from Malaysia was not swift enough. There are loopholes in the work of Malaysia Airlines and security authorities. If it is due to a deadly mechanical breakdown or pilot error, then Malaysia Airlines should take the blame. If this is a terrorist attack, then the security check at Kuala Lumpur airport and on the flight is questionable."

Fear of airborne terrorist attacks had stalked the aircraft industry since 9/11. However, Flight MH370 had gone missing, while the fate of the three planes that hit the Twin Towers of the World Trade Center in New York and the Pentagon in Virginia was all too evident. However, the fourth plane was downed in rural Pennsylvania. The question was asked whether MH370 had been taken over by hijackers and resistance by the crew or the passengers had caused the plane to crash in the sea.

United Airlines Flight 93 had taken off without a hitch from Newark Liberty International Airport in New Jersey heading for San Francisco on 11 September 2001. The Boeing 757-222 had reached its cruising altitude of 35,000ft (10,668m) before the terrorists struck. Once they had taken over the cockpit, they switched off the transponder; that had been done on two of the planes. On the third, Flight UA175, which hit the south tower of the World Trade Center, the transponder's code was repeatedly changed to confuse air traffic controllers.

The passengers were then herded to the back of the plane. There they used cellphones and the on-board phones to call 911 and contact loved ones. Only then did they discover that the hijacking of UA93 was not an isolated incident. The World Trade Center was already in flames. Four passengers in particular – Todd

Beamer, Tom Burnett, Mark Bingham and Jeremy Glick – would be hailed as heroes because their phone conversations provided the most detailed account of the passengers' plan for a life-or-death charge on the cockpit after the terrorists had seized control.

Beamer, a 32-year-old account manager for a Silicon Valley software firm, made a lengthy 911 call to Lisa Jefferson, a veteran GTE (General Telephone & Electronics Corporation) operator outside Chicago. As the plane lurched and passengers screamed, Beamer, a devout Christian, and his seatmates recited the Lord's Prayer. Jefferson joined in. More screams were heard while Beamer and others recited the Twenty-third Psalm: "Yea, though I walk through the valley of the shadow of death, I will fear no evil…"

Then Beamer said: "Are you guys ready? Okay, let's roll!"

The cockpit voice recorder that records the last 30 minutes of every flight was recovered at the crash site. Most of the tape was taken up with the howling wind created by a plane travelling fast at low altitude but the recording also includes the seven-minute death struggle in which muffled voices are heard screaming and cursing in both English and Arabic as the plane plunged toward the earth. The families of the victims were permitted to listen to the tape, something that is not normally made public. The recording opened the possibility that some of the victims were killed before the plane hit the ground. Investigators who recovered remains from the crash site brought possible stab wounds and lacerations to the attention of FBI pathologists. But the FBI said that "the catastrophic nature of the crash and fragmentation" left them unable to draw conclusions. Could a similar fate have befallen Flight MH370?

There are other cases of hijacking going wrong. On 23 November 1996, Ethiopian Airlines Flight 961 had just taken off from Addis Ababa when three young men stormed into the cockpit. At least two of them had been hidden in the lavatory before takeoff and they appeared to be drunk. Arming themselves with an axe, they insisted the pilot fly them to Australia, where they would seek political asylum. The two men – unemployed high-school graduates – and a nurse said they were opponents of the Ethiopian regime and had recently been released from jail. They had read in the in-flight magazine that the Boeing 767 could make the trip to Australia on a fuel tank – and the plane had just been refuelled. Forty-two-year-old Captain Leul Abate explained that they had only taken on enough fuel to reach Nairobi, the next leg of their route. It would not take them even a quarter of the way to Australia. But the hijackers did not believe him and threatened to blow the plane up, brandishing what they said was a bomb, but later turned out to be nothing more than a bottle of liquor in a sinister wrapping.

Captain Abate headed out over the Indian Ocean, but instead of heading for Australia, he hugged the coastline. Noticing they were still within sight of land, the hijackers forced the pilot to head east. Abate then headed for the Comoro Islands that lie been mainland Africa and Madagascar.

Meanwhile, the hijackers took little interest in the passengers, who remained calm. If they were going to rush their captors, they figured, it would be better to wait until the plane was on the ground in case the hijackers detonated the threatened explosives. Running short of fuel, one engine stopped, causing the aircraft to drop from 39,000ft (11,887m) to 25,000ft (7,620m). The hijackers were enraged that their instructions were not being followed.

At this point the pilot made an announcement on the intercom, telling passengers to put on their life jackets, but not to inflate them. A second announcement told them to assume the crash position with pillows on their heads, braced for a hard landing. There was some panic.

The plane was now out of fuel and the second engine stopped. Flight 961 had been given clearance to land at Moroni Airport on Grand Comoro. Knowing they were not going to make it, Captain Abate decided to ditch the plane in shallow waters off the beach at Mitsamiouli at the north end of the island, but the hijackers fought to wrest control of the plane from the pilot. Suddenly the plane banked to the left; the wing tip and the engine hit the water and the plane somersaulted and broke up. Both pilot and co-pilot survived; the hijackers did not. Eight of the crew died, along with 122 of the 160 passengers. Many died because they had inflated their life jackets, which prevented them from swimming out of the water-filled fuselage. Until 9/11, Flight 961 was the deadliest hijacking in history.

While terrorism could not be ruled out, the police were investigating whether any passengers or crew on the Flight MH370 had personal or psychological problems that might shed light on the mystery, along with the possibility of a hijacking, sabotage or mechanical failure.

"Maybe somebody on the flight has bought a huge sum of insurance, who wants family to gain from it, or somebody who has owed somebody so much money," Malaysian police chief Khalid Abu Bakar said. "We are looking at all possibilities. We are looking very closely at the video footage [taken at Kuala Lumpur International Airport]. We are studying the behavioural pattern of all the passengers."

There was also a chance that one of the ground crew had smuggled a bomb on board. Or could a hijacking have been pulled off by a stowaway? Security specialist Philip Baum cited two known incidents of stowaways who dressed as aircraft staff and boarded planes as recently as 2012 – two in Iceland, and another who went from Shanghai to San Francisco hidden in an electrical compartment. He said: "At almost every major international airport, criminal activity of one type or another takes place in what are supposed to be sterile zones. It is certainly a possibility that, in an airport the size of Kuala Lumpur's, individuals, with or without the knowledge of the crew, could have managed to secrete themselves on board."

Meanwhile, the authorities continued to take an interest in the pilot Zaharie Ahmad Shah. It was not unknown for a pilot to commit suicide by crashing his plane and killing his passengers. On 31 October 1999, EgyptAir Flight 990, a scheduled flight from Los Angeles International Airport to Cairo with a stopover at JFK, crashed into the sea, some 60 miles south of Nantucket, killing all 217 on board. While the Egyptian Civil Aviation Authority claimed that the crash was due to mechanical failure, America's National Transportation Safety Board maintained that it was suicide. The crash occurred while the captain was out of the cockpit and the 59-year-old co-pilot Gamil al-Batouti was heard on the cockpit voice recorder saying farewell prayers. As the Boeing 767 plunged into the Atlantic he concluded "*Tawakilt ala Allah*" (or "I put my faith in God"). His precise motives remain a mystery.

On 19 December 1997 SilkAir Flight 185 from Jakarta to Singapore crashed into the Musi River near Palembang in southern Sumatra, killing all 97 passengers and seven crew members on board. Using computer modelling, the National Transportation Safety Board (NTSB) concluded the crash was the result of deliberate movements of flight control, most likely by the captain.

Royal Air Maroc Flight 630, bound for Casablanca on 21

August 1994, crashed approximately 10 minutes after takeoff from Agadir-Al Massira Airport. All 44 passengers and crew on board were killed. Investigators found the plane's autopilot was disconnected by the aircraft's 32-year-old pilot, Younes Khayati, who then went on to deliberately crash the aircraft.

LAM Mozambique Airlines Flight 470 from Maputo International Airport, Mozambique, crashed into the Bwabwata National Park in Namibia on 29 November 2013, en route for Quatro de Fevereiro Airport, Angola, killing all 33 people on board. The cockpit voice recorder captured several alarms going off during the descent, as well as repeated loud bangs on the door from the co-pilot, who was locked out of the cockpit until shortly before the crash. The conclusion was that Captain Herminio dos Santos Fernandes had manually changed its autopilot settings with the "clear intention" of crashing the plane. The plane's intended altitude was reportedly changed three times from 38,000ft (11,582m) to 592ft (180m). In Caprivi Strip, which is over 3,280ft (1,000m), this is below ground level.

Then on 9 February 1982, Japan Airlines Flight 350 on a domestic scheduled passenger flight from Fukuoka crashed on the approach to Haneda Airport in Tokyo Bay. The cause of the crash was traced to 35-year-old Captain Seiji Katagiri's deliberate engaging of engine number two and three's thrust-reversers, which slow the plane, in flight. The first officer and flight engineer tried to restrain him and regain control of the aircraft. Despite their best efforts, the McDonnell Douglas DC-8's descent landed down in shallow water, some 908ft (277m) short of the runway. Twenty-four of the 174 people on board died.

Katagiri was one of the first on the rescue boat (he told rescuers that he was an office worker to avoid being identified as the captain). Later he was found to be suffering a mental illness prior to the incident (he had been experiencing hallucinations and feelings of depression). Ever since he was granted one month's leave in November 1980 for a "psychosomatic disorder", his wife had worried about his neurotic behaviour. He once summoned police to his two-storey house near Tokyo, saying he was convinced it was bugged, but a thorough search turned up no eavesdropping devices. On three occasions, his employers had urged him to see a psychiatrist. Charged with murder, he was found not guilty by reason of insanity.

However, MH370's pilot, 53-year-old Zaharie Ahmad Shah, could have hardly been less like Katagiri. His friends described him as an "aviation tech geek" who loved his job so much, he even spent his days off tinkering with the Boeing 777 flight simulator he had set up at his gated property in a suburb on the outskirts of the Malaysian capital, where many airline staff live as it provides quick access to the Kuala Lumpur International Airport.

"We used to tease him. We would ask him, 'Why are you bringing your work home?'" said a fellow pilot, who had known him for 20 years. "He knew everything about the Boeing 777. Something significant would have had to happen for Zaharie and the plane to go missing – it would have to be total electrical failure."

Friends who saw him the day before the flight told the *New Straits Times* that he had been in a "jovial" mood.

Pictures posted by Shah on his Facebook page show a simulator with three computer monitors, a tangle of wires and several panels. On YouTube, it appeared he was a fan of cross-dressing British stand-up comedian Eddie Izzard. Videos he has "liked" included one entitled *How To Cut a Glass Bottle in Half With Fire and String* and another entitled *The God Delusion* – the title of one of a series of books by British atheist Richard Dawkins. In his spare time, he followed Dawkins' Foundation for Reason and

Science, along with academic and technical lectures, and videos on how to make balloon animals and one about cycling.

According to his friend Peter Chong, while Shah was a Muslim, he was not especially committed or pious, but he attended mosque for Friday prayers as most Malaysian men do. Neither disaffected nor marginalized, he certainly did not fit the profile of an Islamic terrorist.

Shah had been a keen footballer at school, a promising science student and had trained as a pilot in the Philippines before joining Malaysia Airlines in 1981. He had no financial difficulties, no obvious enemies, and, as an instructor, devoted students.

"Everyone who knew him, liked him," said one 43-year-old captain who has known Shah for nearly 25 years. "I flew as his co-pilot many times. He has always been a good pilot, very professional."

Ritzeraynn Rashid, who flew with Shah in the 1980s and 90s, said that he was "always smiling and very cheerful. We shared a lot of good memories. We were like brothers."

Shah's passion for aviation went beyond the Boeing 777, though. Other photos posted by him on Facebook show he was an avid collector of remote-controlled, miniature aircraft, including a lightweight twin-engine helicopter. Additionally, he was certified as an examiner to conduct simulator tests for pilots by Malaysia's Department of Civil Aviation.

"You could ask him anything and he would help you – that is the kind of guy he is," said a Malaysia Airlines co-pilot who had flown with Shah.

Officials from Malaysia Airlines said it was impossible to believe that he would in any way be to blame for the disappearance of the aircraft. A respectable family man and a grandfather, a mild-mannered social and political activist who raised money for the poor and loved his job so much that he badgered friends into using his flight simulator to share his pleasure, he was also known for turning up to community events with large quantities of food he had cooked, and had volunteered to be a poll monitor at recent elections.

But it was not just suicidal pilots that the authorities had to watch for. On 29 May 2003, onboard Qantas Flight 1737 from Melbourne to Launceston, passenger David Robinson, a computer engineer from Britain, produced two sharpened wooden stakes from his pocket. He stabbed flight attendant Denise Hickson and flight purser Greg Khan. Despite repeated blows to the back of the head, Khan tackled Robinson and unbalanced him. Passengers including Canadian ex-soldier Derek Finlay held Robinson down and tied him up, and the plane returned to Melbourne Airport, where Robinson was duly arrested. He was also found to be carrying aerosol cans and cigarette lighters, which could have been used as a rudimentary flamethrower.

Robinson admitted attempting to hijack the plane, which he intended to crash into the Walls of Jerusalem National Park in Tasmania. This, he said, would release the Devil from his lair and bring about Armageddon. He also admitted that he had intended to hijack aircraft on two previous occasions. Due to mental impairment, he was found not guilty of attempted hijack of an aircraft, attempted murder and grievous bodily harm and was committed for psychiatric treatment. There were 50 people on board the plane.

Clearly the passengers and crew on board Flight MH370 had to undergo the utmost scrutiny.

In March 2015, British pilot Simon Hardy, a senior Boeing 777 captain who flew the Asian air routes for seventeen years, claimed to have solved the mystery. After seeing television coverage of a woman and child in China "waiting for Daddy to come home", he began his own investigation. According to Hardy, the last voice from the cockpit was that of the captain, Zaharie Ahmad Shah, despite earlier communications having been handled by the first officer Fariq Abdul Hamid. This was a crucial clue.

"The person flying doesn't operate the radio," said Hardy. "The radio calls are done by the first officer all the way through until the last one, which is done by the captain – three minutes before the transponder went off. The plane is up and running. Shah has to do the radio because he's told the other pilot to check something in the cabin."

The transponder was turned off and air traffic control lost contact with MH370 at a point over the China Sea where four flight information regions (FIRs), divisions of airspace, intersect.

'Then it did something quite remarkable," continued Hardy. "It did a U-turn and reached landfall exactly at the border between Malaysia and Thailand. Then it flew along the border. It went in and out of those two countries' airspace eight times. I've never seen anything like that, but it is a good way to cause confusion between the controllers."

Hardy was convinced that this did not happen by accident.

"This is probably very accurate flying rather than just a coincidence," he said. "As both air traffic controllers in both those countries would probably assume that the aircraft was in the other country's jurisdiction and not pay it any attention."

Hardy believed that the aircraft may have been depressurised by this time and the passengers had lost consciousness.

After flying along the border, the plane headed to Penang, but made three turns in quick succession at the island.

"It does a strange hook," he said. "I spent a long time thinking about this and eventually I found that it was a similar manoeuvre to what I'd done in Australia over Ayers Rock."

As the airway goes directly over Ayers Rock you don't actually see it otherwise because it disappears under the nose of the aircraft.

"The clue was Ayers Rock," he said. "I have done the same manoeuvre there, to look down and get a great view. Somebody was taking a last emotional look at Penang."

Then things fell into place.

"I thought of this at 5 a.m., went downstairs and researched where the air crew were from. Hamid came from Selangor and Shah from Penang. Someone did a nice long turn and looked down on Penang. It's perhaps the only clue to the perpetrator."

The last military radar fix, at 18.22 GMT, put MH370 over the Andaman Sea heading towards the navigation waypoint Anoko, not far from the Andaman Islands. Hardy then went to work on the seven Inmarsat "handshakes", each of which put the plane somewhere on an arc. He analysed the ratio of the distances between the most reliable arcs and calculated the speed needed to cover the distances. The points where MH370 crossed arcs four, five and six lay on a heading of 188. Extending the line northwards brought him to a point just two nautical miles from Anoko.

"This was the eureka moment," he said.

The final handshake – on the seventh arc – was at 00.19 GMT on 8 March. At this point, the fuel must have been nearly exhausted. While the ATSB thought that MH370 then crashed, Hardy believed that the plane was landed on the water then sank close to a trench in the seabed. This would explain why no debris has been found, and could happen only if someone were at the controls. And the plane had been ditched, Hardy calculated, some one hundred nautical miles from where the ATSB were searching.

David Learmount of *Flight Global* spent weeks checking Hardy's calculations before posting them on the website.

"Nobody has argued with it," he said.

An ATSB spokesman commented: "We can confirm we have been in telephone and email contact with Captain Hardy." He described the pilot's work as "credible".

Shah's family dismissed this as a smear. His elder sister Sakinab Shah released a statement, branding these claims "disgusting" and claimed that "none of you have the right to blame Captain Zaharie Ahmad Shah for any wrongdoing." She also accused people of pouncing like "hungry starved wolves with their twisted and conniving interpretations."

But the "rogue pilot" theory has continued to gather pace. Even Nik Huzlan, a retired Malaysian Airlines pilot who knew Captain Shah for thirty years, believes someone in the cockpit caused the plane to cease communications and turn around from its scheduled flight path, saying, 'your best friend can harbour the darkest secrets.'

CHAPTER NINE

DEATH WISH

The idea that pilot suicide could have been responsible for the loss of Flight MH370 and the deaths of the 239 people on board gained new credence on 24 March 2014 when Germanwings Flight 4U9525 from Barcelona to Düsseldorf smashed into the Alps, killing all 150 on board. It soon became clear that the co-pilot, twenty-seven-year-old First Officer Andreas Lubitz, had crashed the plane deliberately.

Born in 1987, Andreas Günter Lubitz grew up in Neuburg an der Donau, Bavaria and Montabaur in the German state of Rhineland-Palatinate. He was the son of a nice middle-class family. His father was a successful business executive, and his mother was a piano teacher. As a boy Andreas had dreamt of flying and his ambition had always been to become a pilot.

"He was a real fanatic," said a friend. "His room was plastered with pictures of planes and the Lufthansa logo everywhere. Pictures of old planes, new planes, of the largest planes – everywhere you could see aviation stuff, even over his bed."

He turned up at his local glider club at the age of fourteen or fifteen, saying he wanted to learn to fly. Club member Peter Rueker remembered him as "rather quiet but friendly". His wealthy parents could afford to pay for lessons.

The club's chairman, Klaus Radker, said: "It was his dream to fly from an early age and it was a dream he began to fulfil here, so when he went on to gain his commercial licence and fly planes like the Airbus he was very happy and proud."

After one year of lessons under dual control, he was able to fly a glider on his own, then to pilot light aircraft. By then a commercial pilot, he renewed his light aircraft flying licence only months before the fatal incident and, soon after, attended the club's barbecue with his girlfriend. Nobody at the club noticed anything strange in his demeanour.

"He seemed normal. Proud of his job after so much training. He seemed happy," described Radker. "I always found him a friendly, if very reserved, person. Open and polite … I find it hard to believe that Andreas, who dreamt of flying and of being a pilot, would deliberately fly his plane into a mountain and kill all those people. If that is true it also means that the results of all the psychological tests he would have had to take to be a pilot were wrong."

After obtaining his glider pilot's licence as a teenager, Lubitz was accepted as a Lufthansa trainee once he had finished the tough German preparatory exams at the town's Mons-Tabor High School. He then had to pass a number of rigorous assessments – including psychometric testing of a candidate's ability to work under pressure and handle stress – to be accepted on its pilot training programme. Only between 4 and 8 per cent of those who apply are offered a place. Lubitz was one of them.

In 2008, he started pilot training at the Lufthansa Flight Training

School in Bremen, moving on to the Lufthansa Airline Training Center at Goodyear, Arizona, between July and November 2010. Training lasts between twenty-nine and thirty-three months. Throughout that time more vetting takes place. Rigorous checks are scheduled throughout a Lufthansa pilot's flying career. However, while standard psychometric assessments were made, no information was gathered by speaking to friends and relatives or piecing together the candidates' life stories. This was thought to be too intrusive and something that could possibly deter potential trainees.

A year into his flight training, Lubitz took several months off. It appeared he had suffered some sort of a breakdown and he informed the Flight Training Pilot School that he had had a previous episode of severe depression.

"During his training at Lufthansa flight school, Andreas was listed as unsuitable for flight duties, because he spent one-and-a-half years in psychological treatment, and so he had to repeat courses," a source told *The Times*. "The reason was evidently depression."

"Apparently he had a burnout, he was in depression," said the mother of a classmate.

A special coding, "SIC", was entered on his licence, meaning that he needed a "specific regular medical examination", according to Germany's federal aviation office.

Lufthansa twice refused to renew Lubitz's medical certificate over concerns about his mental health. He took an extended break from his pilot's training for "medical reasons" after November 2008. The following April, Lufthansa declined to renew his medical certificate because he was taking medication for depression, and again refused Lubitz's request to renew his medical certificate three months later. However, just two weeks after that, the company did renew his certificate.

Around that time, Lubitz flew gliders over the area where the crash would later occur. Dieter Wagner, a senior member of the Luftsports Club Westerwald, said: "Andreas took part in a training course with my niece, who was a good friend of his, in the Alpes-de-Haute-Provence region. He was passionate about the Alps, obsessed even."

After his break in training, Lubitz was deemed fit to resume. Lufthansa Chief Executive Carsten Spohr stated: "He not only passed all medical tests, but also his flight training, all flying tests and checks. A hundred per cent fit to fly, without any limitations."

Lubitz went on to complete his training and spent an eleven-month waiting period working as a flight attendant at Lufthansa before gaining his commercial pilot's licence. This earned him the nickname "Tomato Andi", teased for handing out the tomato juice. For a young man who wanted to fly transatlantic jets, finding himself working as a "trolley dolly" was demeaning.

Nevertheless, in 2013, he went on to become a first officer, not with Lufthansa but with the flag-carrier's less glamorous short-haul budget airline Germanwings, and moved into an apartment in Düsseldorf, the airline's hub. He had clocked up only 630 hours of flying before his final flight, compared with the six thousand hours flown by the captain of the fatal flight, father of two, Patrick Sonderheimer.

Nobody suspected anything was wrong. Even Lubitz's girlfriend, a twenty-six-year-old teacher, was aghast when she heard what he had done. However, a previous girlfriend described him as "tormented" and "able to hide secrets" during their five-month relationship. A twenty-six-year-old airline hostess living near Frankfurt indentified only as Maria W., she said they had met on a flight. There followed a tempestuous romance, comprised of largely fleeting assignations in hotel rooms around Germany and the rest of Europe.

According to Maria, Lubitz was a man who appeared "nice and open-minded" in public, but needed constant reassurance in private.

"He was a good man who could be very sweet," she said. "We spoke a lot about work, and then he became another person. He became agitated about the circumstances in which he had to work, too little money, anxiety about his contract and too much pressure."

They split up when she felt unable to deal with his growing problems and his increasingly volatile temper.

"During conversations he'd suddenly throw a tantrum and scream at me," she explained. "I was afraid. He even once locked me in the bathroom for a long time."

Maria said she thought he had crashed the plane because he knew his illness would prevent him progressing to Lufthansa jets. It was later revealed that he had problems with his eyesight.

"He did it because he realized that because of his health problems his big dream of a job with Lufthansa, a job as captain and as a long-haul pilot, was as good as impossible," she said.

When she heard about the crash she recalled that he had told her the previous year that he was going do "something that will change the whole system and then all will know my name and remember it".

"It didn't make sense at the time but now it all does," she commented. She also revealed that he would wake up at night in a sweat, screaming in terror: "We're going down."

It also emerged that, after they had split, he made a desperate attempt to win her back, buying her a new Audi only weeks before the crash. She declined the gift, but he had bought another Audi for himself, putting his finances into a precarious condition.

Despite concerns about his health, Lubitz was a fitness fanatic. Johannes Rossbach, who lived two doors away from him in Montabaur, said he would regularly see the pilot jogging through the neighbourhood's quiet streets.

"He was very polite. He would always say hello and goodbye. There certainly seemed nothing out of the ordinary about him," said Rossbach. "I can't believe someone like that would kill 149 other people. It's something that absolutely needs investigating and proving before we can believe it."

Lubitz regularly ran half-marathons alongside his father Günter. But he was becoming increasingly unwell. In the weeks before the crash, he was being treated in Uniklinik hospital in Düsseldorf, but he hid his condition from his employer.

After Lubitz's flat had been searched, the prosecutors' office in Düsseldorf said: "There are sick notes saying he was unable to work, among other things, that were found torn up, which were recent and even from the day of the crime, supporting the assumption based on the preliminary examination that the deceased hid his illness from his employer and his professional colleagues."

And there were serious causes for concern.

"Several years ago before obtaining his pilot's licence the co-pilot was in a long period of psychotherapeutic treatment with noticeable suicidal tendencies," the prosecutors' statement reported. "In the following period and more recently more visits to specialists in neurology, psychiatry and psychotherapy occurred, with corresponding sick notes." However, there was no record of "suicidal tendencies or aggression" in his more recent visits, the statement said.

It was also reported that Lubitz had lost 30 per cent of his vision, possibly caused by stress. Problems with his eyesight were thought to have affected his mental stability, but he did not want to take time off sick for fear that it might endanger his career.

Dr Samuel Lepastier, the head of research at Paris Diderot University, said it was highly likely that Lubitz was suffering from schizophrenia, given the strong medication he was taking – notably Olanzapine, an antipsychotic drug whose side effects include "changes in personality, thoughts or behaviour; hallucinations and suicidal tendencies". Dr Lepastier thought that Lubitz's initial severe depressive episode "could have been the first manifestation of schizophrenia, which often first strikes in one's early twenties".

"Patients can then feel they have fully recovered only to discover years later that their condition is worsening and they require treatment that could be very long," he explained. "It is at this stage that the temptation to commit suicide is greatest. What we don't know is if Lubitz had been told he might require hospitalization and realized his career was over."

Dr Lepastier also said that there was a "documented desire" among schizophrenics with suicidal tendencies to "end their life by breaking their body into pieces".

In the run-up to the crash Lubitz kept a diary recording how disturbed he was – ironically it was called his "happiness diary", which was supposed to be part of his psychotherapy. Between its pages were found prescriptions for powerful antidepressants and tranquillizers. Lubitz had also been prescribed mirtazapine, an antidepressant whose side effects can include suicidal thoughts, yet not one of the amazing total of forty-one doctors who saw him before the disaster thought to contact the airline. They were, of course, bound by oaths of confidentiality and were under an obligation to respect their patients' privacy.

Investigators also found a sheet of paper that Lubitz had left. Dated 22 March, it was headed "Decision Sunday", followed by "BCN" – the airport code for Barcelona. Two days later, he flew a plane from Barcelona into a mountainside.

In the days before the crash, Lubitz had researched three topics on the internet – "medical methods of treatment", "ways to commit suicide" and "cockpit doors and their security provisions". He also seems to have had a practice run on the outbound leg of the journey. On the flight from Düsseldorf to Barcelona, Lubitz was ordered to descend to 35,000 feet by French air traffic control, but set the autopilot to descend to 100 feet – the same setting he would later use to crash the plane. Seconds later, he changed the setting to the maximum altitude of 49,000 feet. In the minutes that followed, he repeatedly changed the setting to different altitudes. None of the changes had a noticeable effect on the aircraft's trajectory, the director of the BEA Rémi Jouty, said.

"Air traffic control had given the descent order and the plane had already commenced its descent," he commented. "I can't speculate on what was happening inside his head; all I can say is that he changed this button to the minimum setting of 100 feet and he did it several times."

The captain was out of the cockpit at the time and Lubitz alone was in control of the Airbus A320.

The fatal return flight began with jovial exchanges in German between the two airmen. But Lubitz's mood had suddenly changed, becoming more laconic as the captain began to discuss the landing checklist. Chillingly, when Captain Sonderheimer tried to brief Lubitz on plans for a routine landing in Düsseldorf, the first officer replied: "Hopefully" and "We'll see".

Sonderheimer then made a routine announcement to passengers, apologizing for the late departure. In the twenty minutes that follow, Captain Sonderheimer told Lubitz that he had not had time to go to the lavatory during their stopover in Barcelona. It was at this point that Lubitz suggested that the captain leave him alone in the cockpit and offered to take over.

"You can go now," he told him.

It was a full two minutes before Captain Sonderheimer took him up on the offer. The captain's last message to the Marseille air traffic control said: "*Merci* Germanwings one eight Golf." That was at 10.30 am. Twenty-seven seconds later, he left the cockpit, saying to Lubitz: "You can take over."

Once he had gone, Lubitz flicked a switch on the central console, locking the door behind him. Doing this ensured that even the supposedly fail-safe emergency override system could not be operated.

Half-a-minute later, Lubitz switched off the autopilot and changed the altitude setting from 38,000 feet to 100 feet. Almost immediately, the aircraft began its descent. An automated alarm then sounded, announcing "sink rate" – a warning to pilots that the plane was descending too fast.

Passengers were probably aware that something was seriously wrong. Conditions were clear below 15,000 feet and they would have been able to see the mountains rapidly coming up towards them. According to the preliminary crash report: "The rest of the descent was performed outside of any clouds in visual flight conditions with visibility greater than 10 kilometres."

Meanwhile Lubitz sat in silence, ignoring the pleas of the captain and air-traffic controllers during the eight-minute descent.

"For God's sake, open the door!" shouted Sonderheimer above the screams of passengers behind him.

In the final two minutes before the crash, "noises similar to violent blows on the cockpit door were recorded on five occasions," the crash report stated. It was thought that the captain tried to break down the door with a crowbar, but the door was armoured against terrorist attacks, making this impossible.

Another automated warning went off, saying: "Terrain! Pull up! Pull up!"

Captain Sonderheimer shouted again: "Open the damn door!"

On the tape, the passengers could be heard screaming once more. The final catastrophic crash was followed by a terrible silence.

The report found no technical fault with the plane and said both pilots were "above standard" in terms of proficiency. The French prosecutor, Brice Robin, concluded that the co-pilot crashed the plane intentionally. Listening to the cockpit voice recorder, he said: "We heard the captain ask the co-pilot to take control, then we hear the noise of a seat that goes back and a door open, we can assume he went to relieve himself. The co-pilot was alone. It is at this moment that the co-pilot manipulates the buttons of the flight monitoring system to action the descent of the plane. The action of this selection of altitude can only be deliberate."

With the autopilot off, Lubitz set a new flight path to descend to 100 feet on a steady descent of 3,500 feet per minute.

Captain Sonderheimer returned from the bathroom and typed in the code alerting his colleague that he wished to return to his seat. He got no response. Fearing his co-pilot might be incapacitated, he entered emergency code, intended to override the locking mechanism. This failed because Lubitz had set the system to block the override, an innovation that had been introduced following 9/11, to keep terrorists out of the cockpit.

"We hear the captain then speaks via an interphone to speak to the co-pilot," reports Robin. "No response of co-pilot, he taps on door, no response of co-pilot, all we can hear is the sound of breathing until impact suggesting the co-pilot was alive until impact. Apparently he was breathing normally, so this is not someone having a heart attack, for example."

Concerned by the unexplained alteration to the flight plan and loss of altitude, air traffic control operators attempted to contact the flight deck on its assigned radio frequency. After getting no response, they tried the international distress frequency, but again without success. At 10.35 an international emergency was declared by air traffic control.

For Lubitz, the crash could not come fast enough. He accelerated the plane as it plummeted towards the mountainside.

"Several times during the descent, the pilot changed the automatic pilot settings to increase the aircraft's speed," said the BEA.

The passengers realized something catastrophic was happening when they saw Captain Sonderheimer trying to break through the cockpit door. As panic spread throughout the aircraft, the captain made one last effort to smash through the door. Passengers began screaming, knowing that they were on a collision course with the Alps.

In the cockpit, an automatic alarm sounded to warn that the plane was too close to the ground. Lubitz ignored it. At a height of 6,175 feet, Germanwings Flight 4U9525 disappeared from the air-traffic controllers' radar screens. By now the passengers and cabin crew were fully aware of the imminent disaster. The aircraft clipped the tip of a ridge, then crashed into the face of the remote mountain Les Trois Eveches, between the communes of Digne-les-Bains and Barcelonnette. At 10.42 am, air traffic control informed the French search-and-rescue national control centre.

Robin concluded: "The most plausible and realistic conclusion is that the co-pilot, through a deliberate decision, refused to open the cabin door to the captain and activated the button to start the descent. There was a deliberate desire to destroy this plane."

The result was mass murder.

"When you have 150 people in your responsibility, I can't call this suicide," he said.

In the wreckage, mobile phones were found that recorded the last few moments of the tragic flight by passengers at the back of the plane. Footage included scenes of chaos and passengers screaming "My God" in several languages. *Paris Match* said: "We have checked and rechecked its authenticity." However, according to the magazine the scene was "so chaotic that one cannot distinguish anyone, but the screams of passengers reveal that they were perfectly conscious of what was about to befall them. One can also hear metallic blows, at least three times, suggesting the captain tried to break down the cockpit door with a heavy object," *Paris Match* reported. "Towards the end after a stronger shock, the screams intensify. Then nothing."

Paris Match also reported that Lubitz "had put an oxygen mask on" in the final minutes and was breathing steadily.

The ghastly business of the collection of the victims' remains and belongings then began. Forensic experts identified 150 genetic profiles from more than two thousand body parts recovered from the crash site at Le Vernet in the Provence Alps. These were matched to DNA samples provided by victims' families, so at least their loved ones had some remains to bury. That may be scant consolation for these unfortunate people, but they are still better off than the relatives of those on board Flight MH370.

It was only when the bereaved families arrived at the crash site that they were told that their loved ones had not died in a tragic accident, but had been the victims of a mass murderer. Lubitz's parents, Günter and Ursula, learnt that their son had deliberately caused the disaster as they arrived at the press conference organized by French prosecutors. They were devastated and were quickly separated from the relatives of the victims. Bernard Bartolini, mayor of a town near the crash site, said he had spoken to Günter.

"He is carrying on his back the entire weight of the drama. He is a man whose life has broken down," pointed out Mr Bartolini.

Back in Germany, Lubitz's elderly aunt later condemned her nephew for causing the crash.

"He did that on purpose, flying into the ridge. It is difficult for the family to deal with it," stated his seventy-nine-year-old Aunt Brigitte. "I knew nothing of mental health problems or eye problems. When we celebrated family occasions, he was happy. He never spoke about stress at work. We were proud that he had fulfilled his childhood dream."

The father of one of the British victims said that: "if there was a motive or a reason for the act we don't want to hear it." Phillip Bramley, whose twenty-eight-year-old son Paul died in the disaster, warned airlines to do more to look after their pilots.

He said: "I believe the airlines should be more transparent and their pilots looked after properly. We put our lives and our children's lives in their hands."

The three British victims included seven-month-old Julian Pracz-Bandres, who was travelling to Manchester with his Spanish mother, Marina Bandres Lopez-Belio. She had bought tickets for the Barcelona-Düsseldorf flight at the last minute because there were no direct flights available.

Also among the victims were sixteen children from Joseph

Koenig School, who had texted their friends shortly before take-off to tell them how much they were looking forward to coming home. Fourteen girls, two boys and two teachers from the school in Haltern am See, in North Rhine-Westphalia, died. At an emotional press conference held at the town hall there, Bodo Klimpel, the mayor, announced: "For many families in Haltern am See the world has stopped turning today. We stand speechless before a tragedy in which eighteen young people – sixteen schoolgirls and boys from the tenth grade and their teachers – have not come back from their exchange programme in Spain."

Bass-baritone Oleg Bryjak and contralto Maria Radner, singers with Deutsche Oper am Rhein, were also on the flight.

"I think that the victims only realized what was happening at the last minute," said prosecutor Robin. "We only hear screams in the last seconds. Death was instant."

A woman called Sandrine, whose uncle died in the crash, said that Robin's conclusion came as something of a relief.

"You can hear screams, but they didn't live through eight minutes of total horror," she said.

Robin confirmed: "The victims only realized what was happening at the last minute. We only hear screams in the last seconds."

Three days after the crash around three hundred families were driven to a memorial chapel at Le Vernet, within sight of the crash site. As they stepped off their coach in the shadow of the mountain, an elderly couple burst into tears and were quickly offered assistance by Red Cross counsellors. Dozens of police vans shielded the mourners from the world's media as they held hands and walked past the flags of the fifteen countries whose nationals were among the dead, before attending a brief commemorative ceremony. Each family placed a rose at the base of a memorial plaque. After they returned to the coaches, a helicopter ferrying recovery workers to the crash site flew overhead, continuing their difficult and dangerous search on the rocky slopes. They had first arrived at the crash site within hours of the crash to find that the plane had disintegrated. No piece was larger than a car and debris was spread out over two kilometres of rocky mountainside. They found no survivors and no single body was found intact. As referred to earlier, the victims' remains would undergo DNA tests to help identification in the following weeks, hopefully granting families some kind of closure.

At the same time, around forty relatives of the five crew members gathered in Seyne-les-Alpes, the medieval mountain town that has become an operational headquarters for emergency services. Then the two convoys switched locations without ever crossing paths.

"I would like us all to spare a thought for the co-pilot's family," said Stephane Gicquel, of the National Federation of Victims of Collective Attacks and Accidents. "They are going through an unbearable tragedy. It was right to separate them from the others but it is devastating."

The European Aviation Safety Agency afterwards issued instructions to airlines that there must be two airline crew in the cockpit at all times, including one qualified pilot. This would bring European regulations into line with those in the US. Aviation doctors also called for pilots to undergo more frequent and comprehensive laboratory tests, particularly those designed to establish whether there are traces of psychotropic drugs and narcotics in their systems.

Soon a chilling warning about the dangers of flying came closer to home. Forty-seven-year-old British Airways pilot Robert Brown was convicted after using a claw hammer to hit his estranged wife

Joanna at least fourteen times, following a bitter and costly divorce battle. He had been due to fly a Boeing 747 jumbo jet from Heathrow to Lagos the next day, but rang in at the last moment to say he was too sick to work. Brown stated at his trial: "I didn't want to be another husband who kills his wife and then himself and nobody cares. I thought if I got to work I could crash an aircraft, or fly to Lagos and crash it there. I wanted to make a statement."

He was convicted of manslaughter rather than murder after the jury concluded that he had been suffering extreme stress due to his marital breakdown. Like Lubitz, Brown was a competitive runner, whose disturbed mental state had passed unnoticed.

CHAPTER TEN

OFF THE MAP

The nightmare continued for relatives in the Metropark Lido Hotel, who were kept away from the prying eyes of TV crews and press photographers behind the well-guarded double-doors of the hotel's second-storey ballroom. More than 100 of them were corralled there, while others hid in the corners of the hotel's atrium, quietly weeping.

Groups of helpers from the California-based Buddhist charity Compassion Relief Tzu-Chi Foundation tried to comfort the families and friends of those missing on the flight. Leading a team of more than 20, Yun Jizeng said: "We will give psychological comfort to these families at this terrible time. We hope that through our comfort we can bring some peace to these families and help them feel the warmth of society in this most difficult time of their lives."

One young man approached local journalists to ask for the latest news, complaining that the airline had not told them anything.

Asked if he was a family member, he said: "Yes – all my family is up there, except for me." Then he burst into tears.

Zhang Zhilin, from the nearby metropolis Tianjin, was found on a stairway. He was awaiting news of his 26-year-old cousin.

"I don't understand," he said. "We have all the technology in the world these days, and how is it that we can't locate them?"

A widely forwarded post on the messaging app WeChat said: "MH370, we hope the radar can see you. If you copy, keep flying at your current height until you reach your destination. We'll clear the way for you. Everybody is more than happy to let you be the first to land. The sky is clear, with temperature in Beijing at five degrees Celsius, a little bit cold. Please wear your coats to keep warm. Remember to hug your family and friends after you disembark. They love you, they really do."

Not everyone was so optimistic. The trending topic on Sina Weibo, China's most popular microblog, was "Pray for Malaysian Air". Many users posted emoticons of flickering candles and beating hearts.

As the hunt for wreckage continued, the Malaysian Maritime Enforcement Agency sent a patrol ship to gather a sample from an oil slick off Vietnam to determine whether the oil came from the flight or a passing ship as no debris was found nearby. The search in the South China Sea widened.

Speculation began that the aircraft had broken up at 35,000ft (10,668km), spreading the debris over a wide area. Otherwise, if the plane had plummeted intact from its cruising altitude, breaking up only on impact with the water, search teams would have expected to find a fairly concentrated debris field. Dozens of military and civilian vessels have been criss-crossing waters beneath the aircraft's flight path, but have found no confirmed trace of the lost plane and the search area was being widened to a circle of 50 nautical miles (58 miles or 92km) from where it was last seen on radar.

Andrew Charlton, an aviation consultant at Geneva-based Aviation Advocacy, said: "The 777 is a very reliable aircraft, Malaysia is a very good airline and it had cleared takeoff and landing. For the aircraft not to have been able to talk to the ground is really most alarming and concerning. It just disappeared off the face of the map. When this happens it's catastrophic and instantaneous, and it's very difficult not to assume an explosion was involved at that point."

However, such a scenario did not necessarily involve foul play. Mechanical failure could have caused the plane to break up. But one source drew parallels with the Air India Flight 182 lost over the Atlantic in June 1985 and the Pan Am Flight that crashed at Lockerbie in December 1988. Both planes had been downed with bombs and both were cruising at around 31,000ft (9,448km) at the time.

There was a false alarm when a Singaporean search plane spotted a yellow object, some 7–8 miles (11–12km) southwest of Tho Chu island, resembling a life raft. Rescue helicopters and ships searching for the jet rushed to investigate, but it simply turned out to be moss-covered debris floating in the ocean. Ships had failed to find the rectangular object previously seen that was thought to be one of the missing plane's doors. Debris plucked from the South China Sea by a Vietnamese helicopter proved to be cable from a ship and the oil taken from the slick in the South China Sea came from a ship, not the missing aircraft.

The following day the radius of the search area was doubled to 100 nautical miles (115 miles or 185km). Searchers had found nothing in the initial search area. Earlier claims that an oil slick and piece of debris that had been seen came from the plane appeared to be untrue.

Malaysia's Department of Civil Aviation chief Azharuddin Abdul Rahman said: "Unfortunately we have not found anything that appears to be objects from the aircraft, let alone the aircraft. We are looking at the possibility of a stolen passport syndicate. As far as we are concerned, we have to find the aircraft. We have to find a piece of the aircraft, if possible. There are many experts around the world who have contributed their know-how and knowledge… we are equally puzzled."

Rahman also said that the luggage of five passengers who had checked in to the flight but did not board was removed before departure. They were looking at "every angle" to explain the plane's disappearance.

Four other passengers had failed to check in. One, named Kaiden, said he was angry at his girlfriend and co-worker because "she'd gotten sick and I had to cover her. I was working on that, missed my flight to China. Grew angrier. But for the grace of God we'd be on that flight."

Malaysia Airlines then revealed that the two passengers using stolen passports were Iranians. An old school friend who lived in Kuala Lumpur said that they had stayed with him after arriving from Tehran a few days earlier, though intelligence sources thought the pair had begun their journey in Qatar. He added that they had bought fake passports in Iran because they wanted to migrate to Europe. One of them had dyed his hair before the flight in an attempt to look more like his fake passport photograph.

Both Malaysia and neighbouring Thailand, where the passports were originally stolen, host large and established Iranian communities.

Meanwhile, Thai police were hunting another Iranian named Khadim Ali, who had bought the tickets for the two passengers who boarded Flight MH370 using stolen passports. He had purchased them from a travel agent after insisting on inexpensive flights and paid in cash. Benjaporn Krutnait, owner of Grand Horizon Travel, said she had been asked to book flights for Europe on 1 March 2014. Initially, she arranged tickets on Etihad and Qatar Airways flights for two customers but when they did not fly that day, Ali asked her to book the cheapest flights to Europe – in this case, a Malaysia Airlines' flight from Kuala Lumpur connecting through Beijing and on to Amsterdam.

Eventually Krutnait purchased the two tickets for the doomed flight, which would have arrived in time to make a transfer from Beijing to Amsterdam. From there, the men would have caught separate connecting flights to Copenhagen and Frankfurt. When she tried to contact Ali on 10 March on the Tehran-based cellphone number he had provided, the line was dead.

It was long suspected that Iranians were responsible for the downing of Pan Am Flight 103 in retaliation for the Iranian Airbus shot down in Iranian airspace over the Persian Gulf in July 1988. Iran Air Flight 655 was taking off from Tehran on its way to Dubai when it was blown apart by a surface-to-air missile fired from United States Navy guided missile cruiser USS *Vincennes*. The US government said that the crew incorrectly identified the Iranian Airbus A300 as an attacking F-14 Tomcat fighter – a plane made in the United States and operated at that time by only two forces worldwide, the United States Navy and the Islamic Republic of Iran Air Force. The *Vincennes* was signalling warnings on a military channel which the civilian plane could not receive. Consequently, the airliner was unable to respond to several requests for it to change course. However, some analysts have blamed the captain of the *Vincennes* for reckless and aggressive behaviour in a tense and dangerous environment – the previous year Iran had tried to close the Persian Gulf to stop the flow of oil and the US Navy had been sent to keep it open.

In 1996, the United States and Iranian governments reached "an agreement in full and final settlement of all disputes, differences, claims, counterclaims" relating to the incident at the International Court of Justice. As part of the settlement, the United States agreed to pay US$61.8 million (£36.7 million) in compensation to the families of the Iranian victims. However, the United States has never admitted responsibility, nor apologized to Iran for the incident.

As the downing of Pan Am Flight 103 took place over land a lot is known about it. The Boeing 747 had takeoff from London's Heathrow at 6.25 pm on 21 December 1988, 25 minutes behind schedule. It was carrying 243 passengers and 16 crew members.

The plane was bound for New York; on board were both Britons and Americans heading for the States for the Christmas holiday, among them 35 of a party of 38 students from Syracuse University, who had been studying abroad and were going home to spend the holiday with their families. Others were on more serious business. Brent Carisson, a Swede and chief administrative officer for the United Nations Council for Namibia, was flying to New York to sign an accord on Namibia's independence from South Africa.

Thirty-seven minutes after takeoff, Flight 103 was cruising at 31,000ft (9,500 m) – six miles high – over the Scottish border. The plane was flying at 434 knots (500 mph or 804 km/h). James MacQuarrie, the 55-year-old American pilot, and his 52-year-old co-pilot Raymond Wagner, switched on the autopilot and settled down for a routine transatlantic flight. As they gave their instruments one final check, the air traffic controller at Shanwick gave them radio clearance for their flight out over the Atlantic.

Outside it was cold and dark. During the climb intermittent rain had splattered against the cockpit's reinforced windscreen. Now the 115-knot (132-mph or 213-km/h) jet stream was creating light turbulence. Below them clouds at round 16,000ft (4,877m) covered the Scottish landscape.

A precisely 7.02 and 50 seconds pm, over the tiny village of Castlemilk, three miles south of Lockerbie, a terrorist bomb planted in a Toshiba radio-cassette recorder in the plane's baggage hold exploded. It weighed less than a pound.

The baggage hold was in front of the plane's left wing. The bomb went off just 25 inches (63.5cm) from the skin of the fuselage. The shock wave punched a hole in the side of the plane, sending burning baggage out into the freezing air. It ripped through the jumbo's main electrical cables. Captain MacQuarrie had no chance to make a Mayday call. The flight recorder only recorded the sound of the explosion before its power failed.

Then came the full force of the blast. It stretched the fuselage skin. Within a second, it had blistered and busted; around the 5ft (1.5m) hole, the edges "petalled" outwards in a starburst. The blast was also channelled upwards, causing the passenger compartment to buckle and break. Everyone on board had heard the explosion. Shockwaves also travelled down the air-conditioning, reverberating through the cabin. Those in the forward section and on the left-hand-side of first class on the upper deck suffered minor injuries from the blast.

People sitting directly over the left wing felt the plane disintegrating beneath them. The starburst around the hole was rapidly unzipping. One petal tore back as far as the wing. A second ripped forward 43ft (13m) and a third tore around under the belly of the plane, almost up to the windows on the starboard side. A passenger plane is held together only by its thin skin; unlike a car it does not have a metal chassis. With such severe damage, the forces on it will rip it apart.

Amid the sound of tearing metal and popping rivets, the aircraft nose-dived. The flight control cables had been severed by the explosion and it rolled to the left. The left side of the forward fuselage ripped open and the entire nose section twisted upwards and to the right. The cockpit turned all the way around until it was facing the back of the plane, then broke way. It hit the right wing, knocking the inner engine off its stanchion. The nose hit the tailplane, causing extensive damage. From there the body of the plane travelled in an increasingly steep flight path until, by 19,000ft (5,791m), it was travelling vertically downwards.

On the way down, both the nose and the fuselage spilled their contents. The aerodynamic effects of the plane's steep dive tore the remaining three engines off the wings. Around 9,000ft (2,743m), the rear of the cabin broke away and disintegrated, scattering bits of the cabin floor, the rear baggage hold and the landing gear across the fields and houses below.

It was a quiet Wednesday evening in the small Scottish village of Lockerbie when Myra Bell looked out of the window of her flat. As she gazed out at the southern edge of the village, she saw a huge black object falling from the sky. She realized that it was a passenger plane and all those on board were going to die.

A wing filled with more than 200,000 pounds (91,000kg) of aviation fuel crashed into Sherwood Crescent at 200 miles an hour (322 km/h). It crashed into the houses at the end of the crescent, leaving a huge crater 100ft long and 30ft deep (30m x 9m). The fireball could be seen 6 miles away (10km). Those living in the remainder of the crescent felt the terrible heat and air being sucked out of their houses. The force of the blast sent Robert Jardine flying across his living room. When he looked out of the window he saw that the home of his neighbours, the Flannigan family, had disappeared completely. The body of 10-year-old Joanne Flannigan was found in the wreckage of their home. Those of her parents, 44-year-old Thomas and 41-year-old Kathleen, were never found. The home of John and Rosaleen Somerville and their children, 13-year-old Paul and 10-year-old Lyndsey, had disappeared too. Their bodies had been vaporized in the impact. Eleven residents of Lockerbie died in the disaster.

The main body of the fuselage landed 350 yards (320m) from the Townfoot service station, which went up in flames. Now the ball of fire that had been number three engine hit the town. The nose section buried itself in a hilltop 3 miles (5km) from the east of the Lockerbie; the other engines hit the Netherplace area. One hit the water main.

Nearby, the seismic station belonging to the British Geological Survey registered 1.6 on the Richter Scale. The main impacts occurred at 19.03, 36.5 seconds and 46 seconds after the bomb had gone off. Some local residents thought there had been an earthquake; others that two low-flying fighters had collided. Keith Paterson thought that the Chapelcross nuclear power station had exploded. He only discovered what had really happened when he grabbed a torch and went outside. In the dark, he saw two eyes looking up at him: they belonged to a dead body. All 259 people on board Flight 103 were dead – or soon would be. It was later discovered that some people had miraculously survived the crash and may have lived for some time after they hit the ground, but by the time they were found, it was too late.

The first fire engine arrived at 7.10 pm, eight minutes after the bomb went off. Soon, rescuers were combing the area for survivors. It was an impossible task. Wreckage from the plane was spread over an arc 80 miles (129km) long. The local police and volunteers, including a police surgeon from Yorkshire named Dr Fieldhouse, continued the search for survivors for 24 hours. All those they found were dead. Captain MacQuarrie's body was discovered on the grass outside the cockpit. Inside the nose section rescuers found another 15 bodies, nearly all of them cabin crew or first-class passengers.

Christine Copeland found the body of a young woman in her garden; it turned black before her eyes. The body of a young man landed on the front doorstep of Esther Galloway. For the next three days she had to step over it while the accident investigators went about their work. But most of the bodies were not intact and the emergency services had to set about the grim task of finding body parts.

Every body part had to be examined by a doctor, photographed, numbered and tagged before it could be removed. Some pieces had to be dug out of the rubble or cut from the wreckage of the aircraft. This was a gruesome and laborious business. Some bodies were not removed until five nights after the crash.

From the beginning, it was clear that the crash site was also a crime scene. One week before Flight 103 was blown from the skies, the American Embassy in Finland received a message from an anonymous caller, saying: "There will be a bombing attempt against a Pan American aircraft flying from Frankfurt to the United States." After the downing of Iran Air Flight 655, Tehran Radio said that the passengers and crew would be avenged in "blood-splattered skies". The US air force command warned that the Iranians would strike back in a "tit for tat fashion" producing "mass casualties". They went on to say: "We believe Europe is the likely target for a retaliatory attack due to the large concentration of Americans and the established terrorist infrastructures in place."

As the bomb had gone off when the plane was at cruising altitude, wreckage was scattered over 850 square miles (2,200 sq km). A singed page from the instruction manual for the Toshiba radio-cassette player had been found in a field, 60 miles (96.5km) away. Even so, large pieces of fuselage – memorably half the cockpit – were found. If MH370 had exploded at a high altitude, it may be possible to find similar pieces of wreckage.

In a gruesome coincidence, while the search of MH370 was going on a new report by Al Jazeera, the satellite TV channel based in Qatar, established that the Pan Am bombing was organized by the Iranians. This had long been suspected, but the new evidence seemed to confirm that Tehran conspired with Syrian-linked terrorists to target the American airliner in revenge for the accidental shooting-down of the Iranian Airbus in the Persian Gulf, earlier that year. The only man to be jailed for the bombing, Libyan security officer Abdelbaset al-Megrahi, may after all have been innocent of planting the bomb. He stoutly maintained he was innocent before he was controversially released from prison on compassionate grounds in 2009 and died at home in Tripoli in May 2012. The new investigation indicated that while Colonel Gaddafi's regime may have been involved in the planning, and Libya accepted responsibility for the bombing and paid compensation in order to get sanctions lifted, it was Iranians who planted the bomb. Had Pan Am 103 not been delayed and had exploded over the Atlantic as planned, its fate could well be as mysterious as that of Flight MH370.

Air India Flight 182 blew up over water. On 23 June 1985, the Boeing 747 was on its way from Montreal-Mirabel International Airport to Heathrow, before flying on to Indira Gandhi

International Airport, New Delhi. The transponder had been picked up by Shannon air traffic control when the aircraft disappeared. A bomb in a Sanyo tuner in a suitcase in the forward hold had exploded, causing rapid decompression and the break-up of the aircraft in mid-air. No Mayday call was heard. The wreckage plunged into 6,700ft (2,042m) of deep water off the southwest Irish coast, 120 miles (193km) off the shore of County Cork. All 329 people on board were killed.

Fifty-five minutes before the explosion on Flight 182 a second bomb aimed at Air India Flight 301 exploded at Narita International Airport, Tokyo, killing two baggage handlers and injuring four others. Sikh militant Inderjit Singh Reyat, a Canadian national, was convicted of the bombing. In 2003, he pleaded guilty to manslaughter and was sentenced to 15 years.

Flight 182 was on radar when it was blown up. Two hours later a cargo ship spotted bodies floating in the water. They showed signs of hypoxia, caused by lack of oxygen. Eight exhibited "flail pattern" injuries, indicating they had left the plane before it hit the water. Twenty-three bodies showed evidence of receiving injuries from a vertical force; they had been killed when the plane hit the water. Twenty-one bodies were found with no clothing, including three children. Some had suffocated; others had drowned. Within two-and-a-half weeks the black boxes had been located and recovered.

Like Air France Flight 447, Air India Flight 182 had disappeared at its cruising altitude without a Mayday, but its debris was quickly spotted. But where was the debris of Flight MH370?

While air investigators were considering the possibility that MH370, too, had fallen prey to terrorists, a group calling themselves the Chinese Martyrs Brigade claimed responsibility.

The outfit, unheard of before then, sent an email that read: "You kill one of our clan, we will kill a hundred of you as payback." Officials believe it to be a hoax. The message was delivered through an encrypted Hushmail service, which made it virtually impossible to trace. However, it emerged that Taiwan had received a warning about potential terrorist attacks on China three days before the Malaysia Airlines' plane vanished. Authorities on the island were told of plans for atrocities at Beijing Airport and the city's subway system. This was reminiscent of Lockerbie.

CIA Director John Brennan said the possibility of a terror link could not be ruled out but "no claims of responsibility" over the missing jet had "been confirmed or corroborated".

"Clearly this is still a mystery, which is very disturbing," he added.

CHAPTER ELEVEN

A CHANGE IN DIRECTION

The Malaysian police quickly established that one of the passengers travelling on stolen passports was 19-year-old Pouria Nourmohammadi Mehrdad, who was planning to seek asylum in Germany and was not thought to have been a member of a terrorist group. His mother was waiting for him in Frankfurt and had been in contact with police. She called the Malaysian authorities to inform them of her concern when her son did not get in touch with her. The second man, 29-year-old Delavar Seyed Mohammadreza, was also thought to have been an asylum-seeker with no terrorist connections.

CCTV footage showed them boarding the plane. One was wearing a short-sleeved blue T-shirt, the other was dressed in a long-sleeved black shirt.

"The more information we get, the more we are inclined to conclude it is not a terrorist incident," said Interpol's Ronald Noble at a press conference in Lyon, France. "Eventually, we'll able to exclude that they were involved in conduct that might have involved the plane to disappear and focus on eliminating the human trafficking ring that allowed them to travel."

Sanctions against Iran have plagued the economy and high unemployment led many young Iranians to travel to Europe, North America or Australia – legally or illegally. The two Iranians on Flight MH370 were well educated and, it was said, were "looking for a place to settle". It seems they were travelling to Europe to try and find work and boarded the doomed plane in search of a better life.

They had travelled from Doha, the capital of Qatar, boarding the plane with their Iranian passports.

"We know that once these individuals arrived in Kuala Lumpur on 28 February, they boarded Flight 370 using different identities, a stolen Austrian and a stolen Italian passport," said Noble.

Malaysia, Indonesia and Thailand were popular stop-off points for Iranians looking to settle in the West. Many arrive on tourist visas and contact local travel agents and people-traffickers.

"Thanks to everyone who has prayed for me," Mehrdad posted on his Facebook page after he arrived in Malaysia. When a friend in Tehran asked what he was doing there, the excited 19-year-old replied with a winking icon and a cryptic line. "Bro, Mohsen, I am leaving too."

According to his Facebook page, Mehrdad had studied software engineering at the Islamic Azad University of Parand, in the suburbs of Tehran. His mother left a message of her own on his page.

"Hopefully you all have a few days' rest and then come home. Have fun," she said.

He and Delawar did just that. Pictures added to the page show they visited the Petronas twin towers and other tourist sites in Kuala Lumpur. These were his last posts on the site.

Swedish police had been contacted by a relative of Delawar who lived in Malmo, saying that he was travelling on a false passport in the hope of claiming political asylum in Sweden.

Mehrdad's friend who had put them up for a week in Kuala Lumpur told the BBC: "I met him the first day he arrived in Malaysia. He said he was staying for three to four days but was eventually going to Germany. His final destination was Frankfurt. We went together to book the flights, and I even had his booking number and was checking his flight status online all the time. That's why I remember which flight he was taking: I had seen his flight number. I accompanied them to the airport."

Then the two asylum-seekers began their preparations.

"The last night before the flight, they stayed at mine," he continued. "Mehrdad's friend was dying his beard and hair, and was checking the colour to match with the picture of a passport. He was making himself look like the photo in the passport."

Mehrdad's friend was evidently puzzled.

"When we printed the tickets, I realised that the passports were fake," he explained. "My friend's passport belonged to Austria and my friend's friend had a passport belonging to Italy… They had three flights to take: from Kuala Lumpur to Beijing, from Beijing to – I think – Amsterdam, and from Amsterdam my friend was heading to Frankfurt and his friend was going to another country."

It was then time to bid them farewell.

"My last contact with the two was 11.30 pm, when they had passed the immigration gate," he said. "I wanted to make sure they found their way. They said they were waiting to get on the plane. I have informed the airline, and this is how I've made sure they were aboard the flight."

In Kuala Lumpur, police confirmed that they did not believe the two passengers were linked to any militant groups. Police chief Khalid Abu Bakar told reporters that Mehrdad was apparently heading to Frankfurt to join his mother. When he failed to arrive in Germany, she had contacted the authorities in Kuala Lumpur.

"We believe he is not likely to be a member of any terrorist group, and we believe he was trying to migrate to Germany," said Khalid. "His mother was expecting him to arrive. She contacted us here, so that is how we know he is the one."

Then, as darkness fell in Malaysia after the fourth day of a massive search for any sign of the missing plane, news came of a change in direction of the investigation. The focus had shifted to the Straits of Malacca, on the western side of the Malay Peninsula, and 400 miles (644km) from where they had been searching before. The Malaysian military reviewed radar evidence showing that the missing Boeing 777 plane changed course and made it to the Malacca Strait. Malaysian air force chief General Rodzali Daud said radar at a military base in Penang had detected a plane near the island of Pulau Perak, at the northern approach to the strait.

Meanwhile, Vietnam had moved its planes northward, searching the dense jungle and uninhabited mountain areas along its borders with Laos and Cambodia. Army units along the border had also been given orders to search for the plane.

"So far we have found no signs so we must widen our search," said Lieutenant General Vo Van Tuan, deputy general chief of staff of the Vietnam People's Army.

There were a number of reasons why the search may have been directed in the wrong place. First, radar coverage was patchy in that part of the world and MH370 might have been in a "radar gap" at the time of its loss. Second, air traffic control authorities rely on information broadcast from transponders on aircraft, which boost the performance of ground radar surveillance. These transponders also help ground controllers positively identify any aircraft on cluttered radarscopes. If there was a technical problem with the plane's transponder, air traffic control might have received erroneous data. This would have led the authorities to start their initial searches in the wrong area.

Ten countries and six navies were now involved in the search, including some that had formerly been hostile. The US Seventh Fleet, based in the Japanese island of Okinawa, sent a P–3C Orion surveillance plane that can sweep about 1,500 square miles (3,885 sq km) every hour. It was equipped with sensors that could detect small pieces of debris in the water. Adding to the mystery was the failure of US spy satellites to turn up any sign of the plane.

It is very difficult to hide a plane the size of Boeing 777 from satellite surveillance and the lack of any demands from hijackers seems to suggest that the aircraft is not hidden away on a remote island airstrip – though it was always possible negotiations were going on in secret. Conspiracy theorists hold that the passengers are still alive and the plane has been escorted to a secret location by Vietnamese fighter jets, who forced the airliner down to a remote military airfield as part of a counter-terrorism investigation. They claim the search was simply a cover-up to buy more time.

A second theory said that a Vietnamese fighter plane accidentally crashed into the Boeing 777 while on a training mission. Fearing China would see the accident as an act of aggression, Hanoi had hidden all the evidence. A slightly different take was that the Vietnamese Army blasted the airliner out of the sky. They had fired a ground-to-air missile to knock down the jet and then hide the wreckage. A surprisingly popular theory was that the aircraft was downed by a missile from North Korea, even though the rogue state was 2,000 miles (3,218km) away from the area in which the aircraft was lost.

Others believe the plane was hijacked by terrorists using stolen passports. They suggest the Boeing landed safely at an abandoned Vietnamese airport, where the passengers and crew are being held hostage. Some claim the jet was abducted by aliens, while others believe the 100-ton plane was blown to atoms by a massive explosion.

If the aircraft did break up at high altitude, then the large debris field should have been relatively easy to spot and the radio beacons inside the black box data recorder would have activated. This led some to believe that the aircraft dived into the sea at high speed and sunk virtually intact. Even so, some wreckage should have been left on the surface.

Some of the families of the missing still held out hope. Nineteen relatives claimed that they had called cellphones of their missing loved ones and they had rang out, suggesting the devices are still intact even though the recipients themselves are not able to answer.

"If I could get through, the police could locate the position, and there's a chance he could still be alive," said Bian Liangwei, the sister of one of the missing passengers. A number of relatives passed on the phone numbers to authorities and asked them to track the signals, but a Malaysia Airlines spokesman said the company had tried one of the numbers given to them and had failed to get through. However, it was reported that some of the crew's phones did ring out, leading relatives to believe the company was hiding something.

One explanation is that the phones were not actually ringing. With some providers, the cellphone may sound as if it is ringing before it goes to voicemail, when actually the battery is down or the phone is otherwise unreachable.

One man claimed that his brother-in-law was still logged into his social network profile. And while the Chinese authorities tried to bury the story, domestically at least, the relatives resorted to the social media, where their misery had triggered broad condemnation of a Communist Party leadership as wildly out of touch with its people.

Others showed their concern. A shopping mall in Beijing suspended advertising on its large outdoor LED screen to display a search timer. It showed an image of a plane along with a digital clock marking the time since the last contact with the flight.

While some clung to the belief that the plane had landed safely in some remote place, most experts were of the view that it had been lost somewhere at sea. It took a week for debris to be spotted from an Indonesian jet lost in 2007, close to the area between Malaysia and Vietnam where Flight MH370 had gone missing. The largely intact fuselage of that flight still sits on the bottom of the sea. And some planes do disappear completely.

In 1979 a Boeing 707-323C belonging to Varig, the Brazilian airline, left Narita International Airport bound for Galeão International Airport in Rio de Janeiro, with a stopover at Los Angeles International Airport. It was a cargo flight carrying 153 paintings by Japanese-Brazilian Manabu Mabe, returning from a Tokyo exhibition, valued at US$1.24 million (£736,000), and a crew of six. The pilot, 56-year-old Captain Araújo da Silva, had logged 23,000 hours of flying time. Radio contact was lost 30 minutes after takeoff. Neither the plane nor the paintings have ever been found.

In 1974, a newly converted Lockheed WC-130 Weatherbird was transferred to the 54th Weather Reconnaissance Squadron, the "Typhoon Chasers", at Andersen Air Force Base on Guam to investigate Typhoon Bess. The crew departed Clark Air Base in the Philippines on 12 October. Radio contact with the aircraft was lost as it was heading into the typhoon's eye over the South China Sea to make a second position fix. There were no radio transmissions, indicating an emergency on board. Search teams could not locate the aircraft or its crew. All six crew members were listed missing, presumed dead.

In 1956, a Boeing B-47 Stratojet carrying a crew of three and nuclear weapons took off from MacDill Air Force Base in Florida for a non-stop flight to Ben Guerir Air Base in Morocco. After completing its first airborne refuelling without incident, it missed the second. It was thought to have come down in the Mediterranean, but no wreckage was ever found. The Royal Navy abandoned its exercises in the Mediterranean to search for the plane. On land, troops in French and Spanish Morocco did likewise – to no avail.

In September 1990, a Boeing 727 owned by Faucett Airlines of Peru ditched into the North Atlantic after running out of fuel on its way to Miami. The plane was never found and the loss attributed to poor pilot planning.

More mysterious was the disappearance of another 727 that was being used to transport diesel fuel to diamond mines in Africa. One day, just before sunset, the plane took off without clearance and with its transponder turned off. It disappeared and is thought to have crashed in the Atlantic. One theory is that it was stolen so the owner could collect insurance (the owner had financial troubles). Flight MH370 might have done that sort of disappearing act too.

"The world is a big place," said Michael Smart, professor of aerospace engineering at the University of Queensland. "If it happens to come down in the middle of the ocean and it's not near a shipping lane or something, who knows how long it could take them to find?"

However, the Straits of Malacca is one of the world's busiest shipping lanes. If Flight MH370 had gone down there, it would have been spotted.

As the frustration of the family and friends of the 154 Chinese passengers on board MH370 came to the boil, the Chinese authorities split them up into three different locations. In China any sort of protest is discouraged and by separating the friends and families, it was easier for the authorities to keep control.

While the pilot, Zaharie Ahmad Shah, was given a clean bill of health, suspicions emerged about his co-pilot, Fariq Abdul Hamid. Two years earlier he had picked out two blonde teenage backpackers from the check-in queue and invited them up into the cockpit. They sat in the jump seat for the whole flight, including takeoff and landing. Hamid chatted them up and asked them out on a date.

South African tourist Jonti Roos said Hamid and the pilot smoked virtually non-stop at the controls while flirting with her and a friend. Roos was flying back to Kuala Lumpur after a two-week holiday in Phuket with her best friend Jaan Maree in December 2011.

"Throughout the entire flight they were talking to us and they were smoking throughout the flight, which I don't think they're allowed to do," Roos said. "They were taking photos with us in the cockpit while they were flying the plane. At one stage they were pretty much turned around the whole time in their seats talking to us. They were so engaged in conversation that he took my friend's hand and he was looking at her palm and said 'your hand is very creased, that means you're a very creative person' and commented on her nail polish."

The young South African described the pilots as "possibly a little bit sleazy".

"They asked us if we could arrange our trip to stay in Kuala Lumpur for a few nights, they could take us out," she said.

The authorities were concerned because passengers have been prohibited in cockpits since 9/11. Normally, the flight crew are protected by a reinforced steel door with a solid-locking mechanism; these are supposed to be so strong that six highly motivated terrorists could not knock them down.

The girls took pictures, but said they were not concerned about the pilots' misconduct.

"I did feel safe," Roos admitted. "I don't think there was one instance where I felt threatened or I felt they didn't know what they were doing. The whole time they were very friendly. I felt they were very competent in what they were doing. We wished they would stop smoking because it is such a confined space but you can't exactly tell a pilot to stop smoking."

Roos, who moved to Australia, was shocked to learn Hamid was at the helm of the ill-fated Flight MH370.

"When I realized it was the same co-pilot that was quite shocking," she said. "I thought it was crazy. I couldn't believe it. When I saw all his friends and family posting on his [Facebook] wall, my heart really broke for them and my heart broke for the families of the passengers."

If Flight MH370 had been hijacked by terrorists, it seems they would have had no difficulty getting into the cockpit. Plainly security was lax.

Malaysia Airlines said it was taking the report seriously, but did not have more information.

"We are shocked by these allegations," said a spokesman. "We have not been able to confirm the validity of the pictures and videos of the alleged incident."

When he went missing, Hamid was preparing to marry his 26-

year-old girlfriend, Nadira Ramli, a pilot with the budget airline AirAsia and the daughter of another Malaysia Airlines' pilot. The couple studied at the same pilot school. Before the flight, he posted the online comment: "Time to take passion to next level."

The eldest of five children, Hamid lived with his parents in a smart two-storey detached family house in Kuala Lumpur's Shah Alam middle-class enclave, 40 minutes from the airport. Neighbour Ayop Jantan said Mr Hamid's father, a high-ranking civil servant in Selangor state, was proud of his son.

"To be a pilot is a very high status job in Malaysia, like a doctor or lecturer," he explained.

Hamid's grandmother, Halimah Abdul Rahman, described him as "a good son, obedient... and a pious man".

His brother, Afiq, told the *New Straits Times*: "This is just heart-breaking. I do not know what to tell you. I am not doing okay. Sorry, I cannot really think right now. My parents are very sad right now."

According to Ahmad Sarafi Ali Asrah, head of the nearby Surau Al-Mawaddah mosque which Hamid attended regularly, he was a "good boy, a good Muslim, humble and quiet." Secretary of the mosque committee Azlan Azmi said: "I saw him with his father, usually. They are certainly a good family." And friends said Hamid was "religious, not reckless." He regularly played five-a-side football with local youths and paid for their football shirts. His other interest was cars. He had a new BMW and a four-year-old Audi.

Asrah said the co-pilot's parents were distraught and the community solidly behind them, supporting the family in prayers.

"His father still cries when he talks about Fariq. His mother too," said Asrah.

Hamid had joined Malaysia Airlines in 2007. With just 2,763

hours of flight experience he had only recently started co-piloting the sophisticated Boeing 777.

CNN correspondent Richard Quest was pictured in the cockpit when he visited Flight MH370 while Hamid was training. Quest watched him land the plane and described it on television as "textbook perfect".

A neighbour of the Hamid family, a taxi driver, said: "I don't think Fariq can hijack the plane. He loves cars so much, just like I do. I didn't see anything strange happening in his family, for example before the plane went missing."

Again, he seemed nothing like a hijacker or a terrorist.

CHAPTER TWELVE

UNIDENTIFIED FLYING OBJECT

On 12 March 2014, Malaysian authorities spelt out the reason for the shift to the new search area. It seems that, after Hamid's last transmission, the plane had veered off to the west, travelling over Malaysia and Thailand. By then its transponder and other location systems were off. Its last tracked position on radar recorded the flight about 250 miles (402km) off course over the Malacca Strait, near the island of Pulau Perak, at 2.40 am.

Air force chief General Tan Sri Rodzali Daud said: "It changed course after Kota Bharu and took a lower altitude. It made it into the Malacca Strait. After that, the signal from the plane was lost."

The contact was made by military radar which was operating that night. Unlike civilian radar, it did not depend on interrogating a transponder. The radar was of a simple World War II vintage. It beamed a radio signal that bounced back off any metallic object, effectively "painting" the surface with radio waves. But it could not identify a plane. That depends on the expertise of radar controllers, who were trained to interpret speed, height and mass of the blip that appears on their screens. Without a signal from the plane's transponder it was impossible to be certain that what the radar operator saw was MH370 and the contact remains, officially, an unidentified flying object.

The military were reviewing the data. General Rodzali Daud said: "I am not saying it's Flight MH370, we are still corroborating this. It was an unidentifiable plot. We are working with the experts."

American analysts had also been called in to examine the radar data.

If it was MH370, the pilots should have informed air traffic control of their change of course, but no message was received from the doomed airliner. Aviation expert Ross Aimer said the lack of distress call or emergency locator signal may be due to a "black spot".

"There are spots in the world where you cannot communicate," he explained.

It had also flown across Malaysia and should have been picked up by civilian radar, so its transponder must have been knocked out or switched off.

Asked why news of the sighting over the Malacca Straits had not been released before, civil aviation chief Azharuddin Abdul Rahman told reporters: "There are some things that I can tell you and some things that I can't."

Plainly the US and Chinese military who were guiding the search efforts were not eager to share the information for fear of revealing secrets about their surveillance capabilities.

News that the plane had turned west and flown over the Malay Peninsula and the Straits of Malacca led relatives to believe that Flight MH370 had been hijacked and that their loved ones were now being held in the Sumatran jungle, forcibly prevented from answering their phones.

"I hope it is a hijacking, then there will be some hope that my young cousin has survived," one relative said. "My uncle and aunt had an emotional breakdown: they are not eating, drinking and sleeping and could not face coming here."

In response, Malaysia Airlines issued a statement, saying: "We regret and empathize with the families and we will do whatever we can to ensure that all basic needs, comfort and psychological support are delivered. We are as anxious as the families to know the status of their loved ones."

Adding to the confusion, a spokesman for the Malaysian Prime Minister's office said that he had checked with senior military officials, who told him there was no evidence that the plane had recrossed the Malay Peninsula, only that it may have attempted to turn back.

"As far as they know, except for the air turnback, there is no new development," he said, adding that the reported remarks by the air force chief were "not true".

It also emerged that the Federal Aviation Administration in Washington drew up a new airworthiness directive relating to Boeing 777s in November 2013. This was prompted by reports of cracking of the fuselage skin under the aircraft's satellite antennae. The FAA, which supervises the safety of American-made aircraft such as Boeings, told airlines to look out for corrosion in that area. If a crack opened it could lead to rapid decompression, which in turn could cause the plane to break up.

During a maintenance inspection, one 14-year-old 777 was found to have a crack 16 inches long (40cm) under its antenna. The report said: "Cracking and corrosion in the fuselage skin, if not corrected, could lead to rapid decompression and loss of structural integrity of the aeroplane."

The FAA directive was issued just two days before MH370 took off. The missing aircraft was serviced on 23 February 2014, just two weeks before it went missing. Further maintenance was scheduled for 19 June, so there would have been no further opportunity to spot any cracking. But Boeing said that the FAA alert did not apply to the missing jet as it did not have the same antenna as other Boeing 777s.

However, Mary Schiavo, a former Inspector General at the US Department of Transportation, said: "Boeing put out a warning back in August, and it said the 777 had a problem with fuselage cracking. I wonder what didn't get done. If this plane had a problem and it had cracking or some sort of a rapid decompression and lost the ability to communicate, it would make perfect sense."

While the search for the black box was on, investigators from Malaysia and the National Transportation Safety Board in Washington were combing through live data stream broadcast during the flight provided by ACARS, a system that is sometimes considered the equivalent of an "online black box".

Despite the shift of the focus of the search, satellite images on a Chinese government website showed suspected debris floating off the southern tip of Vietnam, near the plane's original flight path. The images, taken at around 11 am on Sunday, 9 March appeared to show "three suspected floating objects" of varying sizes, the largest being about 79 x 72ft (24 x 22m). Their co-ordinates put them in the sea off the southern tip of Vietnam and east of Malaysia. This conflicted with the information the Malaysians were giving out.

"There's too much information and confusion right now," said the Chinese foreign ministry in Beijing. "It is very hard for us to decide whether a given piece of information is accurate. We will not give it up as long as there's still a shred of hope."

Global Times said in an editorial: "We do not know what information the Malaysians are releasing is real and what is not. We must say that information provided by Malaysia is very chaotic. They released contradictory information about how many people got on board and how many people used fake passports. We worry that Kuala Lumpur may not be capable of effectively handling the information."

There were at least nine eyewitnesses to something that might have been a plane crashing there. One report came from a New Zealander on an oil rig off Vung Tau in southern Vietnam. He sent an email saying he had seen a "burning object" in the sky about 200 miles (322km) out to sea at the time of the crash.

Mike McKay told his employers that he had observed the plane burning at high altitude.

"I believe I saw the Malaysia Airlines plane come down. The timing is right," he said. "I tried to contact the Malaysian and Vietnam officials several days ago but I do not know if the message has been received."

McKay said he was on the oil rig *Songa Mercur*, off southeast Vietnam. When he observed the plane it appeared to be in one piece, he said – "From when I first saw the burning plane until the flames went out was 10 to 15 seconds." It was still at high altitude.

"It is very difficult to judge the distance," he said, "but I'd say 50–70km [164–230ft] along the compass bearing 260–275 degrees."

Vietnam officials confirmed they had received the email but found no wreckage in that area. However, others still believed this was the area where the search should be concentrated.

"There was always great scepticism about this 90-degree turn," said Peter Goelz, former director of the US National Transportation Safety Board. "There have been misinformation and corrections from Malaysian authorities on the whereabouts of MH370. At best, Malaysian officials have thus far been poor communicators; at worst, they are incompetent."

But the Malaysian government was also adamant.

"We have nothing to hide," said acting transport minister Hishammuddin Hussein. "We owe it to the families to tell the truth."

The shift of focus to the Andaman Sea added another dimension to the search. In parts, depths there exceed 14,500ft (4,420m). In contrast, much of the Gulf of Thailand is less than 300ft (91m) deep. Plainly it was much easier to locate and salvage wreckage from shallower water.

Meanwhile, some 43 ships and 39 aircraft from at least eight nations were scouring an area of 35,800 square miles (92,721 sq km) in an unprecedented effort to find the missing plane.

"There are emotions and frustrations but they will not distract us from the search," said Hishammuddin Hussein. "It's not something that is easy. We are looking at so many vessels and aircraft, so many countries to co-ordinate, and a vast area for us to search. But we will never give up – this we owe to the families."

As they extended the search area into the Andaman Sea, India joined in the hunt since the islands there are Indian territory. The Indian Ministry of External Affairs offered Malaysia all the help that may be required to find the aircraft, including naval ships, aircraft and other military support. A Dornier aircraft from India's coastguard was sent to scour the eastern side of the Andaman Islands. Five Indians are among Flight MH370's 239 missing.

General Rodzali Daud, head of the Royal Malaysian Air Force, then gave out more information about the last sighting of the unidentified plane thought to be Flight MH370. He said that the aircraft was plotted on military radar at 2.15 am on Saturday, 8 March 2012, 200 miles (322km) northwest of Penang, off Malaysia's west coast. That would place it somewhere in the south Andaman Sea, east of India's Nicobar Islands, between the Thai resort of Phuket and the tip of Aceh province in Indonesia. It had taken the Malaysian authorities more than four days before their admission that the jet may have been picked up by military radar 45 minutes after it disappeared from civilian screens over the Gulf of Thailand. Extending the search area still further, they warned that the search might take months. Already it had grown to 35,800 square miles (92,721 sq km) – about the size of Portugal. Concern had also spread to India. On the beach at Puri, in the eastern state of Odisha, an Indian sand sculptor Sudarsan Pattnaik built a monument dedicated to Flight MH370 and its passengers.

Following news of the radar contact of an unidentified flying object over the Straits of Malacca, it seemed that the missing plane may have flown on for another four hours after voice contact was lost. A Pentagon official said: "We have an indication the plane went down in the Indian Ocean."

Fuelled to fly to Beijing, the plane could have flown far out into the Indian Ocean. The guided-missile destroyer USS *Kidd* was sent to the region to help the search. It carried two Seahawk helicopters that could be deployed for an aerial hunt, but would take 24 hours to get on station. Other assets were brought into play. Commander William Marks of the US Seventh Fleet on board the command ship USS *Blue Ridge* said: "Ships alone are not going to get you that coverage, helicopters are barely going to make a dent in it and only a few countries fly P-3s. So this massive expanse of water space will be the biggest challenge."

The P-3 Orion is a long-distance surveillance plane, which the US uses alongside an updated P-8 Poseidon, an ultra-sophisticated version of the Boeing 737.

The Indian Ocean is the third largest ocean, covering some 28 million square miles (72 million sq km) and some of it is more than 24,000ft (7,315m) deep. The winds and currents on this enormous stretch of water could shift any surface debris tens of nautical miles within hours, dramatically widening the search area with each passing day.

Already five days of searching had taken its toll on the 700 sailors from the Pacific-based US Seventh Fleet involved.

"Fatigue starts to become a factor," admitted Commander Marks.

Even Malaysian air teams combing the Andaman Sea were feeling the strain. After another frustrated rescue mission over the Andaman Sea, members of one air force unit said they were losing hope.

"Of course, we can't rule anything out," said acting transport minister Hishammuddin Hussein. "This is why we have extended the search."

If the task of finding the missing plane was not already hopeless enough, reports then came in that the plane had been "pinged" several hours after it disappeared from radar. The 777 carried another automated transmission system that sent back technical data regularly to the plane-maker Boeing and Rolls-Royce, who made the engines. The *Wall Street Journal* reported that Rolls-Royce Trent engines had received a transmission from the plane hours after it lost contact with air traffic control. If true, this would widen the radius of the search zone by more than 2,000 nautical miles (2,300 miles or 3,704 km), an area stretching from India to Australia.

All modern Rolls-Royce engines automatically transmit data by radio or satellite link from antennae on the aircraft to a ground station in Derby. The data is routinely transmitted at takeoff, during the climb, when the aircraft begins its cruise and on landing. Further transmissions can be made if there is an anomaly in flight. Sensors inside the engine measure oil pressure, temperature, shaft speed and vibration levels. The data is collated in Britain and analyzed by computer to help with maintenance.

The electronic "pings" picked up would suggest that automatic systems relaying flight data via satellite to ground monitoring stations were switched on and ready to communicate with satellites. The pulses were not in themselves proof that the jet was in the air or on the ground. Indeed the signals could have been sent even if the jet had crashed. The only catastrophic failure involving Trent 800 engines came in 2008, when ice crystals clogged the fuel-oil heat exchangers in two engines, restricting the flow of fuel and causing British Airways Flight BA38 from Beijing to crash just short of the runway at Heathrow.

British air accident investigators flew to Kuala Lumpur, along with experts from the engine-makers Rolls-Royce, to help the Malaysian authorities try to establish what happened to Flight MH370. US specialists were also on the case. These included Scott Dunham of the National Transportation Safety Board, a leading interpreter of radar data. He was accompanied by teams from the National Transportation Safety Board (NTSB), the Federal Aviation Administration and Boeing, the plane maker. In aviation terms, the missing plane was already middle-aged. It was delivered to Malaysia Airlines in 2002 and had made 7,525 cycles of takeoffs and landings, clocking up some 53,465 hours in the air.

Investigators in the US were now examining whether the missing plane was intentionally diverted from its planned route.

US counter-terrorism officers were looking into the possibility that the route had been changed "with the intention of using it later for another purpose" and its transponders were intentionally turned off to avoid detection. A hijacker may not have known about the system that downloads data automatically as part of a routine maintenance and monitoring programme. This suggests the plane flew on for a total of five hours. Its final confirmed location was at 1.31 am on 8 March, about 40 minutes after it took off from Kuala Lumpur International Airport. At that point it was heading north across the mouth of the Gulf of Thailand on what should have been a six-hour flight to Beijing.

If the plane had flown on for another four hours, it could have covered up to another 2,000 miles (3,218km) and reached as far as India and Pakistan, or even the northwest coast of Australia. In practical terms the search area became almost limitless.

The *Wall Street Journal* said the new data raised a "host of new questions and possibilities about what happened" to the plane and those on board. It also caused confusion in Malaysia, where transport minister Hishammuddin Hussein immediately rejected it.

"Engine data transmission reports are inaccurate," he insisted, "Both Boeing and Rolls-Royce have told us they did not get any ACARS transmission after 1.07 am last Saturday. There is no real precedent for a case like this – the plane vanished."

Both companies had been assisting in the investigation.

"Rolls-Royce and Boeing teams are here in Kuala Lumpur and have worked with investigation teams since Sunday," he continued. "This issue has never been raised. Since today's media reports Malaysia Airlines has asked Rolls-Royce and Boeing specifically about the data. As far as Rolls-Royce and Boeing are concerned, those reports are inaccurate."

Asked if it was possible that the plane had kept flying for several more hours, the minister said: "Of course, we can't rule anything out. This is why we have extended the search. We are expanding our search into the Andaman Sea."

Neither Boeing nor Rolls-Royce were willing to comment at that point.

Hussein also denied reports in the Malaysian media which claimed police had raided the home of Captain Zaharie Ahmad Shah to find out whether the pilot was suffering any psychological problems.

"The pilot's house has not been searched," he said.

However, he confirmed that the Malaysian government were asking for radar data from India.

There was further confusion when General Rodzali Daud released a statement denying remarks attributed to him in a local media report, saying that military radar had confirmed that aircraft flew west and had made it to the Malacca Strait. The Associated Press then contacted a high-level military official, who confirmed the remarks.

Colonel Umar Fathur of the Indonesian air force said the country had received official information from Malaysia that the plane was above the South China Sea, about 12 miles (19km) from Kota Bharu, Malaysia, when it turned back and then disappeared. That would mean its last confirmed position was closer to Malaysia than has previously been publicly disclosed.

Confusion over whether the plane had been spotted flying west prompted speculation that different arms of the Malaysian government had differing opinions over where the plane was most likely to be, or that authorities were holding back information.

"There is only confusion if you want to see confusion," said Hishammuddin Hussein.

Of course this was of little comfort to the relatives of those missing. Airline staff were pelted with water bottles at a news conference in Beijing by 400 relatives, all shouting: "Tell us the truth!" During a two-hour meeting with the Malaysian envoy, one relative demanded: "Is the envoy asleep?"

He assured relatives that Malaysia was doing all it could and that he would pass on their concerns to the authorities in Kuala Lumpur but there was very little more he could tell them.

Questions were also being asked as to why the Chinese had waited three days to release satellite pictures of the debris in the South China Sea. The Chinese authorities explained that verification was in progress.

With the search already taking place on both sides of the Malay Peninsula, the search area was gradually expanded to include everywhere the plane could have reached with the fuel it had on board.

It was a vast area in which to locate something as small as a piece of an aircraft.

CHAPTER THIRTEEN

SIGHTINGS

The story that MH370 had travelled westwards gained further ground when a number of people reported several sightings of a low-flying aircraft in the Kelantan Province of northeast Malaysia, just south of the Malaysian-Thai border. One fisherman, at sea at about 1.30 am on 8 March 2014, was reported to have seen unusually bright lights at about the time the airliner is thought to have changed course. The plane was flying "so low its lights were as big as coconuts," he said. Others told the local press they heard a boom and saw a flame in the sky but when questioned by the police, they came up with nothing to confirm the fate of the missing plane.

Nevertheless 55-year-old fisherman Azad Ibrahim remained adamant.

"I was walking towards the rear of my house when I saw the light and wondered where it was heading to," he recalled. "The airspace here is like a highway for aircraft and they usually travel in routine patterns. However, the light I saw was moving towards a completely different direction. It was going towards the sea."

This appeared to rule out that the plane had been lost due to sudden catastrophic mechanical failure as it would mean that the aircraft flew around 285 nautical miles (328 miles/528km) after its last contact with air traffic control.

But there was another sighting by a Malaysian eyewitness who believed she had spotted a plane in the water as she travelled on another airliner across the Indian Ocean on her way home from Jeddah in Saudi Arabia. Fifty-three-year-old Latife Dalelah, a housewife from Kuala Lumpur, said she saw a silvery object in the sea, close to the Andaman Islands.

"I was staring out of the window as I couldn't sleep," she explained. "I was shocked to see what looked like the tail and wing of an aircraft on the water. I woke my friends but they laughed me off. But I know what I saw. I am convinced that I saw the aircraft – I will not lie."

Later, residents on the remote Maldives island of Kudahuvadhoo, nearly 2,000 miles (3,219km) away off the southern tip of India, claimed to have seen a low-flying jumbo jet the day Flight MH370 disappeared at around 6.15 am local time, that is 9.15 am Malaysian time. It was heading south. Ibrahim Sarih, manager of the Blue Leaf Guesthouse on Kudahuvadhoo, said: "I've never seen a jet that size flying so low. We've seen seaplanes, but I'm sure that this was not one of those. I could even make out the doors on it quite clearly. It's not just me either, several other residents have reported seeing the exact same thing. Some people got out of their houses to see what was causing the tremendous noise too."

It was said to be a big plane, white with blue-red stripes across it. The description was consistent with the missing Malaysian

Boeing 777. Islanders said they did not recall ever seeing a plane there, and at that height, before, making it unlikely that what they had seen was a normal takeoff or landing by another passenger jet.

If a Boeing 777 had flown direct from the Gulf of Thailand to the Maldives, it should have arrived much earlier – 3 am local time, well before sunrise. However, it may have flown at very low level to avoid detection, which would have slowed it considerably. It may also have been flying at a reduced speed to conserve fuel, perhaps because whoever controlled the plane wanted to maximize its range.

As the plane did not land at the airport of the Maldives' capital Malé, which is to the east of Kudahuvadhoo, the closest airport big enough for a 777 to land was Mahé in the Seychelles, 1,400 miles (2,253km) further on, but the missing jet would not have had enough fuel to get there anyway. The US and British airbase at Diego Garcia is closer, 800 miles (1,290 km) away. It had a runway long enough for a 777 to land, but had not reported sighting the aircraft. However, there have been no civilians there since the last of the plantation workers and their families were removed in 1971, and from the surrounding islands the following year. After 9/11, the British government allowed the CIA to run a "black" jail, where they tortured al-Qaeda suspects as part of their "extra-ordinary rendition" programme.

Lawless Somalia, on the coast of Africa, also 2,000 miles (3,219km) beyond the Maldives, was the ideal place for a hijacked plane to land. Again, that would probably have been too far for Flight MH370 to go and it was also among the first places that spy satellites would have scoured for signs of a giant plane. However, as we have seen in the case of Ethiopian Airlines Flight 961, hijackers make mistakes and Flight MH370 could have crashed into the sea after running out of fuel in a failed bid to reach the home of modern-day piracy. A plane full of hostages would easily fetch as good a ransom as an oil tanker.

Assessing news of the sightings of a low-flying plane over Kelantan Province, one investigator said: "It's possible that the aircraft hugged the terrain in some areas which are mountainous to avoid detection."

It was flying perhaps as low as 5,000ft (1,524m) using a technique known as terrain masking, also used by military pilots to avoid being spotted by radar.

"Radar goes in a straight line. If you are in the shadow of a mountain or even the curve of the earth – if you are under the radar beam – you can't be seen," explained Jason Middleton, head of the aviation department at New South Wales University. "The further [radar beams] go out, the weaker they are and the further they need to come back. Radars have dead zones which are low and also which are far away."

The passengers would have noticed a sudden dive to 5,000ft (1,524m), but it would not have harmed them. Speculation began that it had flown low over three countries. Flying undetected at a low altitude would have used more fuel, travelling through denser air, but the plane could still have had enough fuel to fly for eight hours.

"It is likely that the distance it could fly would be as much as halved, compared to a normal cruising flight. But technically, there is no reason why the aircraft could not fly at a low altitude for a long time," said aviation expert Chris Yates.

A Boeing 777-200ER could be flown at a lower altitude, but surely that was a dangerous thing to do?

"If you try to do something like flying at low altitude over land there are going to be obstacles in your way that a large commercial airliner cannot avoid quickly," explained Yates.

So it was easier to fly at low altitudes over water. And at that time in the morning, while being invisible to radar, over land a large plane would surely have alerted people beneath its flight path. But who would have been flying a plane at such a low altitude? An investigator told the *New Straits Times*: "The person who had the control over the aircraft has a solid knowledge of avionics and navigation and left a clean track."

Over the sea, it was easy to avoid radar beams. Sidney Dekker, of the Safety Science Innovation Lab at Australia's Griffith University, an expert on aviation safety, said: "Particularly over oceanic areas, radar coverage is extremely unreliable and partial."

So it was possible that the plane had been spirited away under the ceiling of radar detection, but that did not explain why.

"I'd be prepared to accept at this stage any possibility," said Professor Graham Braithwaite, head of Transport and Safety Engineering at the Cranfield University Safety and Accident Investigation Centre. "OK, we may have ruled out the guys with two stolen passports but that is not the same thing as saying we have ruled out sabotage or suicide and all those other things are still on the table."

The loss of communications from the plane remained a puzzle but could have a simple explanation. According to Professor Braithwaite: "You can lose communications for a whole series of reasons: a loss of power or just the data not being picked up by something that's able to collect it."

One theory was that a sudden decompression caused everyone on board to black out and the undamaged plane continued on automatic pilot until it ran out of fuel. This could have happened if the plane had undetected cracks such as those found under the antenna on other 777s.

"After a few seconds everyone would become unconscious,"

explained Jim Hall, a former chairman of America's National Transportation Safety Board (NTSB).

Small cracks could lead to a slow decompression of the cabin, which would go unnoticed until lack of oxygen began to disorientate the crew and passengers. A semi-conscious crew might have tried to turn the aircraft around and head back to Kuala Lumpur, before losing consciousness completely.

"It could have been a small leak and the oxygen was leaving the plane before the crew really noticed it," said Paul Cousins, president of the Australian Licensed Aircraft Engineers Association (ALAEA).

Larger cracks on the plane's fuselage would have caused "massive depressurization".

"Immediately everyone on board would be unconscious," Cousins added.

The cracks could have enlarged and cut connections to the communications antennae, cutting the transponder and the ACARS and so preventing the pilots from making a Mayday call. Eventually they could have led to structural failure of the aircraft. Indeed, larger cracks in the fuselage might have caused a sudden decompression, leading to a catastrophic disintegration of the aircraft in mid-air.

Such decompressions do occur. The Boeing 747-122 of United Airlines Flight UA811 left its stopover at Honolulu International Airport on a flight from Los Angeles to Auckland on 24 February 1989. As it climbed toward its cruising altitude, it began a detour around a thunderstorm. Anticipating turbulence, 59-year-old Captain David Cronin, who had logged more than 28,000 flying hours with around 1,650 on 747s, left the seatbelt sign on. After being airborne for approximately 16 minutes, they were at about 23,000ft (7,000m) when a grinding sound was heard in the

Business Class section, followed by a loud thud that shook the whole plane. The noise came from the forward cargo door, which had blown out. It slammed into the side of the fuselage, tearing it open. Pressure difference caved in the cabin floor. Ten seats were sucked out. Two of them were unoccupied, so eight passengers were lost. A ninth passenger in the next seat was also lost when the armrest failed. A flight attendant was nearly pulled out of the plane. She was seen clinging to a seat leg and pulled to safety, though she was badly injured. Another flight attendant clung onto the stairs leading to the upper deck during decompression.

The pilot thought a bomb had gone off (Pan Am Flight 103 had gone down over Lockerbie just 10 weeks earlier). The plane made an emergency descent to an altitude where the air was breathable, while making a 180-degree turn to head back to Honolulu. Debris blown out of the plane during decompression damaged engines Number Three and Number Four, which caught fire. They were shut down and the crew began dumping fuel in readiness for an emergency landing.

The control surfaces on the leading edge of the right wing, the horizontal stabilizer and the tailfin were also damaged. The intercom had also been knocked out, so Flight Engineer Randal Thomas went back to tell the flight attendants to prepare for an emergency landing. It was only then that he saw that there was a large hole behind the first exit door. Returning to the cockpit, he advised the Captain not to exceed the stall speed by more than a small margin, otherwise the whole plane might break up.

Coming in to land, Captain Cronin found that the flaps stuck, forcing him to land at high speed – some 200 knots (230 mph or 370 km/h). Nevertheless, he managed to bring the 747 safely to a halt. An emergency evacuation of the plane took 45 seconds. During the scramble, every one of the flight attendants was injured. However, the plane was repaired and went back into service. The cargo doors on 747s were subsequently redesigned so they could not open during flight.

A Boeing 737-297 on Aloha Airlines Flight AQ243, between Hilo and Honolulu in Hawaii on 28 April 1988, also suffered an explosive decompression in flight. Nothing unusual was spotted in the routine inspection of the aircraft before departure. On board were 89 passengers and six crew. As the aircraft reached its normal flight altitude of 24,000ft (7,315m), about 23 nautical miles (26 miles or 42.5km) south-southeast of Kahului, Maui, a small section on the left-hand side of the roof ruptured with a "whooshing" sound and 58-year-old flight attendant Clarabelle Lansing, who was standing by the fifth row, was sucked out of the hole. Fortunately, the passengers were seated with their seat belts on at the time, preventing further fatalities. One passenger reported seeing Ms Lansing's legs disappearing through the roof.

The first officer, 36-year-old Madeline "Mimi" Tompkins, who had logged 3,500 of her 8,000 flying hours on 737s, was flying the plane at the time. She felt the aircraft roll to the left, then right, and then the controls went loose. Behind her, the door to the cockpit had disappeared, and when the captain, 44-year-old Robert Schornstheimer, looked back, he could see blue sky. Captain Schornstheimer had 6,700 of his 8,500 flying hours on the 737. He took over and the two of them flew the plane to the closest runway at Kahului Airport on Maui, where Schornstheimer made an emergency landing.

Sixty-five people were injured, eight of them seriously. The entire roof of the plane, from the back of the cockpit to the front of the wings, had been blown off. The plane was a write-off and had to be dismantled where it stood. Neither Clarabelle Lansing's body nor the roof of the plane were ever found. It was thought that her body, plugging the initial hole, had caused a much larger section of the roof to tear away.

The rear cargo hatch door blew off the McDonnell Douglas DC-10-10 of Turkish Airlines Flight 981 on 3 March 1974. As the plane was climbing out of Paris's Orly International Airport bound for London Heathrow, air traffic controllers heard the pilot say, in Turkish, "the fuselage has burst". The aircraft had disintegrated. When the wreckage hit the ground there were few small fires as there were not many pieces of aircraft left large enough to burn. The aircraft crashed into a forest near the town of Meaux some 20 miles (32km) away at 430 knots (495 mph or 796 km/h). There were 346 people on board, but only 40 bodies were visually identifiable and nine passengers were never identified. Among the dead were an amateur rugby team from Bury St Edmunds, Suffolk, who were returning from a Five Nations match between France and England, and the Olympic-medal-winning hurdler John Cooper.

On the cockpit voice recorder the sound of rushing air could be heard as the cabin underwent decompression. It was discovered that six passengers were sucked out of the cabin while the plane was still airborne. The rear cargo hold hatch beneath the floor, portions of the interior floor and six passenger seats, still holding dead passengers, were found in a turnip field near the town of Saint-Pathus, approximately 9.3 miles (15km) from the main crash site. French investigators determined that the rear cargo hatch had failed in flight, and the cargo area had decompressed. The resulting difference in air pressure between the cargo area and the pressurized passenger cabin above it caused a section of the cabin floor above the open hatch to fail. This blew out through the hatch, along with the passenger seats attached to the floor section. Control cables that ran beneath that section of floor were severed, and the pilots lost control of the plane's elevators, rudder and Number Two engine.

Earlier in the history of flight, little was known about metal fatigue such as that which led to the cracking of the fuselage around the 777's external antenna. Then, in 1954, two De Havilland Comets fell out of the sky. The first production commercial jetliner, the Comet, was enormously successful at the time. On 10 January 1954, British Overseas Airways Corporation Flight 781 was flying from Rome to London on the final leg of its flight from Singapore when it experienced explosive decompression over the Mediterranean, killing the 29 passengers and six crew on board. BOAC engineer Gerry Bull led a team that inspected the plane's pre-takeoff in Italy.

During the flight 31-year-old Captain Alan Gibson was in communication with Captain Johnson on a passing BOAC four-engine propeller-driven Argonaut. They were talking about weather conditions ahead when the conversation suddenly ceased. Around that time fishermen saw wreckage falling into the sea.

With no black boxes – cockpit voice recorders and flight data recorders were only installed in the 1960s – it was difficult to tell why a previously reliable plane had broken up in such a catastrophic fashion. However, autopsies found that victims had ruptured lungs, indicating the cabin had depressurized. The wreckage was collected and, as there was no evidence that a bomb had gone off on board, it was assumed that an engine turbine had exploded, severing the fuselage and modifications were made.

Then, on 8 April 1954, there were problems when South African Airways Flight 201 from London to Johannesburg took off from Rome en route to Cairo. It had been chartered by BOAC. Again the plane had been inspected by Gerry Bull and his team. They found a faulty fuel gauge and 30 loose bolts on the left wing, which delayed the departure by 25 hours. That night, after Flight 201 had reached its cruising altitude of 35,000ft (10,668m), the plane suddenly vanished. The following day, a patch of oil and some wreckage and bodies were found 70 miles (113km) off Naples. The water was so deep there that a salvage operation was considered impractical. After that all Comets were grounded.

During a year-long investigation it was discovered that cracking had occurred around the windows by repeated pressurizing and depressurizing of the cabin. The windows had been riveted, rather than bonded as the plane's original specification had called for. This had been done with a rivet punch that made a less accurate hole than a drill. The windows also had square corners, where the cracks began. Since then jetliners have had windows with rounded corners, spreading the stress more evenly. After design modifications, the Comet returned to the air in 1958.

While decompression was one theory for the loss of Flight MH370, investigators had not ruled out terrorism or a bungled hijacking. Indeed the very week it disappeared, convicted British bomb plotter Saajid Badat told a New York terror trial he gave a shoe bomb to a group of Malaysian terrorists who were planning a 9/11-style hijacking in December 2001.

Over 10 years had passed since then, but "these spectaculars take a long time in the planning," a British security expert noted.

Giving evidence by video link against Osama bin Laden's son-in law, 48-year-old Sulaiman Abu Ghaith, who was accused of conspiring to kill Americans and supplying terrorists, Badat told the court that he had been given two shoe bombs during a visit to Afghanistan. One he took to Britain; the other he gave to the Malaysian terrorist cell. The plan was for them to use it to breach a cockpit door, but Badat believed it was powerful enough to bring down a jet.

He told the court: "I gave one of my shoes to the Malaysians – I think it was to access the cockpit."

According to Badat, the Malaysian terror cell comprised "four to five individuals including a pilot". He also said that the Malaysian plot was being masterminded by Khalid Sheikh Mohammed, the principal architect of 9/11 and currently a denizen of Guantanamo Bay. According to Badat, Mohammed kept a list of the world's tallest buildings and crossed out New York's Twin Towers after the September 11, 2001 attacks with hijacked airliners as "a joke to make us laugh". Also on the list were the Petronas Twin Towers in Kuala Lumpur. Badat said he believed the Malaysians, including the pilot of the suicide mission, were "ready to perform an act".

During Badat's meeting with the Malaysian terrorist cell, details of the operation were discussed and the possibility was raised that the cockpit door might be locked.

"So I said, 'How about I give you one of my bombs to open a cockpit door?'" he told the court.

The disclosure that Malaysians were plotting a 9/11-style attack raised the prospect that both pilots were overpowered and the plane intended for use as a fuel-filled bomb, like the planes that had hit the World Trade Center and the Pentagon on 9/11. Clearly one possible target would have been the Petronas Twin Towers in Kuala Lumpur, a symbol of Malaysia's modernity and the world's tallest buildings from 1998 until 2004, when the Taipei 101 was completed.

Although Flight MH370 had been heading away from Kuala Lumpur when contact was lost, radar spotted it turn back and Badat had told the story of his meeting with the Malaysia terrorists to investigators long before Flight MH370 went missing. During the 2011 trial of Adis Medunjanin, a Bosnian-born American citizen who was subsequently convicted of conspiring to blow up New York subways, Badat first told prosecutors of the Malaysian shoe bomb plot.

Asked what he knew of the Malaysian group, he said: "I learnt that they had a group ready to perform a similar hijacking to 9/11."

Had he helped them?

"I provided them with one of my shoes because both had been… both had explosives inserted into them," he explained.

Thirty-four-year-old Badat, from Gloucester, was a co-conspirator with shoe-bomber Richard Reid, who tried to detonate explosives packed in his soles on American Airlines Flight 63 from Paris to Miami in December 2001 and is currently serving three consecutive life sentences plus 110 years without parole in the US. Badat did not go through with the plot and was therefore sentenced to 13 years.

Professor Anthony Glees, director of the University of Buckingham's Centre for Security and Intelligence Studies, said the possibility of an Islamist plot offered one explanation for why the Malaysian authorities "have not been telling us the whole truth". He believed the disappearance of Flight MH370 was a hijacking as soon as he heard that the plane had altered its flight path.

"Evidence that it turned back to Malaysia means that this could easily have been a Malaysian Islamist plot to turn the plane into a 9/11-style bomb to fly it into a building in Kuala Lumpur," he said. "Now we know there is evidence of a Malaysian terror cell with ambitions to carry out such an attack and so this makes it even more credible."

The Malaysian government want to keep quiet about it because "Islamist terrorists in Malaysia present the country with a really serious political problem," Professor Glees added.

Others also had good reason to keep quiet. According to Professor Glees: "The global repercussions of another 9/11 attack, including grounded aircraft and stock-market crashes, is something no government would want to face."

James Healy-Pratt, head of aviation at Stuarts Law solicitors, who represented 50 families in the 2009 Air France crash, agreed that there had been a cover-up.

"Compared to Air France there has been very little information given out," he noted. "Serious questions need to be asked about how this has taken a week to get so little information. If it is terrorism, that will have an effect on the Malaysian stock market and local economy."

According to the passenger manifest, there were four Malaysian Muslim men aged between 29 and 33 on board, but reports circulated that the CIA and other intelligence agencies had screened the passengers and crew and found no connections to terrorism. Nevertheless, inside Bukit Aman, Kuala Lumpur's police headquarters, officers were reopening old files and investigating a group of high-profile extremists resident in Malaysia.

While New Zealand and Japan joined the search for the missing plane, in China passengers' families furiously rejected offers of US$5,000 (£3,000) "comfort money" from Malaysia Airlines. Despite assurances to the contrary, they feared the cash – close to a year's income for a Chinese farmer – was a trap that would later rob them of more substantial compensation. Instead, they were determined to get their pound of flesh from the Malaysians. A woman from Zhengzhou, whose niece was on the flight, said that the Ambassador was questioned about the many discrepancies in the official narrative. Why had the military taken so long to come forward with its radar records? What was being hidden? Was the airline trying to conceal a hijacking?

"There were so many questions, and so many denials," the woman said. "Many families seemed to think that the Malaysian Government knows where the plane is and won't say. There were many, many questions about the mental state and qualifications of the pilots. Some asked if they bore a grudge against the airline and this was their revenge."

One man at the meeting said it was "ridiculous" that the Malaysians seemed to have no information and could not get their story straight about even the most basic of facts. Another insisted: "We are definitely going to sue them – this is really bad."

A young woman added: "I really want to see President Xi. I don't know what could possibly be more important than the lives of these 200 people."

In Beijing some 315 family members registered to travel to Malaysia on a flight provided by the airline.

"The majority of us won't go," said a man whose son was on the missing aircraft. "They are offering us a flight on Malaysia Airlines and we don't trust it any more."

There was distress in Kuala Lumpur too. Choi Tat Sang, a 74-year-old Malaysian, said that his family was still holding out hope that the plane and all on board were safe. His 45-year-old daughter-in-law, Goh Sock Lay, was the chief flight attendant. Her 14-year-old daughter, an only child, had been crying every day since the plane's disappearance.

"We are heartbroken," he said. "We are continuing to pray for her safety and for everyone on the flight."

Meanwhile, a cyber-search was underway as Internet surfers around the world joined an online hunt for the missing plane by scanning high-resolution satellite pictures. More than half a million volunteers logged onto the *tomnod.com* website, which uploaded images of a thousand square miles of sea the day after the disappearance of Flight MH370. Each surfer was allocated a tiny square to scan in minute detail – a technique known as "crowd-sourcing".

The project had been made possible by DigitalGlobe, a Colorado company that own one of the world's most advanced commercial satellite networks. The satellite images, taken from 400 miles (644km) above the ocean, should be able to depict an item as small as a suitcase.

"This is a real needle-in-the-haystack problem, except the haystack is in the middle of the ocean," said Luke Barrington, of DigitalGlobe.

The company asked online volunteers to mark "anything that looks interesting, any signs of wreckage or life-rafts".

Crowd-sourcing projects have become a familiar part of the response to emergencies. DigitalGlobe ran a similar campaign after Typhoon Haiyan struck the Philippines in November 2013. Within a day, thousands of volunteers tagged more than 60,000 sites of interest where aid could be directed. After the Boston Marathon bombing of April 2013 police asked the public to submit cellphone footage to help trace suspects. This very quickly proved successful.

The response to the missing aircraft initially overwhelmed the DigitalGlobe website after 500,000 visitors logged onto the system on the first day. After that, up to 100,000 people an hour visited, viewing the images 6 million times in the first three days. And on 12 March 2014 one US volunteer claimed to have spotted the hazy outline of a plane lying beneath the sea. Mike Seberger, a 47-year-old IT expert from Chicago, sent the image to official investigators for further examination.

Later, Taiwanese university student Xie Meng Xiu claimed he had found a photograph of the plane flying off-course above an unknown jungle. The picture, found by scouring websites, had yet to be verified, though some commentators said it appeared to be a different model to the missing Boeing 777.

But few held out any hope that anyone would be found alive. Malaysia's acting transport minister Hishammuddin Hussein admitted: "As time passes I fear that the search and rescue will become just a search, but we will never give up hope. We will do whatever it takes to find it."

By then the search area had grown to nearly 27,000 square nautical miles (37,000 square miles or 95,000 sq km). Clearly searching so huge an area would take some time.

"We are looking at the long haul," Hishammuddin Hussein said. "I think in all cases of this nature eventually it will be found. If you look at Air France, it took weeks to find the location."

He expected the search to take weeks, even months.

At that time, the search was still taking place in two areas. One covered 14,440 square nautical miles (20,000 square miles or 50,000 sq km) of the South China Sea, to the east of the Malaysia Peninsula. The other was 12,425 square nautical miles (17,000 square miles or 44,000 sq km) in the Strait of Malacca, the congested shipping lane that lies between its western coast and the Indonesian island of Sumatra. Azharuddin Abdul Rahman, director general of Malaysia's Department of Civil Aviation, said that searches were being conducted further northwest in the Andaman Sea.

"This is bizarre. I think they are searching the wrong area," complained one user of Weibo, the Chinese micro-blogging website. Others used the site to urge users to pray for Li Jie, with one girl called Lu posting: "Can you all pray with me please? There are so many things we haven't spoken of yet, we haven't finished, and I still hope that the dreams we shared together can come true."

CHAPTER FOURTEEN

ACT OF PIRACY

In Malaysia, people expressed their grief in traditional ways – folding paper cranes, lighting candles, burning incense and joining vigils at mosques, churches, Taoist temples and Buddhist pagodas. But the complaints continued. The deputy chairman of the Beijing-based Aviation Law Society, Zhang Qihuai, accused the Malaysians of reacting too slowly.

"Emergency action should have been taken immediately after this sudden occurrence," he insisted. "If the Malaysians had deployed planes to search for the missing flight the minute the flight was found to be out of contact, it might have saved a lot of time and effort."

Amid the confusion, Vietnam briefly scaled down search operations in waters off its southern coast, saying it was receiving poor information from Malaysia.

Malaysia's acting transport minister Hishammuddin Hussein played down the growing criticism.

"It is normal in a crisis of this magnitude, as time passes by, for there to be emotions and frustrations," he said.

The hunt for the missing plane continued regardless. Tom Philips, a reporter for the *Daily Telegraph*, joined the six-man crew of a C-130 Hercules search plane from Kuala Lumpur's Subang air force base that swept out over the Strait of Malacca. It was still dark when the plane took off at 5.15 am local time on the sixth day of the search. As the sun rose, they headed northwest toward a sector of the Andaman Sea, just west of the Thai island of Phuket: the area designated Section E. It was hundreds of miles west of Flight MH370's planned route to Beijing. Captain Syansul, the co-pilot, said that to have been lost there the plane would have needed to fly between 300 and 400 nautical miles (345–460 miles or 556–741km) in the wrong direction.

Reaching the search area, the Hercules descended to 2,000ft (609m), where tiny white birds could be seen skimming the surface of the sea and flying fish were gliding above the water. By then it was 9 am and rays of sunshine turned the Andaman Sea a spectacular shade of orange.

"We hope we can find it but it is beyond our control," Syukri Bin Abd Mutalib, the navigator, told Philips.

"Yes, we will find it," insisted 34-year-old observer, Sergeant Zulfamy Bin Sulaman. The crew had been putting in gruelling 15-hour shifts since Flight MH370 went missing. Sergeant Sulaman was armed with a pair of hefty black marine binoculars and a Nikon D3X SLR camera.

The plane's second observer, Sergeant Zulhelmi Bin Hasam, who sat on the other side of the galley, told Philips: "We are looking for oil, for pieces of the aircraft, even for human bodies."

But there was nothing to be seen. Already they had searched Sections A, B, C and D, and seen nothing but blue water, with the

174

occasional white flicker of cresting waves. Sergeant Zulfamy admitted you have to be mentally strong – after two hours staring at the sea you became light-headed and can no longer focus – but he forced himself to go on as it was their responsibility to find the plane.

Sergeant Zulfamy added that he had yet to tell his two young sons, aged two and six, about his part in the search for the plane.

"They are very small," he said, but they had noticed their father's increasing workload. "They say, 'Dad, you come home very late'. I'm very tired."

Already, by 10.02 am, the observers' eyes were weary ones, glazing over from the featureless seascape beneath. They perked up momentarily when patches of white foam appeared to the East, then settled back into torpor.

"It's pollution," said Zulfamy. "If it was the plane there would be more of it."

The only thing of note was a small boat passing underneath. Half an hour later Section E had been fully swept. Then they headed back to Kuala Lumpur, where reports were circulating that wreckage had been found in the original search area on the other side of the Malay Peninsula in the South China Sea.

A Singapore air force C-130 took another party of reporters on hair-raising search flights that skimmed the waves at 170 mph (275 km/h). The observers peered through large window panels at the vast expanse of empty ocean, once again finding nothing of note.

A dead body was found in the sea off the west of Malaysia, but it turned out to be that of drowned fisherman Abdi Samita. A bright orange and black life-raft was hauled out of the water by fishermen near Port Dickson, also on the west coast of Malaysia, an hour from Kuala Lumpur, but it had no connection to the missing plane.

The Chinese satellite photographs, purportedly showing large pieces of debris roughly 200 miles (322km) from where the plane last made contact, were now dismissed. But the Chinese Ambassador to Malaysia said the photographs should not have been released – they were "a mistake" and did not show any debris from Malaysia Airlines Flight MH370. The area had been searched, but no wreckage found.

"There is nothing," said Hishammuddin Hussein. "We went there, there is nothing."

This left the Chinese in a reflective mood. An editorial by the country's official news agency, Xinhua, asked: "After six days of searching, can we still expect a modern version of the happy ending in Robinson Crusoe?"

Chinese premier Li Keqiang stepped in, saying he would like to see better co-ordination among the countries involved in the search.

"Families and friends are burning with anxiety, the Chinese government and Chinese people are all deeply concerned about their safety," he said. China alone had deployed eight ships and was using 10 satellites in the search.

The satellites were looking for the plane, he said, not just debris. However, the only instance of such a satellite picture being of any use in a crash investigation was when TWA Flight 800 blew up over Long Island in 1996. Just 12 minutes after the Boeing 747-131 took off from John F. Kennedy International Airport on its way to Paris and Rome it suddenly exploded, killing all 230 on board. Investigators found an image from a US weather satellite that caught the aircraft the instant it came apart.

The cockpit voice recorder was recovered. Seconds before the crash, the pilot was heard to say: "Look at that crazy fuel flow indicator there on number four... see that?"

The captain of an Eastwind Airlines Boeing 737 following said: "We just saw an explosion up ahead of us here... about 16,000 feet (4,800m) or something like that, it just went down into the water."

Like the families of those on board Flight MH370, relatives of the victims were put up in a hotel. The Ramada Plaza JFK Hotel became known as "Heartbreak Hotel" and acted as a "makeshift grief-counselling center," according to the New York *Daily News*. It took some time to retrieve the corpses of those killed. Delays and conflicting information provided by various agencies again provoked anger. Families became suspicious that investigators were not being truthful, or withholding information. In the end, remains of all 230 victims were recovered and identified, the last of them over 10 months later.

At first, it was thought that Flight 800 had been the victim of a terrorist attack, but after 16 months the FBI had found no evidence of criminal activity. It took the National Transportation Safety Board (NTSB) four years to conclude that the accident had been caused by an explosion of vapour in the fuel tanks, probably ignited by a short circuit. There were many alternate theories, of course, including that it was brought down by a missile from a US Navy vessel, resulting in a government cover-up. Similar theories surrounded the fate of Flight MH370. Some were even more bizarre.

The Sun reported that the Malays had brought in a witch doctor to solve the mystery of lost Flight MH370. Shaman Ibrahim Mat Zin performed a series of bizarre rituals in Kuala Lumpur Airport to ward off evil from the Malaysian jet. The medicine man smashed coconuts together over his head and mimed rowing with a bamboo stick, saying: "It weakens bad spirits so rescuers can find the plane."

In another twist, spoon-bender Uri Geller claimed he had been asked by a "significant figure" to use his psychic powers to help. Meanwhile, hundreds of uninhabited islands in the Indian Ocean were being searched in case the plane crash-landed near them, as if the story of Flight MH370 was a sequel to *Lost*.

"A normal investigation becomes narrower with time – as new information focuses the search, but this is not a normal investigation," said Hishammuddin Hussein. "In this case, the information has forced us to look further and further afield."

However, there were new clues regarding its whereabouts to be followed up. Although the Malaysian government had at first denied it, more signals had been received from the doomed plane. While the ACARS data reporting system had been closed down at 1.07 am and the transponder turned off 14 minutes later, just before the pilots' last contract with air traffic control, the plane continued to send faint electronic signals to satellites run by British firm Inmarsat for five hours.

A company spokesman explained: "Routine, automated signals were registered on the Inmarsat network from the Malaysia Airlines' flight in its flight from Kuala Lumpur. This information was shared with Malaysia Airlines. Since being advised that the plane was missing we have afforded urgent priority to the provision of data to those participating in the search and rescue activities."

Even if no data was being exchanged, Inmarsat's satellite sent out a "ping" to the plane every hour to check that the system was still switched on. If it was, the onboard system responded with a handshake.

As the signals continued long after other communication ended, it seemed that the plane had not simply blown up in mid-air and a police source said: "We're looking at sabotage, with hijack still on the cards."

It now seemed that the plane had been deliberately flown

toward the Andaman Islands, either flown manually or someone had programmed the autopilot. The fate of Flight MH370 was now dubbed an "act of piracy" with the plane still being piloted long after it had lost contact with the ground. Officials were examining the possibility that Flight MH370 had been deliberately steered off course by an unknown hijacker. Investigators believed "human intervention" could have played a role in the disappearance. The Andaman Islands seemed its most likely destination, could the plane or its wreckage be hidden under the dense forest there? The Indian air force and navy sent Dornier reconnaissance planes equipped with heat sensors to find out.

It was then revealed that, when tracked by military radar, the plane climbed to 45,000ft (13,716m), well above the approved altitude ceiling of 43,100ft (13,137m) for a 777, and then fell unevenly to 23,000ft (7,010m) in less than a minute as it approached Penang. But investigators do not believe the readings are accurate because the aircraft would normally have taken longer to complete such a reduction in altitude. There is no explanation for intentionally flying in such an erratic fashion as it would harm the passengers and raise suspicion among anyone scanning the area on radar.

Nevertheless Malaysian authorities said that only someone with "significant flying experience" could have done this. But why would the plane climb to such an altitude? Was the pilot trying to evade ground radar systems as the plane started out for its new destination? Why then did it drop low before making its second turn, this time to the northwest, taking it up the Straits of Malacca and out into the Indian Ocean? However, the changes in course and altitude suggested that someone – either the pilot or a hijacker – remained in control of the aircraft for several hours after contact with the ground was severed.

Inmarsat's hourly pings also indicated the plane had continued to fly beyond its last known point of contact. However, the plane's handshake did not transmit its location, but satellite communications expert Professor Mischa Dohler, of King's College London explained it should be possible to use the signal strength to work out roughly where the plane was.

"They were lucky because it was just on the junction of two satellites' coverage areas," he said. By comparing the relative strength of the two signals, it made it easier to get a better fix on the jet's position.

Data wizards at Inmarsat provided the vital satellite information to the UK Air Accidents Investigation Board, as well as to the Malaysian authorities. Unfortunately, Flight MH370 was not fitted with one of the updated versions of the Inmarsat system that would have allowed investigators to get a GPS fix and know exactly where it was. It was using the old Swift 64 system that provided only the most basic information. This could give a guide to a rough direction of travel. The signals continued for another four or five hours, and would still have been transmitted if the plane was on the ground. US officials discounted the idea that the 250-ton airliner could have landed safely and undetected. They concluded it was more likely to have crashed into the Indian Ocean.

Meanwhile, the Indian Navy stepped up their search of the Andaman Islands. They had a population of 380,000, but only 37 of the 572 islands in the archipelago are inhabited so it was perfectly possible that the aircraft crashed there without anyone seeing it. Many of the islanders have little contact with the outside world and some of the Andaman tribes are considered among the most isolated people on the planet.

"We have many radar systems operating in the area, but

nothing was picked up," said India's Rear Admiral Sudhir Pillai, chief of staff of Andamans and Nicobar Command. "It is possible that the military radars were switched off as we operate on an as-required basis. So perhaps secondary radars were operating which may not have the required range to detect a flight at an altitude of 35,000 feet."

However, Denis Giles, editor of the *Andaman Chronicle*, said there was nowhere to land a Boeing 777 in the archipelago without attracting attention.

"There is no chance that any aircraft of this size can come towards Andaman and Nicobar Islands and land," he insisted.

If the aircraft had continued to fly to the northwest and headed over Indian territory it would have been detected. India has strong air defences and radar coverage should have allowed authorities there to see the plane and, if necessary, intercept it.

While investigators had become convinced that the disappearance of Flight MH370 was an act of piracy, it was then revealed that it was carrying a cargo of lithium-ion batteries. These are used in laptops and cellphones and have a poor safety record. Ten million Sony batteries used in Dell, Sony, Apple, Lenovo, Panasonic, Toshiba, Hitachi, Fujitsu and Sharp laptops were recalled in 2006 when it was found that contamination by metal particles during manufacture could cause a dangerous short-circuit. In March 2007 computer manufacturer Lenovo recalled some 205,000 batteries due to the risk of explosion. And in August 2007 cellphone manufacturer Nokia recalled over 46 million batteries that risked overheating and exploding. A Nokia N91 blew up while being recharged in the Philippines that July.

There was a possibility that the batteries in the cargo hold could have overheated and burned through the aircraft's frame. Lithium-ion batteries have been responsible for 140 incidents on planes over 23 years and were blamed for the crash of a UPS cargo plane in Dubai in 2010. The Boeing 747-400F had just taken off from Dubai International Airport when the crew reported a fire in the cockpit. They were 120 nautical miles (138 miles or 222km) from the airport when an emergency was declared. Returning to Dubai, they made their approach too high. Turning for a second approach, the plane crashed, barely missing Dubai's Silicon Oasis technology park. The two crew members were killed. The batteries also caused a fire on a UPS flight that made an emergency landing in Philadelphia in 2006.

Boeing's 787 Dreamliner aircraft suffered a series of setbacks when lithium batteries suffered electrical fires. On 16 January 2013, on All Nippon Airways Flight NH-692, en route from Yamaguchi Ube Airport to Tokyo's Haneda Airport, a battery warning light showed, accompanied by the smell of burning as the plane climbed from Ube. It diverted to Takamatsu and the passengers were evacuated via the slides; three suffered minor injuries – the incident was caused by a battery fire.

Another battery fire occurred on a Japan Airlines 787 parked at Boston's Logan International Airport, leading the Federal Aviation Administration to ground all Boeing 787s in service at the time while modifications were made. The grounding was estimated to have cost US$93 million (£55 million) in lost sales.

The FAA also issued a restriction on the carrying of lithium batteries in bulk on passenger flights and they were also classed as "dangerous goods" by the International Civil Aviation Organization. However, Malaysia Airlines said that the batteries on board Flight MH370 were packed and carried in accordance with regulations and were unlikely to have posed a threat.

"We carry lithium-ion batteries but they are approved," said head of Malaysia Airlines Ahmad Jauhari Yahya. "These are not regarded as dangerous goods and were packed as recommended by the International Civil Aviation Organization. We check them several times and make sure the packing is right."

He had previously said the cargo contained only three to four tons of mangosteen fruits.

"Any energy storage device will always have a remote possibility that it could start a fire," said Peter Bruce, professor of Chemistry at St Andrews University. "But in my view it is extremely unlikely."

Another possible cause of the loss of Flight MH370 had been discounted.

The mystery deepened. After a week, there was no sign of the plane and no explanation as to what had happened to it. All likely scenarios were proposed and rejected. If the 777 had suffered a catastrophic mechanical failure, why had no debris been found in the area where the plane lost contact with air traffic control?

If the cabin had depressurized and the pilots had passed out due to lack of oxygen, leaving the plane to fly on for several hours on autopilot, why had the aircraft's transponder and data transmission system been turned off? So again attention turned to terrorism.

South-east Asia was home to a number of al-Qaeda-linked groups. There were 30 terrorist attacks there in 2012 alone. In Indonesia, there was Jamaah Ansharut Tauhid, who were behind a suicide bombing in a church in 2011, and Jemaah Islamiyah, the terrorist organization behind a series of bombings, including the Bali nightclub massacre, which killed 202 people in 2002, and the bombing of the Marriott Hotel in Jakarta, which killed 12 and injured another 150 people in 2003.

In 2000, biochemist and former army captain Yazid Suufat had played host to two of the 9/11 hijackers, Khalid al-Mihdhar and

Nawaf al-Hazmi, at an al-Qaeda summit in Kuala Lumpur. In 2001 he was jailed under the Internal Security Act for seven years on suspicion of being part of the Jemaah Islamiyah network. Since his release in 2008, Suufat has publicly revelled in his connections with Osama bin Laden and his own jihad in Afghanistan. On Facebook and in media interviews he lavished praise on the 9/11 hijackers.

A charismatic figure, Suufat attracted a circle of young admirers, some of whom were just children in 2001. He was rearrested early in 2013 for inciting terrorist acts, but freed by a court. In May 2013, he was arrested again, this time under a section of the penal code covering membership of a terrorist group. He has since been released, and his whereabouts could not be established at the time Flight MH370 went missing.

Another Jemaah Islamiyah fanatic named Mas Selamat bin Kastari was extradited from Malaysia to Singapore over a plot to hijack a plane and crash it into an airport in 2010. Born in Indonesia, Selamat grew up in Singapore. In the 1990s he joined Darul Islam, a precursor movement to the Jemaah Islamiyah. By 1992, he had joined the Singapore Jemaah Islamiyah cell. The following year he was sent to Afghanistan for training. In 1998, he studied the Taliban system of government and returned home "deeply impressed".

According to Singapore security services, Selamat has met Riduan Isamuddin Hambali, the leader of Jemaah Islamiyah and al-Qaeda's military commander in southeast Asia. They discussed various terror tactics, including a proposed plot to hijack a plane from Bangkok and crash it into Singapore's Changi Airport. He fled from Singapore in 2001 before authorities clamped down on Jemaah Islamiyah and arrested 13 suspected members.

Selamat was arrested on the island of Bintan, Indonesia, in

February 2003 by police looking into bombings in Indonesia in 2001 and 2002. Literature on bomb making and the virtue of suicide were found in his possession. He had assumed the name of Edi Heriyanto to obtain an Indonesian passport. In 2003 he was jailed for 18 months for immigration offences. On his release he was not handed over to Singapore since Indonesia and Singapore did not have an extradition treaty.

On 20 January 2006, he was arrested again for using a fake identity card in Java, where he was visiting his son, who was studying at a religious school there. This time he was handed over to Singapore, where he was held without trial under the Internal Security Act. The Malaysian authorities also wanted to question Selamat, who had made frequent visits to the southern state of Johor before fleeing to Indonesia.

However, on 27 February 2008, Selamat escaped from a high-security detention centre by squeezing through a toilet window and climbing over a fence. Nine officers and guards were disciplined over the escape; two were sacked and three were demoted. Interpol was alerted and a reward of US$1 million (£594,000) was put on Selamat's head. On 1 April 2009, he was captured in Johor. Hishammuddin Hussein, then Malaysia's home minister, said that Selamat was being held under the Internal Security Act, adding that he was "planning something, which allowed us to arrest him". The following year he was returned to Singapore, where he was again held under the Internal Security Act. Though this effectively put him out of circulation, he was still able to incite others to acts of terrorism.

Two Malaysian men were arrested on 10 March 2013 for suspected links to a branch of al-Qaeda, while two further Malaysians were arrested the previous October in Lebanon, trying to get to Syria to join the revolt against President Bashar al-Assad.

In a separate incident in May 2013, two Malaysian men were arrested for links to al-Qaeda and charged with joining the Tanzim al-Qaeda Malaysia terrorist group.

Director of the Jakarta-based Institute for Policy Analysis of Conflict Sidney Jones said: "Jemaah Islamiyah has not been involved with violence in the region since 2007. The other groups that are active in Indonesia are all not very competent. I would be extremely surprised if any group from Indonesia, the Philippines or Malaysia would be directly involved."

Most of the Indonesians on board were aged between their mid-forties and late-fifties – not the usual age group despatched on suicide missions. And none of the radical Muslim groups in Indonesia or Malaysia had claimed responsibility.

There was always the East Turkestan Islamic Movement, an umbrella group wanting a homeland for ethnic Uighurs in China's Xinjiang region and thought to have been behind the Kunming railway station attack. However, intelligence sources monitoring extremists said that there was a lack of "chatter" normally involved with the planning of a terrorist attack. They also doubted that local groups had the level of organization to commandeer a plane and fly it undetected. This, experts insisted, would involve "something beyond the mission planning for 9/11". And ETIM had no history of this type of attack.

But China has its own problems directly with the Taliban. In 2008, the Chinese Metallurgical Group and Jiangxi Copper Co bought a 30-year lease on the site of Mes Aynak in Logar province, east Afghanistan for US$3 billion (£1.8 billion). It is thought to be the largest copper deposit in the world. But after Taliban attacks, the mine was closed. Beijing now views Afghanistan more as a security problem than an economic opportunity.

In September 2012, the then Chinese public security chief,

Zhou Yongkang, visited Kabul and China began security co-operation with President Hamid Karzai's regime, training 300 Afghan police officers. Since then the US and China have collaborated in training Afghan diplomats, health workers and agricultural engineers. Ambassador James F. Dobbins, the US Special Representative for Afghanistan, has thrice-yearly meetings with his Chinese counterpart to discuss future areas of co-operation.

Barnett Rubin, former US Special Representative for Afghanistan and Pakistan, said: "Taliban militants attacking Chinese mining activities in Logar province are coming from Pakistan. Uighur militants in western China are being trained in Pakistan, and are going back to China. China has found that Pakistan is not effectively stopping those people. This has really affected China's attitude to Pakistan, which it no longer considers a reliable ally. This is one of the reasons why Chinese-Indian relations have started to warm, and that China is seeking co-operation with the US in Afghanistan."

But former FBI assistant director James Kallstrom was not so sanguine. He thought that no one credible had claimed responsibility so far because the terrorists wanted to keep the plane to use as a weapon "for some dastardly deed down the road". It might even have been taken as a dry run for a future terrorist atrocity, testing the terrorists' ability to hide a plane from radar and satellites, he speculated.

Straightforward hijacking was another possibility. This explained the timing of Flight MH370's disappearance, between two air traffic control zones, and the radio silence. It would also explain why the cellphones of some passengers were connecting, but not being answered. The Straits of Malacca was one of the world centres of piracy; three ships had been taken since the beginning of the month. However, pirates from the Straits had not yet turned their attention to stealing planes.

No demand had been received from the hijackers and planes were hard to dispose of. With ships, pirates simply unloaded the cargo, repainted the vessel, renamed it and sold it on. Besides, to disable the communication and location systems, the hijackers would have to be trained. However, the hijackers of the four planes used in the 9/11 attacks turned off the transponders of three of the jets; the settings on the transponder of the fourth plane were changed repeatedly to confuse air traffic controllers. Flight MH370's transponder was switched off around the time the plane reached cruising altitude. This is when hijackers often strike as pilots emerge from the cockpit to take a bathroom or coffee break.

The result was something Siti Sarah Lebai Abu, an air traffic controller at Kuala Lumpur's National Air Traffic Control Centre with 18 years experience, said she had never experienced before – "a total communications breakdown".

Of course, the pilot and co-pilot could have disabled the transponder and the ACARS system. Probably no one on board had more expertise than Captain Shah. There had been grisly precedents of pilots committing suicide by downing their planes in the ocean. If the plane had stayed intact, it could have sunk quickly without leaving a field of debris. Or had they flown the plane to a secret destination? But both men had been profiled by the police and there was no indication that either one was likely to do such a deed. The two men had not asked to fly together, ruling out their collaboration in a well-planned act. If they both diverted the plane, it might have been under duress, or if one was incapacitated and the other could have decided to deliberately crash the plane or fly it to another country.

It has been suggested that Captain Shah might have a political motive, though that looks increasingly thin. And there had been no reports of any suggested mental health concerns for either the pilot or the co-pilot.

Scott Shankland, an American Airlines pilot who spent several years as a co-pilot on Boeing 777s, said that a captain would know how to disable radios and the plane's other tracking systems. But a hijacker, even one trained to fly a plane, "would probably be hunting and pecking quite a while 'Do I pull this switch? Do I pull that?' You could disable a great deal [of the tracking equipment] but possibly not all of it."

Some of the plane's data is transmitted automatically from equipment outside the cockpit, making it even harder to avoid leaving a trail of electronic breadcrumbs, he added.

Aviation consultant Chris Yates said: "It's increasingly clear that the hand of some form of terrorism is at play. The levels of specialist aviation knowledge on display here cause me to cast my eyes back to 9/11, when hijackers had acquired a level of technical and flight training."

Even an experienced pilot would struggle to pull off this vanishing act.

American officials said that, in all, three different pieces of signalling equipment had been disabled. One of them was located outside the cockpit. The implication was that at least two people had collaborated to change the course of Flight MH370 and make it and its crew and passengers disappear.

But Shah and Hamid seemed unlikely hijackers and they did not fit the profile of a terrorist in any way. If the captain and co-pilot have been involved they will have given new meaning to the term "clean skins".

Phil Giles, a former air safety investigator who worked on the

Lockerbie bombing, said: "Unless the hijacker has a fair amount of technical and aviation knowledge, he would have to rely on putting a gun to the pilot's head."

CHAPTER FIFTEEN

IN LIMBO

Professor John Hansman, an aeronautics expert familiar with the Boeing 777, did not believe that Flight MH370 had been hijacked. He said it would be possible for an intruder to turn off the transponder, but knowing how to shut down other systems would be more difficult. Even if 9/11-style hijackers got that far, he insisted that they would have had a hard task to keep flying, make a successful landing, and hide the plane. "If it was a hijacking, it was probably a hijacking gone bad," he surmised.

Instead, Hansman thought there could have been a series of malfunctions or a fire that shut down key systems and incapacitated the pilots. He compared it to the 1999 crash in South Dakota of a Learjet carrying pro-golfer Payne Stewart. Shortly after it had taken off from Orlando, Florida, air traffic controllers found they couldn't contact the crew. The plane failed to make the westward turn toward Dallas, Texas, over north Florida. It continued flying over the southern and midwestern

United States for almost four hours, covering 1,500 miles (2,414km). Pilots of planes sent up to intercept it saw no movement in the cockpit. The plane ran out of fuel and crashed into a field near Aberdeen, South Dakota, after an uncontrolled descent. All six on board were killed. It was thought that they lost cabin pressure soon after reaching cruising altitude. The pilots passed out due to lack of oxygen and the plane flew on on autopilot in a curious limbo until it eventually crashed.

There was a similar, even more lethal air crash in Greece in 2005. A Helios Airways Boeing 737-31s arrived at Larnaca Airport on Cyprus from London Heathrow on the morning of 14 August 2005. The crew had reported a frozen door seal and abnormal noises coming from the right aft service door, and requested a full inspection. To carry out a pressure check on the door, the ground engineer had to switch the pressurization system to "manual". When he had finished, he forgot to reset it to "auto" and the plane was returned to service.

The next crew included, as captain, Hans-Jürgen Merten, a 58-year-old German contract pilot hired by Helios for the holiday flights. He had been flying for 35 years and had accrued 16,900 flying hours. Fifty-one-year-old Pambos Charalambous, a Cypriot who flew for Helios, served as the first officer. Charalambous had accrued 7,549 flying hours throughout his career. And 32-year-old Louisa Vouteri, a Greek national living in Cyprus, replaced a sick colleague as the chief purser.

The cockpit crew overlooked the setting of the pressurization system during the pre-flight procedure and the after-start check. Helios Airways Flight 522 took off at 9.07 am, bound for Prague via Athens, still with the pressurization system set to manual and the outflow valve partially open. The crew missed the incorrect setting again in the after-takeoff check.

As the plane climbed, the pressure inside the cabin dropped. When it reached an altitude of 12,040ft (3,670m), an alarm sounded. This warned the crew to stop climbing. However, they mistook the alarm for the takeoff configuration alarm, which warns that an aircraft is not ready for takeoff and can only sound on the ground.

A few minutes later, cooling equipment warning lights on the overhead panel came on, indicating that there was not enough air flowing through the cooling fans, followed by the master caution light. At 18,000ft (5,486m), the oxygen masks in the passenger cabin automatically deployed.

The captain radioed Larnaca to tell them what was happening and spoke to the ground engineer who had carried out the pressure check on the door. He asked the captain to confirm that the pressurization system was set to "auto". Perhaps already suffering the effects of hypoxia, the captain ignored the question and asked about the cooling equipment. That was the last that was heard from him. Nicosia air traffic control tried to contact the plane, without success.

The 737 climbed to 34,000ft (10,363m). Heading on toward Greece, it failed to contact Athens air traffic control, which also tried unsuccessfully to establish contact. As it neared Athens International Airport, Helios Airways Flight 522 made no attempt to descend and stayed at 34,000ft. Under the control of the autopilot, it remained in the holding pattern for the next 70 minutes.

Two Hellenic air force F-16 fighters intercepted the plane. They saw the first officer slumped motionless at the controls. The captain's seat was empty and, in the passenger cabin, they could see the oxygen masks dangling.

Realizing something was wrong, the flight attendant Andreas

Prodromou entered the cockpit to find no one in control. He sat in the captain's chair. Holding a UK commercial pilot's licence, he tried to take control of the plane. He was not qualified to fly a Boeing 737, but in any case he had left it too late: the plane was out of fuel. The left engine flamed out and the aircraft began to descend. Ten minutes later, the right engine also flamed out.

The plane crashed into the hills at Grammatiko, 25 miles (40m) from Athens, killing all 121 people on board. The passenger list comprised 93 adults and 22 minors; the bodies of 118 were recovered. News media reported that shortly before the crash a passenger sent a text message, saying: "The pilot is dead. Farewell, my cousin, here we're frozen." Police later arrested Nektarios-Sotirios Voutas, who admitted making the story up.

Professor David Allerton of the University of Sheffield said: "Military pilots are trained to detect hypoxia, but generally civilian pilots aren't. It's a very insidious thing, you might not realize at the time it's happening to you, and by the time you've realized it's too late, as you're dopey."

In these two cases, the authorities in Greece and the US reacted quickly when they received no response from the aircraft: this did not happen in southeast Asia.

"If this had happened in Europe or North America within a few tens of minutes people would have worked out there was something very strange going on, and they would have done something, for example, scramble aircraft," Professor Allerton said. "If you lose communication with an aircraft, and certainly if you lose its transponder returns, you assume something quite bad has happened. It doesn't seem to me that the Malaysian authorities were very responsive to what was happening in their airspace. When you ask: 'How could this happen?', if the air traffic controllers haven't been monitoring things very closely then it would be seven hours before somebody realized it hadn't got there."

Since no planes were sent to intercept Flight MH370 and no wreckage was found on the ground or in the sea, it was difficult to dismiss any theory. If it was the work of hijackers, "they would have to be somebody who has detailed knowledge of the plane," said Alan Diehl, a former crash investigator. "Could they get down below the radar and make a beeline to an abandoned airstrip? The short answer is 'Yes'. Even today, satellites don't cover every square kilometre of the Earth."

The investigation was expanded to include people Shah and Hamid had worked or trained with. Police chief Khalid Abu Bakar said: "The four areas of focus on the investigation are hijacking, sabotage, personal problems and psychological problems – that includes the ground staff, everybody."

Malaysia's acting transport minister Hishammuddin Hussein said there were four or five possibilities as to why the plane's communications systems may have been turned off.

"It could have been done intentionally, it could be done under duress, it could have been done because of an explosion," he said. "That's why I don't want to go into the realm of speculation. We are looking at all the possibilities."

He also confirmed that: "If investigation requires searching the pilots' homes, it will be done."

While the Chinese navy now sent ships to the Straits of Malacca, Bernard Loeb, a former head of aviation safety at the US National Transportation Safety Board (NTSB), told *The New York Times*: "We try very hard not to make it look like we are running the investigation, even if we more or less are."

This may have been one motive for US reports being released through unnamed sources.

"There's no sense reminding everyone – especially China – how much better you are at this than everyone else," said James Manicom, a research fellow at the Centre for International Governance Innovation (CIGI) in Waterloo, Canada. "Better to be modest and constructive than turn up and remind everyone how overwhelming your technical and military advantages are."

Under international protocols, the country where a missing aircraft is registered must lead the investigation and the US had a vested interest in not revealing too much about its technical know-how, especially when dealing with the Chinese. Meanwhile, China wanted to show it could protect its citizens overseas and repeatedly urged Malaysia "to report what they have… in an accurate and timely fashion". The Chinese government's Xinhua News Agency accused Malaysia of dragging its feet in releasing news of the missing flight. Information released by the Malaysian leader was "painfully belated", it said, while delays had resulted in wasted efforts and strained the nerves of relatives.

"Given today's technology, the delay smacks of either dereliction of duty or reluctance to share information in a full and timely manner," Xinhua added. "That would be intolerable."

Still awaiting further news at the Lido Hotel in Beijing, relatives of passengers said they felt deceived at not being told earlier about the plane's Inmarsat signals. "We are going through a rollercoaster, and we feel helpless and powerless," said one woman.

Some, though, saw a glimmer of hope that the plane's disappearance was a deliberate act, rather than a crash. "It's very good," said a woman named Wen, who still clung to the hope that her relative was alive and safely on the ground somewhere.

In response, Malaysia had criticized China for releasing satellite images that it had not passed to Kuala Lumpur, and chided

Vietnam for announcing the discovery of possible debris prematurely.

"We should be cheered by the intentions they have of working together [but] their ability to work together has been proved to be wanting," said Taylor Fravel of the security studies programme at the Massachusetts Institute of Technology (MIT). However, a lot of the problem seemed to lie in inter-departmental squabbles in Malaysia. "It seems the Malaysians internally are not talking very well to each other," he added.

"Given existing tensions in the Asia-Pacific region and strained communications between several key regional countries, it is hard to imagine meaningful co-operation or military transparency between them on information such as radar readings in the effort to locate the Malaysia Airlines flight," said director of the Asia-Pacific programme at the United States Institute of Peace, Stephanie Kleine-Ahlbrandt.

The South China Sea – still one of the main areas of the search – was at the heart of a complex six-party territorial row

"Malaysia was supposed to be the country getting along with China among the claimants in the South China Sea, but even that relationship has deteriorated," said Manicom.

Christopher Hughes, a regional expert at the London School of Economics, noted: "This has been the problem since the end of the Cold War and really since the end of World War II. They have entrenched rivalries over so many issues – territorial, historical and so on – that it is almost impossible to get them to move toward any meaningful multilateral system. They are so hung up on issues of sovereignty and non-intervention and suspicion of each other that it stops them working on the issues that really matter."

Hong Nong, a professor at China's National Institute for South China Sea Studies, pointed out: "Actually, this is not a multinational search; each country has searched by themselves. In my opinion, through this event, it will be good if every country could increase the possibility of co-operation in undisputed areas."

Taylor Fravel of MIT had noticed some progress had been made, though. "What's remarkable is that Vietnam has allowed two Chinese electronic surveillance planes to fly through its airspace," he said.

However, one Kuala Lumpur-based diplomat said: "Despite the appearance of friendly co-operation between the countries, I think that there are some big divisions opening behind the scenes. The main suspicion is that nobody is being completely transparent about releasing the data they have because a lot of it has a military aspect."

As the search spread out into the Bay of Bengal, 57 ships, 48 aircraft and 13 nations were involved. Having completed an aerial search of the northwest section of the Straits of Malacca, an American P-3C Orion reconnaissance aircraft flew on nearly 1,000 miles to the west but still found nothing significant to report, and USS *Kidd* moved into the Andaman Sea.

By then, every piece of data received from the aircraft was under scrutiny. However, to all those following the story around the world, it seemed curious that systems for locating an aircraft were less sophisticated than those used for tracking a smartphone and that, given twenty-first-century communication technology, a large US$260-million passenger jet could simply vanish. All that was known, given the fuel on board, was that the Boeing could have flown a further 2,500 miles from its last-known location. This extended to almost all of India and as far as the coasts of Australia and Japan. A circle with a radius of 2,500 miles has an area of almost 28 million square miles (72 million sq km), twice the size of Africa or a tenth of the surface of the Earth. At that point, however, the clues put the missing plane somewhere out over the Indian Ocean. All Malaysia Airlines could do was re-designate their weekly service from Kuala Lumpur to Beijing MH318 as "a mark of respect to the passengers and crew of MH370".

Then came the puzzling news that Chinese seismologists at a state university had posted details of a distinct, short "seabed incident" about 90 minutes after Flight MH370 went missing, which they said could not be explained as an earthquake. The implication was that they had detected the aircraft's fuselage hitting the seabed.

On Sunday, 16 March 2014, another possibility opened up. "It might well be the world's first cyber hijack," observed British anti-terror expert Dr Sally Leivesley.

A former Home Office scientific adviser, Dr Leivesley said the hackers could change the plane's speed, altitude and direction by sending radio signals to its Flight Management System. It could then be made to crash, or even landed at some remote destination, by remote control. In a plot straight from the pages of a James Bond novel, possible culprits included criminal gangs, terrorists, a foreign power – or a megalomaniac living inside a volcano on a remote tropical island.

Dr Leivesley said she believed a framework of malicious codes, triggered by a cellphone, would have been able to override the aircraft's security software.

"There appears to be an element of planning from someone with a very sophisticated systems engineering understanding," she told the *Sunday Express*.

A fly-by-wire aircraft such as the Boeing 777 is controlled by electronic signals. "This is a very early version of what I would call a smart plane," she continued. "It is looking more and more likely that the control of some systems was taken over in a deceptive manner, either manually, so someone sitting in a seat overriding the autopilot, or via a remote device turning off or overwhelming the systems."

This could have been done by something as simple as a cellphone or a USB stick. "When the plane is air-side, you can insert a set of commands and codes that may initiate, on signal, a set of processes," Dr Leivesley noted. She added that the threat of hacking into an aircraft's system had been outlined late the previous year at a science conference in China.

"What we are finding now is that it is possible with a cellphone to initiate a signal to a preset piece of malicious software, or malware, in the computer that initiates a whole set of instructions," she told *Express* journalists James Fielding and Stuart Winter. "It is possible for hackers, be they part of organized crime or with government backgrounds, to get into the main computer network of the plane through the in-flight, onboard entertainment system."

She went on to outline the dangers: "If you have got any connections whatsoever between the computing systems, you can jump across and you can get into the flight critical system. To really protect your computer systems, you do not let anything connect with them and you would keep the in-flight systems totally in their own loop so nothing whatsoever connects. There are now a number of ways, however, in which the gap between those systems and a handheld device like a mobile [cell] phone can be overcome."

Dr Leivesley was not the only one saying this. German security consultant Hugo Teso, who is also a commercial pilot, had already demonstrated an app that allows the user to control a plane from the ground at the Hack In The Box security summit in Amsterdam in April 2013. Called PlaneSploit, it works on an Android phone and hacks into an aircraft's security system. The computer systems on commercial planes lack the security to tell whether data is coming from a legitimate source. By interfering with the data, Teso said he could then send radio signals that could change a pilot's display or alter the plane's speed, direction or altitude.

In his demonstration, Teso used codes from real-world aircraft to start the hijacking sequence, but used virtual planes to simulate the app's hijacking capabilities. Hijacking a real plane electronically would be "too dangerous and unethical," he insisted. The app attacks a plane's autopilot, and it could do terrifying things such as drop passengers' oxygen masks without warning.

Teso worked with the Federal Aviation Administration and the European Aviation Safety Administration, the governing bodies who regulate flight safety procedures in the States and Europe, and his app is not going to be available for download. But despite the demonstrable capabilities of his app, he did not believe that the plane had been hijacked.

That being so, attention was now turned back on the 53-year-old pilot, Zaharie Ahmad Shah. Police had been standing guard outside the father-of-three's home since the flight vanished, but on 15 March 2014 they began an extensive search inside. Diaries, personal papers, computer files, two laptops and the flight simulator that Captain Shah had built himself were all undergoing detailed forensic analysis. It was thought that the simulator could show the routes he had been training on.

It was then revealed that his estranged wife and children moved out of the family home the day before Flight MH370 went missing. He also appeared to have been a dedicated supporter of the country's opposition leader Anwar Ibrahim, who was sentenced to five years for sodomy, just hours before the jet disappeared. A picture of Shah wearing a T-shirt bearing the slogan "Democracy is Dead" emerged. It had been taken on 5 May 2013 – the day of elections, which led to violent protests against alleged poll fraud. Opposition leader Anwar Ibrahim called his activists onto the streets. A rally led by him drew more than 50,000 participants to a sports stadium outside the capital. Many complained that the general election was riddled with fraud and that the political system was rigged toward the Barisan Nasional – or National Front – which had maintained its rule unbroken for 56 years since Malaysia's independence from Britain in 1957. Its continued grip on power had been achieved most recently in 2013, when the election had been fought in constituencies gerrymandered to give BN supporters a parliamentary presence out of all proportion to its following. Eventually the popular vote was not won by the BN, but by Anwar Ibrahim's Pakatan Rakyat or People's Alliance, though it was denied a role in government.

In the eyes of many of his followers, Ibrahim has been legally and politically persecuted for almost two decades for alleged homosexual acts, which he has always denied. His trials and the bitter social schisms they have exposed in the country were matters of supreme sensitivity for the Malaysian Government, but his imprisonment was not seen as a motive for extremist acts.

Ibrahim denied any strong links to Captain Shah. He told the *South China Morning Post* that he had only seen the pilot at party meetings, but described him as an "ardent supporter". Captain Shah "was nice, smart, articulate – but there was clearly a strong passion for justice".

Sivarasa Rasiah, another opposition leader, said it was

"unthinkable" that Captain Shah could have been involved in terrorism. He was "a really likeable guy, a warm guy".

Anwar Ibrahim later claimed that, while he was finance minister in 1994, he had personally authorized the installation of "one of the most sophisticated radar" systems in the world, based near the South China Sea and covering Malaysia's mainland and east and west coastlines. He said it was "not only unacceptable but not possible, not feasible" that the plane had not been sighted by the Marconi radar system immediately after it had changed course. The radar, he insisted, would have instantly detected the Boeing 777 as it travelled east to west across "at least four" Malaysian provinces.

"I believe the government knows more than us," he said. "They have the authority to instruct the air force or Malaysia Airlines. They are privy to most of these missing bits of information critical to our understanding of this mysterious disappearance of MH370."

He added that Chinese complaints about Malaysia's handling of the search were "absolutely justified".

Friends of Shah's 27-year-old daughter, an architect living in Melbourne, said that speculation over her father's involvement in the aircraft's disappearance was "killing the family". At a meeting of Malaysia's parliament, Mahfuz Omar, a prominent opposition MP, said that if the 239 passengers and crew were being held hostage, his party was willing to provide 239 members to exchange places with them.

Further adding to the mystery, Shah had also left a strange online post, saying: "There is a rebel in everyone of us… let it out! Don't waste your life on mundane lifestyle. When is it enough?"

Was there some political message in this? There was speculation that Shah might have hijacked the plane as a political protest. In this scenario the rapid change of altitude after the plane diverted from its original course to Beijing indicated a cockpit takeover, possibly a struggle between Shah and co-pilot Hamid. Or could it have been a deliberate manoeuvre to knock out the passengers and the rest of the crew? Climbing above the plane's service limit of 43,100ft (13,137m) with a depressurized cabin would have achieved this. This might have explained why none of the passengers used their cellphones to alert those on the ground to the danger they faced.

Experts say calls can be made even at high altitude, high above the antenna.

"It is theoretically possible," said Dan Warren, senior director of technology at the GSM Association, an international cellphone organization. "It would depend on the spectrum range you're in with your phone. It also depends on the power output of the cell itself. It would also depend on the landmass and network they were flying over, and the roaming agreement of the various network operators. There's not really a clear cut answer."

However, he added: "If a plane were to fly over the sea, contact would soon stop. It wouldn't take very long to lose any kind of phone signal. It would depend on altitude and the direction you were flying in."

Although calls from 30,000ft (9,144m) do not usually work – the limit is about 10,000ft (3,048m) – text messages sometimes do. In the absence of the latter, however, one can only conclude that the passengers were prevented from using their phones, or that the plane was flying well out of range of cellphone masts. Some planes have systems to enable passengers to make calls using a satellite link, but it was not thought to have been fitted in the missing 777. But, of course, passengers could not have made calls if they were unconscious.

It was only much later that news came that contact had been with Hamid's phone. Apparently, he had turned it off before takeoff. However, a signal was picked up from it when the plane was about 200 nautical miles (230 miles or 370km) northwest of the west coast state of Penang. That was roughly where military radar made its last sighting of the missing jet at 2.15 am local time on 8 March 2014. The *New Straits Times* reported: "The telco's [telecommunications company's] tower established the call that he was trying to make. On why the call was cut off, it was likely because the aircraft was fast moving away from the tower and had not come under the coverage of the next one."

It was not clear if anyone was actually trying to make a call, or whether the phone had simply been switched on again and was making contact with the nearest mast. Hamid's 18-year-old cousin, Nursyafiqah Kamaruddin, said he was probably trying to contact his mother. "If Fariq could make one call before the plane disappeared, it would have been to her," he insisted.

One senior police officer asked whether Captain Shah's background as an opposition supporter was being examined: "We need to cover all our bases."

The police left Shah's house carrying plastic bags. But his friend Peter Chong insisted Zaharie Ahmad Shah would be "the last person" to hijack the aircraft. He told the *Sunday Mirror*: "I would trust that man with my life. He loves people and being involved in something like that would hurt people. I would not believe he was involved in any way at all. If I went on a plane and was allowed the choice of a pilot, I would choose Captain Zaharie."

Mr Chong, a political secretary to a Malaysian MP, last saw his friend two weeks before the flight. They had agreed to meet that week and the pilot had been "his normal, cheerful self", he said.

Chong was a supporter of the Malaysian People's Justice Party and had met Shah as another "social activist", raising money for the underprivileged by organizing fundraising cycle rides. "During the election he was flying most of the time but whenever he was home, he would help out with environmental events," Chong recalled.

He described his friend as "a very caring person who puts people ahead of himself" – hence his interest in politics. "But his passion was for flying," Chong continued. "He built his own flight simulator to share the joy of flying with friends. He used to say it was more difficult than flying a real plane."

In one of the five video clips Shah uploaded to the Internet he was seen speaking to a webcam at home with what appears to be his home-made flight simulator in the background. While fellow pilots have also said it is common for aviators to bring their work home, and rare for would-be hijackers to advertise their simulators on the Internet, police will be examining the simulator for clues.

Shah had a do-it-yourself video channel on YouTube, where he tutored the impractical on how to repair air-conditioners, fix ice-making machines and make other household gadgets more energy-efficient. He was also a proud cook, posting pictures of himself at the stove and of his dishes, and taking home-cooked food to community events. He also "liked" videos by Ibrahim posted on YouTube.

Since the disappearance of Flight MH370, one of Shah's followers posted: "Captain pls come back, we are waiting you for more videos…" Another said: "I'd say we lost a gem of a man … a great mind and a kind heart."

Along with Captain Shah's selfies with his simulator, on his Facebook page was another showing him brandishing a meat cleaver and holding a bowl of mince. But Chong was adamant that Shah would have done everything to ensure his 227 passengers were safe in the event of a hijack. He was angry at the suggestion the pilot could have "gone rogue", hijacked his own plane and crashed it. "I just do not believe it until there is concrete evidence," he said. "What I hope has happened is that it has been hijacked, landed somewhere and negotiations are going on."

A fellow pilot at Malaysia Airlines said: "Zaharie is not suicidal, not a political fanatic as some foreign media are saying. Is it wrong for anyone to have an opinion about politics?" The Malaysia Airlines company has also said it did not believe that Captain Shah would have sabotaged the plane.

CHAPTER SIXTEEN

MORE THEORIES

While the news media around the world had no fresh evidence to report about the fate of Flight MH370, theories multiplied. Struan Johnston, of Caledonian Aviation, told *The Sun*: "The plane went off radar at the most vulnerable moment during handover with Malaysian and Vietnamese air traffic control. There would be a 10- to 15-minute window of opportunity and at 2 am on such a regular flight, no one's going to pay it much attention. Someone obviously knew all about that so it points to someone who's motivated, smart and knows exactly what's going on in a Boeing 777."

The disabling of the ACARS and the transponder was also suspicious. "The fact the telemetry systems had all been shut down also points to that – maybe an engineer who knows avionics or a pilot," he continued. "Certainly someone who is technologically adept. I would think you would need to have the buy-in of at least one of the flight deck to get into the cockpit. A lot of planning and thought has gone into this."

Johnston believed that money might be the motivation: "There's a possibility it could be a hijacking for an insurance fraud – the aircraft itself is worth £600 million [US$1 billion]," he said. "The level of planning would take months, it would be a very complicated heist if that was the case. Anything could be possible – this is unprecedented."

But what he was certain of was that it was not an accident and there was no catastrophic failure of the aircraft structure. "The aircraft will be found at some point but how long it takes is another question," he said. "If they've been clever enough to get this far, I'm pretty sure it won't be found until they want it to be."

An even more bizarre notion concerns the 20 employees of Freescale Semiconductor on the passenger list. They were employed at the Texas firm's manufacturing sites in Kuala Lumpur, Malaysia, and Tianjin, China, and were said to be experts in stealthy technology. Freescale specializes in aviation electronics. Its owners have connections to Inmarsat and the Council on Foreign Relations and the Skull and Bones, Yale's secret society beloved of conspiracy theorists.

The company develops components for stealth weapons systems and aircraft navigation, and works on radar-blocking technology. Website *Beforeitsnews* said: "It is conceivable that the Malaysia Airlines Flight MH370 plane is 'cloaked', hiding with hi-tech electronic warfare weaponry that exists and is used. In fact, this type of technology is precisely the expertise of Freescale, who have 20 employees on board the missing flight."

Meanwhile, in an attempt to damp down speculation and growing international criticism of Malaysia's handling of the investigation, Prime Minister Najib Razak stepped in and took charge. He said his personal belief was that someone on board was responsible for the plane's disappearance. This was indicated by the disabling of the ACARS and the transponder, and the plane's change of course.

"Based on new satellite information, we can say with a high degree of certainty that the aircraft communications addressing and reporting system was disabled just before it reached the east coast of peninsular Malaysia," said Najib. "Shortly afterwards, near the border between Malaysian and Vietnamese air traffic control, the aircraft's transponder was switched off. From this point onwards, the Royal Malaysian Air Force primary radar showed an aircraft believed to be MH370 did indeed turn back. It then flew in a westerly direction back over peninsular Malaysia before turning north west."

He confirmed that the primary military radar, stationed at old RAF bases at Kota Bharu and Butterworth, on Penang, had tracked a "plot", now known to be MH370, far out into the Indian Ocean.

"Up until the point at which it left military primary radar coverage, these movements are consistent with deliberate action by someone on the plane. In view of this latest development, the Malaysian authorities have refocused their investigation into the crew and passengers on board. Despite media reports the plane was hijacked, I wish to be very clear, we are still investigating all possibilities as to what caused MH370 to deviate."

Investigators believed the plane was commandeered by a "skilled, competent and current pilot" who knew how to avoid radar. Najib noted that the search for the plane had reached a "new phase".

"For the families and friends of those involved, we hope this brings us one step closer to finding the plane," he said. "We realize this is an excruciating time for the families of those on board. Our thoughts and our prayers are with them."

He confirmed that there was a final handshake between the plane and a satellite at 8.11 am – seven hours and 31 minutes after takeoff. This was more than five hours later than the previous time given by the Malaysian authorities as the last contact. The airline said the plane had enough fuel to fly for up to about eight hours. "The investigations team is making further calculations which will indicate how far the aircraft may have flown after this last point of contact," he added.

That last successful handshake proved that the aircraft was still in operation at 8.11 am Malaysian time. One hour later, no such connection was made. So the plane's systems died within that 60 minutes. After that last handshake, Malaysia Airlines said Flight MH370 still had enough fuel to fly for another 30 minutes.

Even such scant information brought comfort to some. A friend of missing passenger Norliakmar Hamid said: "At least we know that she was alive up to 8.11 am on 8 March. Because previously I thought the plane crashed when it was lost from the radar. There is still hope."

The handshake involves two signals, one sent out from a satellite in geostationary orbit 22,250 miles (35,808km) above the Indian Ocean, the other sent back from the equipment on the plane. From the delay between when the outgoing signal was sent from the satellite and the incoming signal returned from the plane, it was possible to work out how far it was away. When a line is drawn connecting all points at that distance, you get a circle with a circumference of 18,000 miles (28,968km) with the satellite at its centre, but much of it could be ignored due to the limited range of the plane from its last known position. This left two arcs – the plane would have been on one of those arcs when the last handshake was made but since then, it could have flown 250 miles (402km) in any direction. This put the plane in one of two "corridors".

One arced northwards as far as the border of the central Asian countries Kazakhstan and Turkmenistan. This northern route would have taken the plane over countries inhabited by extremist Islamist groups with unstable governments, as well as remote, sparsely populated areas where it may have been possible to land a plane unnoticed, reviving the slender hope that the passengers might be alive on the ground.

David Gleave, an aviation safety investigator, said there was a possibility the aircraft had been hijacked and landed somewhere. Meanwhile, Malaysian police said that one of the passengers, whom they would not name, was believed to have undergone flight training. However, whoever had taken over the plane would have had to "get all the communication devices off the passengers as well and then there are ransom demands going on that aren't in the public domain," Gleave said. "So the aircraft is worth well over US$50 million [£30 million] and then each of the passengers' lives is, say, US$1 million [£600,000]. There could be negotiations with embassies and the insurance companies and that wouldn't necessarily be in the public domain."

But he added: "However, to hide the aeroplane you would need to have done a lot of planning beforehand for this."

To start with, the hijacked aircraft would have had to fly over a number of countries undetected, and the region of the northern route also contains American military bases with powerful surveillance capabilities. As a result, aviation security consultant Chris Yates suggested another possible fate for MH370: "In theory, any country that sees a strange blip is going to get fighter planes up to have a look," he said. "And if those fighter planes can't make head or tail of what it is, they will shoot it down."

Kazakhstan's civil aviation authority told the BBC it was not possible for the plane to have reached its airspace undetected as it would have had to fly over China, India and other countries. It also said that it had not detected any "unsanctioned use" of its airspace on 8 March 2014. Pakistan's civil aviation authority said checks of its radar recordings found nothing connected to the flight. But military radar systems can be limited in their range and coverage, and may not always be in operation.

The second, southern, route arced over Sumatra and out across the vast Indian Ocean. With a fuel load intended for only a six-hour flight to Beijing, any journey across the thousands of miles of open water could have resulted only in the aircraft ditching in a sea with an average depth of 12,762ft (3,890m) – nearly two and a half miles deep, or the height of 13 London Shards. The Gulf of Thailand, by contrast, has an average depth of 148ft (45m) but by 15 March the search in the South China Sea had been ended.

Although these corridors narrowed down the search area somewhat, finding the plane even using satellite surveillance was still a mammoth task.

"The area is enormous. Finding anything rapidly is going to be very difficult," said the director of the French space centre in Toulouse, Marc Pircher. "The area and scale of the task is such that ninety-nine percent of what you are getting are false alarms."

The southern track was considered the most likely. Going north, the plane would have crashed into the land where wreckage would be seen, unless whoever was flying it had found a suitable runway. A Boeing 777 needs a runway of 3,800 to 5,200ft (1,158 to 1,585m) to land. All official airports are monitored, but that did not make a landing impossible. There are unofficial ones, not least airstrips created and then abandoned during the Second World War and the Vietnam War. Even so, an aircraft the size of a 777 on the ground is a hard thing to hide.

Going south, the plane would have run out of fuel and been swallowed up by the sea. But the northerly route could not be ruled out just because no one had reported contact. "The sensitivity of some of the military radar and satellite information is clearly posing a problem," said Tony Cable, an investigator who worked for the UK Air Accidents Investigation Branch for 32 years. "I suspect there is an awful lot more information that is known but that is not being released."

Flightglobal's David Learmount said: "If it has flown north, why have none of the countries it has flown over said anything? They would have sent up aircraft to investigate. If it's gone south, there's nothing there until you hit Antarctica."

With the Boeing 777s needing a runway the best part of a mile long to land, he thought it was unlikely it had touched down safely on a remote Asian strip.

"I can't think which airfield it would be – and what would they do with the passengers?" he said. Meanwhile, the government of Pakistan was forced to deny rumours that it was hiding it.

The prospect, no matter how faint, that MH370 had been hijacked and was sitting safely on the ground somewhere brought renewed criticism of the Malaysian government. This was hardly quelled when Malaysia's air chief said it was "possible" the jet's last satellite signals were sent from the ground. Learmount said the Malaysian government's "total incompetence is unforgivable".

For the families waiting, every day increased their agony. They found it difficult to keep up with the news without being tormented by every passing rumour or sensationalist headline. Their lives were on hold.

"I don't think I can get anything done," said one man, describing how his thoughts wandered and at times he felt physically sick. "This long wait is taking its toll on everyone. I don't really want to think about it too much. Every time I think of it, it's hard to think through everything."

His sister was on the plane. She was several years older than him and, throughout their childhood, she had been his protector. When circumstances forced their family apart she was only 16, and for years she had brought him up. "It was just the two of us," he explained.

Even when he grew up, she would go out of her way to help him in any way she could. After he moved abroad some years earlier, his daughter returned to China to spend six months with her aunt.

She was a lively woman, he said, "always busy doing things; always going places". Her son told his uncle that she had been in Malaysia on business. At first, no one dared break the news to their elderly mother but when she tried to call her daughter, relatives were forced to explain.

Although his friends had been supportive, he found it difficult to open up to them. "You really feel awkward about talking to anybody," he explained. "You know they want to say something, but there's not much news and it's hard to find the words."

People phoned with words of comfort. But the idea that his sister might be alive somewhere provided little succour. "But I know it's probably not true," he added. "It's hard to plan for the future. It's one week and I don't know what to expect. I am just afraid. I don't know if it will be a week, or two, or a month."

Some still held out hope. *The Beijing Times* reported that a woman had received a missed call from her father, who was on board the plane. The number "powered off" when she rang back. Fifteen-year-old Eric Chen Zhi Yang, whose mum and dad were on board, said: "It means there's still a chance that they are alive."

The idea that the plane had been hijacked was another straw

that friends and relatives clung to, especially when the FBI said that the possibility that the passengers and crew were being held for ransom could not be ruled out.

Sarah, the sister of missing mining engineer Paul Weeks, said: "The possibility the plane has been hijacked rather than crashed does raise your hopes because you think the potential is there that my brother is still alive. But I also find that very scary as well because if someone has deliberately taken this plane then they've taken it for a reason, and I think we know that often that's not good."

Philip Wood's partner Sarah Bajc said: "My gut feeling is that it landed. I still feel his spirit – I don't feel he is dead."

She was convinced that the plane had been hijacked. "Facts point to the scenario that the flight has been taken," she insisted.

Even lack of any certain knowledge was some consolation. "As long as nobody knows where the plane is, we can believe they may be alive," said a man named Liu, whose son was returning from his first foreign holiday on Flight MH370.

Other relatives posted their hopes online. One wrote: "It is the first time it is good news that a plane was hijacked." The parents of one woman passenger added: "There's still hope for my daughter and her husband."

But this theory was not making things any easier for the Malaysian authorities.

"Every day brings new angles, especially as we are focusing and expanding the search area," said acting transport minister Hishammuddin Hussein. "The search was already a highly complex, multi-national effort. It has now become more difficult. The area has been expanded and has changed. We are now looking at large tracts of land, crossing 11 countries as well as deep, remote oceans. The number of countries involved [in the search] has increased from 14 to 25, which brings new challenges. This is a significant recalibration."

Because the idea that the plane had, against all the odds, landed safely somewhere provided the only possible happy outcome, checks were made of all 657 runways within range that were long enough for a Boeing 777 to have landed. There were 30 in Kazakhstan, 78 in Pakistan, 157 in India and 352 in China.

There was even speculation that the aircraft could be on Australian territory. Malaysian officials asked the Australians to search the remote Cocos Islands in the Indian Ocean, southwest of Christmas Island and midway between Australia and Sri Lanka. An Australian possession, the territory consists of two atolls and 27 coral islands. Two of them, West Island and Home Island, were inhabited – total population some 600. There were few other suitable landing strips along the southern corridor.

As the hunt for the missing plane continued, serious questions were asked about Malaysia's air defences. Since the 9/11 attacks on the United States, security across the world had been tightened and new procedures adopted to improve the detection of rogue aircraft and intercept them before they could be used as weapons of terrorism. And yet, apparently, Malaysia had failed to notice when a plane had changed direction and disappeared from the radar. The missing plane had then flown through Malaysian airspace unobserved, showing serious loopholes in the country's air defences. Until then the Royal Malaysian Air Force had been widely respected. Its fleet of Russian-built Sukhoi S30 and American F-16 fighter jets completed regular training exercises with counterparts from Britain, Australia, New Zealand and Singapore.

Most countries with an advanced air force should have detected an incoming and possibly hostile aircraft some 200 miles from its shores and scrambled fighter jets to challenge it. Indian air traffic controller Sugata Pramanik said a plane "can easily become invisible to civilian radar by switching off the transponder but it cannot avoid defence systems".

Western security analysts were also baffled. "There are a lot of questions," said one. "How did it get to the point where it came back and went wherever? You would have thought planes would have been scrambled and the Malaysians would have acted."

Seventy-year-old Jock Lowe, a pioneer of modern flight who helped get Concorde off the ground, agreed. "In European airspace, if an aeroplane goes out of communication, some military aircraft would be sent up very quickly to intercept it," he said. "It is unthinkable that this could have happened in Europe. It just couldn't happen in most places in the world."

The veteran pilot added: "It has to be right near the top of my list of mysterious disappearances. There were no signals to air traffic control and the plane lost contact with Malaysian civil aviation only fifty minutes into its flight. Nor was any distress signal sent. Conditions in the cockpit appear to have been normal and the 12-year-old aircraft was in proper maintained order, having last undergone routine maintenance in February."

Aviation expert James Hall said hijackers could have taken advantage of sloppy air defence in the region. "They could have been looking for the weakest link and found it in Malaysia," he explained. "They may have been trying to hijack the plane for financial reasons or something similar to 9/11."

Crash expert George Bibel said: "The plane changed course – that screams some kind of evil activity."

Meanwhile, Malaysia's Hishammuddin Hussein dismissed the criticisms of his country and said the mysterious disappearance of Flight MH370 was an "unprecedented case" with lessons for all.

"It's not right to say there is a breach in the standard procedures… what we're going through here is being monitored throughout the world and may change aviation history," he insisted.

Malaysia's director general of civil aviation Azharuddin Abdul Rahman concurred. "Many will have lessons to learn from this," he said. "I've been in aviation for 35 years and I've never seen this kind of incident before."

Besides, at that point, criticism of Malaysia's air defences was a distraction. Foreign minister Anifah Aman said: "The focus must be on finding the plane. I don't want to support any of the theories at this juncture. This involves a lot of lives. My worry is where is the plane and what little chance that people are safe so that they can come back… We believe in miracles and like to think they're safe and can return to their families."

Adding to the mystery came the news that the pilot's sign-off, "All right, good night," came after the automatic transmission equipment had been disabled. But the pilot had made no reference to the disablement, nor did he give any indication that the aircraft had been seized.

"This [sign-off] is something not normal that the pilot would do," said Major-General Affendi Buang of Malaysia's air force. He had assumed that the sign-off was made by Fariq Abdul Hamid (communication was usually the co-pilot's responsibility). But no one knew for sure. It could have been Captain Shah, or even a hijacker. The air traffic controller who received the sign-off call said she could not be sure.

"It's a radio communication and can distort voices," said Paul Drechsel, an air traffic control specialist at the University of North Dakota. "You are talking to so many airplanes and pilots that you wouldn't know who that was." This was another mystery that was unlikely to be solved, he added. Air traffic control voice communications were routinely recorded in the US, but that was not the case in Malaysia. Nevertheless officials said: "Whether the co-pilot's voice was distressed in the final transmission, it is part of the investigation."

The hunt was now on in the southern Indian Ocean. It was proving a Herculean task. Far from land, much of this huge stretch of water is not covered by radar, so tracking the aircraft's last-known movements would probably be impossible. The area is torn by huge waves and powerful currents, spreading any debris from a crash.

Even if the approximate location of the wreckage was found, investigators still had to find the Boeing's black boxes. The water in the area of the search is very deep and the sonic ping transmitted by the flight data recorder and the cockpit voice recorder only had a limited range. A search vessel or aircraft would have to be almost directly above the black boxes to hear it. And if the recorders were trapped under the wreckage, the signal would be further attenuated.

The sonic ping from a black box is only transmitted for around 30 days until the batteries run down. Even in the shallower and relatively familiar waters of the mid-Atlantic, it had taken searchers two years to recover the downed Air France Flight 447's black boxes.

Then even if Flight MH370's cockpit voice recorder was found, it was only capable of storing, at most, the last two hours of audio from the flight. If the plane had continued flying until it ran out of fuel, well beyond that two-hour limit, the critical period when it changed course would not have been recorded.

Attention was suddenly switched to the northern corridor again. Nine days after Flight MH370 went missing, the Malaysian authorities sought diplomatic permission to investigate a theory that the Boeing 777 may have been flown under the radar to a Taliban-controlled base on the border of Afghanistan and northwest Pakistan. After all, the 9/11 plot was hatched in this area. Even Rupert Murdoch was tweeting that Flight MH370 might have ended up in Pakistan. Militants there denied taking the aircraft.

"These are matters for the jurisdiction of those regions and Malaysia's armed forces and department of civil aviation," said a spokesman for Malaysia Airlines. "In regard to Pakistan and Afghanistan, we cannot explore those theories without permission. We hope to have that soon."

For a commercial plane to pass undetected through these regions seemed virtually impossible. With war raging in Afghanistan, these regions are highly militarized. Indian and Pakistan have robust air defence networks. The US military was also in operation there and it would be almost impossible to hide a 777 from the prying eyes of American drones. To have reached Taliban-held territory would require a combination of extremely sophisticated navigation, skilful flying, brazen audacity and a calamitous security failure by those monitoring international airspace. But so little was known about the fate of the missing plane that this was yet another line of enquiry that remained impossible to rule out.

Then there was Kyrgyzstan. It borders western China's troubled Xinjiang province, where the ethnic Uighur population is waging its separatist struggle. A planeload of largely Chinese passengers would have made a tempting target after the attack at Kunming station. At least one Uighur group claimed responsibility – although its email to news organizations was dismissed as opportunistic.

Malaysian officials said they had requested help from a dozen other Asian countries and had asked them to provide radar data.

They had also asked for assistance from Vietnam, Thailand, Indonesia, and Australia, as well as France, which administers a handful of islands deep in the southern Indian Ocean.

Aviation enthusiast Keith Ledgerwood published a new theory on his blog – that Flight MH370 might have made its way across several countries' airspace by hiding in the radar shadow of another aircraft. He said its last-known manoeuvres indicate that it may have been trying to follow a Singapore Airlines Boeing 777 from the Bay of Bengal across India, Pakistan and Afghanistan.

Ledgerwood plotted the last-known movements of Flight MH370 on an Instrument Flight Rules map that shows the airways and waypoints used by commercial airliners to navigate the skies. He drew in the plane's path from the point where the transponder had been switched off at 1.21 am to the point where military radar lost contact at 2.15. He then looked for other planes that were in the area and noticed that the Boeing 777 of Singapore Airlines Flight SIA68 was in the immediate vicinity at exactly the same time. What's more, it was on the same airway, heading toward the same waypoint. He deduced that Flight MH370 had manoeuvred itself directly behind Flight SIA68 at 2 am. With MH370's transponder switched off, the Singapore Airlines 777 would not have been able to 'see' the Malaysian plane. However, MH370 would have been able to pick up the signal from SIA68's transponder and follow it.

The Traffic Collision Avoidance System, which alerts the pilot if another plane is coming dangerously close, on board SIA68 would not set off an alarm as MH370 approached it over the Straits of Malacca because it, too, is triggered by the transponder on an approaching plane. But the TCAS on board MH370 would have allowed it to keep precise tabs on SIA68 to intercept it.

SIA68 was on its way to Barcelona, Spain. That meant it would fly over the Andaman Sea, out across the Bay of Bengal, then over India, Pakistan, Afghanistan, Turkmenistan and on to Europe. When SIA68 and MH370 entered Indian airspace, they would appear as a single blip on the radar with the transponder information of SIA68 appearing on both air traffic control and military radar screens.

Once MH370 had cleared the airspace of India, Pakistan and Afghanistan undetected, it would reach an area where there was very little radar coverage. Then it could have broken off and landed in Turkmenistan, Iran, Uzbekistan, Tajikistan, Kazakhstan, Kyrgyzstan or even Xinjiang province in China. Any of these locations would match up with the seven-and-a-half hours' total flying time and would fall within the northern corridor provided by the last-known handshake with Inmarsat at 8.11 am. The head of civil aviation in Malaysia said that the aircraft could have been on the ground when its last data signals were sent, hours after it disappeared from the radar over the South China Sea.

"After looking at all the details," said Ledgerwood, "it is my opinion that MH370 snuck out of the Bay of Bengal using SIA68 as the perfect cover. It entered radar coverage already in the radar shadow of the other 777, stayed there throughout coverage, and then exited SIA68's shadow and then most likely landed in one of several land locations north of India and Afghanistan."

The question was, who was flying the plane?

Another suspect then came to light. There was a passenger on board with flight experience: 29-year-old flight engineer Mohd Khairul Amri Selamat was a Malaysian who had worked for a private jet charter company. "Yes, we are looking into Mohd Khairul as well as the other passengers and crew. The focus is on anyone else who might have had aviation skills on that plane," a senior police official involved in the investigations said.

As a flight engineer, Mohd Khairul was responsible for overseeing the systems on a plane during flights to check they were working correctly and to make repairs if necessary. He would certainly have been knowledgeable enough to disable the ACARS and transponder. But Khairul specialized in executive jets and would not necessarily have the expertise needed to divert and fly a large jetliner.

He had more than 10 years' experience as a flight engineer. For the last three years, he had worked for the Malaysian branch of the Swiss-based ExecuJet Aviation Group, which sells and charters aircraft. According to its managing director, Graeme Duckworth, Khairul was the airframe and engine specialist who repaired Learjet and Bombardier Challenger aircraft. "He is an excellent employee, well-respected," Duckworth said.

Khairul's father, 60-year-old Selamat Omar, had been waiting, sleepless and red-eyed, at the Everly Hotel in Putrajaya, an administrative satellite town south of Kuala Lumpur, where the Malaysian families were corralled. Khairul was the third of his four children. Ten days earlier, he had received a frantic, sobbing call from his daughter-in-law Erny. That morning her husband – his son – had been aboard Flight MH370 flight to China. It had failed to arrive.

"I will stay here until they find the plane," he insisted. He believed his son was still alive. "I'm confident that once they find the plane, everything will be back to normal." Dressed in a short-sleeved pink shirt, he told reporters that police had not questioned him about his son, but that the family was happy to help, if needed. He added that, as a child, his son enjoyed sport, especially football, and supported both Liverpool and Manchester United.

Selamat himself made his living off a small piece of agricultural land given to him under a government scheme in the 1980s. He used the plot to grow palm oil and received a percentage of the profits. Khairul had always wanted to be an engineer, so Selamat took out a loan to put him through school and college. He was now married and had a 15-month-old son, Hizat. Recently he had bought a house on the outskirts of Kuala Lumpur. Selamat said he and other family members were supposed to have been visiting Khairul's new home later that month but the latter had told his father he had to go to Beijing to work on a jet there and that they would have to reschedule the visit. That was two days before Flight MN370 went missing. It was the last time they spoke. "Khairul was doing well in his job and was a good son," Selamat said. "He would come visit us at least once a month."

Again, Khairul did not seem disaffected, nor did he fit the profile of a terrorist.

Selamat, who came from Pahang state, northeast of Kuala Lumpur, said that in the days since Flight MH370 went missing, he had tried to maintain a routine, getting up early and switching on the television news and then going for a walk. "I am waiting for the latest news," he said. "If I go home, I will not be able to get the latest news."

He added that he had left the hotel just once since 8 March. But he feared that Malaysia Airlines, which was currently paying for the family to stay there, would stop these payments soon, though a spokesman for the airline said the matter was still being decided. Meanwhile, the relatives comforted themselves with the thought that, if the jet had crashed, wreckage would have been found by then.

"We still have hope," Selamat insisted. "We are praying that all the passengers are safe."

There were hundreds of relatives in a similar position, all waiting for scraps of information, many trying to contain their anger and grief. By and large the Malaysians had not been as outspoken as the Chinese. However, they had hung a banner on the wall of the Everly Hotel, bearing a prayer for MH370's lost passengers and crew.

As the days slipped by, the number of relatives remaining at the hotel dwindled. Most of those left refused to speak to journalists. "As you know, the other family members are not willing to face the media," said Selamat. "For me, if I'm not talking to the media, nobody will know how I am feeling."

The Chinese families were much more strident, particularly in their criticism of the lack of information coming from the Malaysian authorities. Those who had flown to Kuala Lumpur had been put up at a separate hotel, where police kept reporters at bay. Anger boiled over when two relatives of Chinese passengers unfurled a banner outside a press conference about to be addressed by the Malaysian acting transport minister.

But the morale of the relatives sank to a new low on 19 March when the German insurance company Allianz announced that it had begun making payouts associated with the loss of the aircraft. A company spokesman said that it and other re-insurers had made initial payments based on Malaysia Airlines' "aviation hull and liability policy". For relatives waiting at hotels in Kuala Lumpur and Beijing, the insurance company's announcement was a chilling recognition that their loved ones are almost certainly gone forever.

CHAPTER SEVENTEEN

THE TRUTH

In Beijing, the families of the missing threatened to go on hunger strike unless Malaysia Airlines told them the truth about the fate of their relatives on board. They vented their anger on Chinese representatives sent by the airline to meet them and insisted on seeing the Malaysian ambassador again.

"What we want is the truth," declared one woman angrily. "Don't let them become victims of politics. No matter what political party you are, no matter how much power you have, if there isn't life, what's the point? Where is compassion?"

When he arrived, the Ambassador had to take the blame. "You're always going back and forth," said one man. "I think your government knows in their heart why we want you to answer us. Because you're always tricking us, telling us lies."

The Chinese government had repeatedly called on the Malaysians to do a better job of keeping the relatives informed. "China has all along demanded that the Malaysian side and

Malaysia Airlines earnestly respond to the reasonable requests of the Chinese families," said Beijing Foreign Ministry spokesman Hong Lei.

A Chinese representative of the airline said what information the families got was beyond his control. The responsibility lay in Kuala Lumpur, where the investigation was centred. "I can accept the criticisms and mistakes that you have pointed out," he said. "But the problem is that some information and material we really have no way to access. I really cannot access it. So I beg for your forgiveness."

It seems that if the airline had paid just US$10 (£6) more it would have known where the missing plane was. Along with several other carriers, Malaysia Airlines had opted for a cheap data package for its aircraft that transmitted only minimal information rather than pay an additional small fee to transmit detailed flight data. "For US$10, you could have told within half an hour's flying time where the plane would have gone," a source told the *Daily Telegraph*.

The search area had now shifted to the south, specifically the Indian Ocean west of Australia. Australian Prime Minister Tony Abbott said he had spoken to his Malaysian counterpart Najib Razak by telephone and had offered more surveillance resources in addition to the two P-3C Orion aircraft his country had already committed. Abbott told the press: "He asked that Australia take responsibility for the search in the southern vector, which the Malaysian authorities now think was one possible flight path for this ill-fated aircraft. I agreed that we would do so."

The Malaysian navy and air force were also searching the southern corridor and three French investigators were brought in to help the search. Previously members of the French team that had searched for Air France Flight 447, they had specialist knowledge of deep-sea operations.

Meanwhile, in Kuala Lumpur, the investigators had come to the conclusion that Flight MH370 had been deliberately diverted. However, China claimed that it had "conducted meticulous investigation into all the [Chinese] passengers, and did not find any evidence for sabotage activity". They were cleared of any "destructive behaviour".

"So far there is nothing, no evidence to suggest that they intended to do harm to the plane," said Huang Huikang, China's ambassador to Malaysia. He told a briefing of the Chinese media that Interpol had cleared two Iranians aboard the flight who were travelling on false passports. This left 72 passengers as feasible suspects, he noted, along with 10 crew members, plus the two pilots.

He also admitted that China had begun searching its own territory for the plane but refused to give details, or even say which regions were being searched and which agencies were involved. As a criminal investigation was under way, he said, "the probe into the incident's cause is not suitable to be conducted in a high-profile way."

Meanwhile, Chinese Premier Li Keqiang rang the Malaysian Prime Minister, Najib Razak, asking him to provide Beijing with more detailed data and information in a timely, accurate and comprehensive manner. "As long as there is still a gleam of hope we should continue to do our utmost," he insisted, despite the difficulty of the search.

Until then, the Malaysian authorities had been maintaining that MH370's transponder had been switched off before the pilot signed off: "All right, good night." Now acting transport minister Hishammuddin Hussein said that the transponder had been switched off two minutes after the sign-off. But in fact it was not possible to tell when the ACARS system was switched off as it responds once every half an hour. It made a handshake at 1.07, but failed to respond at 1.37.

Investigators were now combing cellphone records to see if anyone on board had tried to call or had sent a text. So far they had drawn a blank. "The fact there was no distress signal, no ransom notes – there is always hope," said Hussein.

A fresh theory came from US aviation chief Billie Vincent, who had been a forensic witness in the Lockerbie trial. He said the missing Malaysian jetliner may have been brought down after a massive fire broke out in the hold. "The data released thus far most likely points to a problem with hazardous materials," he maintained. "This scenario begins with the eruption of hazardous materials within the cargo hold – either improperly packaged or illegally shipped – or both."

Vincent believed that a fire broke out in the cargo hold. It may have been started by a small bomb that failed to destroy the aircraft, he conjectured. The fire burnt through the wiring of the plane's communications systems, cutting off the transponder and the ACARS antenna. Toxic fumes would have quickly overwhelmed the passengers and crew. "As opposed to being hijackers, the crew were heroically trying to save the airplane, themselves and the passengers when this catastrophe hit," he said.

Vincent believed one of the pilots managed to put on an oxygen mask and tried to turn the plane back to Kuala Lumpur. He attributed the rapid ascent and descent to the crew not being able to see properly due to smoke in the cockpit. They eventually managed to stabilize the jet at 23,000ft (7,010m). By then, the pilots were unconscious too.

"The plane then continues [on autopilot] until no fuel remains and crashes – most likely into the ocean as there has been no report of any Emergency Locator Transmitter signal which can be received by satellite if the crash was on land," he added.

He also took the view that much of the confusion had been caused by the Malaysian government, which had been "too accommodating" under pressure from the media and China, and had rushed into releasing information that it then had to withdraw.

Meanwhile, Malaysian police had a new theory of their own. They were investigating whether a bomb could have been planted in a large consignment of tropical fruit loaded onto the flight just before it took off. Malaysia Airlines confirmed that "three to four tons" of mangosteens were taken aboard. The fruit had been screened as "a matter of routine", but it was the only extra cargo on the flight apart from passengers' luggage.

Police Inspector-General Tan Sri Khalid Abu Bakar said: "We are very thorough in our probe. Even the four tons of mangosteens in the aircraft hold is being investigated. We tracked down who plucked the fruits, who packed and shipped them out, and who put them on the plane. Then, we had to see who was to receive them in China and who paid for it, and how much. That is how in-depth this probe is going."

It was then reported that, at some point during the flight, a new set of co-ordinates had been entered into the Flight Management System. This is the computer system that carries out many of the routine tasks on board as modern planes no longer carry a navigator or a flight engineer. Re-entering the destination co-ordinates is a complex procedure, and would have resulted in reconstructing the entire flight plan. It was unclear whether the new instructions were entered before takeoff or in flight.

Senior US officials said the first turn back to the west was likely programmed into the aircraft's flight computer, rather than being executed manually. This would have to be done by someone knowledgeable about aircraft systems. But Malaysia Airlines' chief executive Ahmad Jauhari Yahya said this was speculation, adding: "Once you are in the aircraft, anything is possible."

Then Thailand admitted that its radar had detected a plane, later identified as MH370, nine minutes after its last contact with air traffic control, but had failed to share the information earlier because Malaysia had not specifically asked for it. The unidentified plane was on a jinking flight path toward the Strait of Malacca. However, Thailand's Air Vice-Marshal Montol Suchookorn said the plane had not actually entered Thai airspace. At 1.28 am, he said, Thai military radar "was able to detect a signal, which was not a normal signal, of a plane flying in the direction opposite from the MH370 plane" back toward Kuala Lumpur. The plane later turned right toward the Malacca Strait. When asked why the data had not been released earlier, he said: "We did not pay any attention to it, and Malaysia's initial request for information was not specific. The Royal Thai Air Force only looks after any threats against our country. When they asked again and there was new information and assumptions from Prime Minister Najib Razak, we took a look at our information again. It didn't take long for us to figure out, although it did take some experts to find out about it."

Police examining the flight simulator at Captain Shah's home found there were programs for landing Boeing 777 on five Indian Ocean runways – at Malé in the Maldives and at the US military airstrip on Diego Garcia, and three other runways in Sri Lanka and southern India.

Again his friend Peter Chong jumped to Shah's defence, insisting that there was nothing secret about this. "He was not hiding it," Chong said. "He was open about it. He loves flying – he wanted to share the joy of flying with his friends."

It was later revealed that some files had been deleted from the simulator and experts were making an effort to restore them in case they shed some light on the whereabouts of the missing plane, or whether Shah had ever sought to practice flying undetected.

Police chief Khalid Abu Bakar said an examination of the flight simulator seized from Captain Shah's home revealed that data logs were deleted on 3 February 2014, over a month before Flight MH370 went missing. The simulator was apparently used to play three games: Flight Simulator X, Flight Simulator 9 and X-Plane 10.

"Some data had been deleted from the simulator and forensic work to retrieve this data is ongoing," said Hishammuddin Hussein. "I would like to take this opportunity to state that the passengers, the pilots and the crew remain innocent until proven otherwise." The FBI had been called in to help and had been given the electronic data to analyse. But other pilots said there was nothing suspicious about deleting data from the flight simulator and likened it to getting rid of unwanted files from a computer. "It takes a bit of memory," said Amin Said, who ran a commercial fight simulator in Kuala Lumpur. "Sometimes it would just conflict."

However, more suspicion fell on Captain Shah when it was then revealed that he had taken a mysterious two-minute phone call in the cockpit, minutes before the plane took off. The call came from an unknown woman and was made from a pay-as-you-go SIM. In Malaysia, anyone buying a pay-as-you-go SIM card must fill out a form giving their identity card or passport number under anti-terror measures brought in after the 9/11 attacks (terror groups have previously orchestrated attacks using untraceable SIM cards bought using fake IDs). The number was traced to a shop in Kuala Lumpur and efforts were made to track down the woman who had made the call. "If we want to eliminate the chief pilot from the inquiry, we must interview her in detail to find out what his state of mind was," a source close to the investigation said.

Electronic equipment used by First Officer Hamid was also being examined.

In another development, former pilot Chris Goodfellow, who had 20 years' experience as a Canadian Class-1 instrument-rated pilot for multi-engine planes, published his theory on his Google+. "There has been a lot of speculation about Malaysia Airlines Flight 370," he wrote. "Terrorism, hijacking, meteors. I cannot believe the analysis on CNN; it's almost disturbing." He added that he "tends to look for a simpler explanation".

According to Goodfellow's theory a fire, possibly electrical or from an overheated tyre on takeoff, sent smoke into the cockpit shortly after the crew signed off with Malaysian air traffic controllers. The pilot executed a sharp left turn and headed for a nearby emergency landing spot, while turning off the electronics to isolate the potential fire hazard. As a consequence the transponder and the ACARS were disconnected.

"Zaharie Ahmad Shah was a very experienced senior captain with 18,000 hours of flight time," said Goodfellow. "We old pilots were drilled to know what is the closest airport of safe harbour while in cruise." He took a quick look at Google Earth and found Pulau Langkawi, an island in the Malacca Strait, had "a 13,000-foot [4,000m] strip with an approach over water at night with no obstacles. He [Shah] did not turn back to Kuala Lumpur because he knew he had 8,000 foot [2,438m] ridges to cross – he knew the terrain was friendlier towards Langkawi and also a shorter distance."

According to Goodfellow, the aircraft climbed to 45,000ft (13,716m) in a last-ditch attempt to put out the fire by starving it of oxygen. Its rapid descent might also have been an attempt to blow out the flames. The pilots were then overcome by smoke, the plane continued on autopilot over Langkawi and headed west into the Indian Ocean, where it eventually ran out of fuel and crashed.

"Captain Zaharie Ahmad Shah was a hero struggling with an impossible situation trying to get that plane to Langkawi," Goodfellow wrote. "There is no doubt in my mind. That's the reason for the turn and direct route."

The loss of Flight MH370 put him in mind of Swissair Flight 111, which had crashed off Nova Scotia on 2 September 1998. The McDonnell Douglas MD-11 had taken off from John F. Kennedy International Airport, New York, bound for Cointrin International Airport in Geneva, Switzerland. Forty minutes into the flight, Captain Urs Zimmermann and First Officer Stephan Loew smelt smoke coming from the air-conditioning system and got a flight attendant to close the vent. Minutes later, the smell returned; the smoke was now visible. They requested a diversion to Boston's Logan International Airport, but air traffic control pointed out that Halifax, Nova Scotia, was closer.

The crew put on their oxygen masks and began their descent. While First Officer Loew flew the plane and tried to dump fuel over St Margaret's Bay, Captain Zimmermann went through the "smoke in cockpit" procedures. According to the checklist, the crew should shut off power to the cockpit. The transponder and other communication systems went off. But this also shut off the recycling fan, drawing the fire into the cockpit. They now put out a "Mayday" call. Captain Zimmermann left his seat and tried to fan back the flames, it is thought using the Swissair checklists found fused together in the wreckage. Meanwhile, First Officer

Loew continued to fly the plane. It crashed into the sea at 345 mph (555 km/h) with a g-force of 350, causing the aircraft to disintegrate. All 229 on board were killed. Heartbreak Hotel – the Ramada Plaza JFK – was used to house the families of the victims. Only one body could be identified by sight. Around 90 bodies were identified using dental records, another 30 by fingerprints and medical X-rays on file. In 100 cases, the medical examiners had to resort to DNA testing.

Goodfellow also compared the disappearance of Flight MH370 to the crash of Air Canada Flight 797 on 2 June 1983. The McDonnell Douglas DC-9/32 took off from Dallas-Fort Worth, heading for Dorval in Quebec, via Toronto, at 4.20 pm. On the flight deck were 51-year-old Captain Donald Cameron and his 34-year-old first officer, Claude Ouimet. Both were experienced pilots – Cameron had accrued approximately 13,000 flying hours and Ouimet had 5,650 hours. While flying over Louisville, Kentucky, a fire began in or near the rear washroom.

The pilots heard a popping sound around 6.51 pm, and discovered that the lavatory's circuit breakers had tripped. An airplane's washroom circuits pop occasionally, especially when a lot of passengers are using them after eating, so Cameron waited around eight minutes to give the tripped circuits time to cool down before reactivating them.

Around 7 pm, a strong, noxious odour coming from the rear of the plane was first reported to the cabin crew. Thirty-three-year-old flight attendant Judi Davidson traced the odour to the lavatory. When she looked into the toilet, she was forced back by thick smoke rapidly filling the small room. Sergio Benetti, the 37-year-old chief cabin crew officer, sprayed the interior with a CO_2 extinguisher, while Davidson reported the fire to the captain. Meanwhile, 20-year-old flight attendant Laura Kayama moved the passengers on the flight, which was less than a quarter full, to come away from the rear of the plane and sit close together near the over-wing exits. First Officer Ouimet went to investigate, but was driven back by the thick smoke. However, Benetti said he thought the fire was out because he doused it with the extinguisher.

Minutes later, though, passengers reported smelling smoke in the cabin again. Two minutes after that, the "master breaker" alarm went off in the cockpit, and electrical systems throughout the plane began to fail, including power for the elevator trim system. This made controlling the plane's descent extremely difficult and strenuous as the pilot and first officer wrestled with the controls. The intercom system also failed, so they were unable to communicate with the passengers. Nevertheless, flight attendants were able to instruct passengers sitting in the exit rows on how to open the doors (this practice was not standard on commercial airline flights at the time).

At 7.20 pm, Captain Cameron and First Officer Ouimet made an extremely difficult emergency landing at the Cincinnati/Northern Kentucky International Airport, across the Ohio River from Cincinnati, Ohio. During the evacuation, when the over-wing doors were opened, the influx of air fanned the fire. First Officer Ouimet escaped through the co-pilot's emergency window shortly after the plane landed, but Captain Cameron was exhausted and passed out. Doused with fire-fighting foam, he came round. He was then able to open the pilot's emergency escape window and drop to the ground, where he was dragged to safety by Ouimet; he was the last person to make it out of the plane alive.

Less than 90 seconds after touchdown, flames in the interior of the plane flashed over, killing 23 of the 41 passengers. The passengers trapped inside the plane died from smoke inhalation and burns from the flash fire. Survivor Dianne Fadley noted: "It was almost like anybody who got out had nothing wrong. You made it and you were completely fine, or you didn't make it."

However, of the 18 surviving passengers, only two were uninjured. Three had serious injuries, while 13 had minor injuries. None of the five crew members sustained any injuries.

Of the 21 Canadians and two Americans who died, many of the bodies were burned beyond recognition. Almost all of the victims were in the forward half of the aircraft between the wings and the cockpit. Some bodies were in the aisles; some still in their seats. Two victims were in the back of the aircraft. It seems they were disorientated, and moved past the over-wing exits before they succumbed. Blood samples from the bodies revealed high levels of cyanide, fluoride and carbon monoxide, produced by the burning component materials of the plane.

A fire downed Nigeria Airways Flight 2120 on 11 July 1991. The Douglas DC-8-61 was taking off from King Abdulaziz International Airport in Jeddah, Saudi Arabia, on its way to Sokoto, Nigeria, when an under-inflated tyre caught fire. This, at once, produced thick smoke. The first officer said: "We gotta flat tyre, you figure?" But the pilot, unable to see the smoke, took off anyway. There was no heat-sensor on the wheel and when the landing gear was retracted it brought the fire inside the hull. The pilot was 47-year-old William Allan, who had logged 10,700 flight hours with 1,000 hours on the DC-8. His 36-year-old First Officer Kent Davidge had logged 8,000 flight hours, 550 hours on the DC-8, and 46-year-old Flight Engineer Victor Fehr had logged 7,500 flight hours, with 1,000 hours on DC-8s.

The experienced crew tried to return to the airport for an emergency landing, but the plane was on fire and started to break up. Eleven miles from the airport bodies began falling out of the fuselage as fuel spilling from the central tanks began to burn through the cabin floor. The plane hit the ground 9,432ft (2,875m) short of the runway, killing all 261 on board.

The National Transportation Safety Board later concluded, "Had the crew left the landing gear extended, the accident might have been averted. Despite the considerable destruction to the airframe, the aircraft appeared to have been controllable until just before the crash." The Canadian company that leased the plane to Nigeria Airways went out of business soon afterwards.

Goodfellow's theory quickly spread across media, both social and mainstream.

"I buy this new MH370 theory of an onboard fire," tweeted *The New York Times*'s Josh Barro.

Business Insider's Henry Blodget said that the theory made sense and "fits the facts". He added that "It requires no fantastically brilliant pre-planning or execution or motives."

James Fallows of *The Atlantic* magazine was also persuaded. "I think there's doubt about everything concerning this flight," he wrote. "But his explanation makes better sense than anything else I've heard so far. It's one of the few that make me think, Yes, I could see things happening that way."

However, Jeff Wise of *Slate* began picking Goodfellow's theory apart, saying: "While it's true that MH370 did turn toward Langkawi and wound up overflying it, whoever was at the controls continued to manoeuvre after that point as well, turning sharply right at VAMPI waypoint, then left again at GIVAL. Such vigorous navigating would have been impossible for unconscious men."

Wise also pointed out that, according to analysis by the Malaysian and US governments, the handshake with the Inmarsat satellite at

8.11 on the morning of 8 March narrowed the location of MH370 at that moment to one of the two arcs, one heading over Central Asia and the other over the southern Indian Ocean. As MH370 flew from its original course toward Langkawi, it was headed toward neither arc. Without human intervention, it simply could not have reached the position we know it attained at 8.11 am.

Former US National Transportation Safety Board crash investigator Greg Feith said there should have been a distress call. "Typically, with an electrical fire, you'll have smoke before you have fire," he noted. "You can do some troubleshooting. And if the systems are still up and running, you can get off a 'Mayday' call."

Despite Henry Blodget's view, *Business Insider* also had second thoughts and ran reaction from pilots. Michael G. Fortune, a retired pilot who flew Boeing 777-200ERs, said it was unlikely the crew would have shut off the transponders to deal with the fire. "The checklist I utilized for smoke and fumes in the B-777-200ER does not specifically address the transponder being turned off," he said.

Another 777 pilot told the website that putting on oxygen masks would have been the first priority for the crew, preventing them from being incapacitated.

Other experts had their own theories. Steven Frischling, a US aviation security expert, said he thought the plane had been taken by force. "Four hours after the aircraft went missing my primary source told me unequivocally that this was a pilot-involved incident," he said. He was told that everything pointed to the idea that the Boeing 777 had not crashed. Certainly, without wreckage, there was no evidence to prove that it had. He also looked to the cargo for an explanation.

"One of the positions on the plane that would be filled with a large metal cargo container is unaccounted for on the manifest," he continued. "So there is unexplained cargo. I don't know who or what was on that plane that they wanted, but they wanted the aircraft. I think it's on the ground, being hidden or dismantled."

Even so, John Cane of Cane Associates Aviation Consultants and former lieutenant-colonel and squadron commander in the US Marine Corps flying Harrier jump jets hedged his bets. He said that MH370 was either at the bottom of the Indian Ocean or in thick canopy jungle in Malaysia or Thailand. "If it flew on for six hours or more after the last communication it's not a malfunction because they would be looking for the first opportunity to land," he reasoned. "That drives you back to the logic that it was a criminal act, especially with the change of direction and changes in altitude."

Aviation lawyer and former US air force pilot Jim Brauchle believed the plane had most likely crashed into the Indian Ocean. "If it had crossed any coastline, even without its communications, it would have been picked up on radar," he said. "The theories of it potentially landing somewhere – is it possible? Sure. Is it probable? I don't think so. It would need a 5,000 feet to 6,000 feet [1,500m to 1,800m] -long decent runway. If it tried to land on some distant aerodrome or literally a field it would crash and we would most likely know about it."

Editor of *Aviation International News Safety* magazine and commercial pilot Robert Mark said: "As time goes on things that seemed outlandish are becoming more plausible. The latest is the theory that MH370 shadowed a Singapore Airlines flight. The Israelis have done this before, shadowing a 747 with a fighter jet so that from the ground radar it looks like one aircraft. We are going to find out ultimately that the people who took this aircraft were as good at planning as the people behind 9/11."

But new theories were no good to the families, who were once again threatening to go on hunger strike. "Progress is too slow, the authorities are hiding information," said the 63-year-old father of Chen Changjun, one of the passengers. "Several relatives want to have a hunger strike to protest."

One woman, who declined to give her name, said the idea of a hunger strike, which had first been mooted a few days earlier, was now gathering momentum. "Since they haven't given us the truth about those people's lives, all of us are protesting. All the relatives are facing mental breakdowns," she said.

Another relative displayed a sign, reading, "Hunger strike protest. Respect life. Return my relative. Don't want become victim of politics. Tell the truth." However, Mr Chen said that a large number of relatives felt that the proposal was too extreme.

At a press briefing in Beijing on 19 March, relatives of the passengers on the missing plane were forcibly ejected. One woman was carried out, screaming, "Where are they, where are they?" Another shouted: "They are just saying wait for information, wait for information. Why won't they give us an explanation? My son, it's been 12 days. I have been here 10 days. Every time we ask a question they don't give us answers." She was then bundled away by police.

A third woman, who disguised her identity with sunglasses and a face mask, said: "There is no information, just endless searching. We call on the Malaysian government to give us information immediately [...] We are not satisfied with the Malaysian government's conduct. What we need is the truth. We need to know where the plane is... The Malaysian government is a liar."

Others cried: "We can't stand any more!" and "Find our relatives!" as they were dragged away. "You are traitors to us, you have let us down. Tell us the truth!" one screamed.

THE TRUTH

The airlines had been wasting their time, they said. "We wanted to see you in the first 24 and 48 hours, so that we wouldn't have had to bear the suffering of the last 13 days!" shouted one anguished relative, his voice quivering with emotion.

Meanwhile, 17-year-old Maira Elizabeth Nari touched the hearts of millions. Her father Andrew, the plane's chief steward, was a Liverpool Football Club fan. While the team was playing Manchester United that weekend, Maira tweeted: "Daddy, Liverpool is winning the game. Come home, so you can watch! You never miss watching the game. It's your very first time." The touching message was retweeted 6,000 times.

The club responded, saying: "We are thinking of your father & all those still missing from flight #MH370 Be strong. YNWA. [You'll Never Walk Alone]"

Maira replied: "If dad sees this, he'll be so happy! He'll be smiling, he'll be laughing. I can imagine how happy he'll be. Dad's a big fan of LFC!"

In the game, Liverpool beat Manchester United 3-0.

The club also sent a Liverpool shirt signed by the manager Brendan Rodgers and the players ahead of their crucial match against Manchester City on 13 April. Maira wrote on Twitter: "Thank you so much for this priceless gift. I am going to frame this jersey. Dad, this is for you. I bet you're the happiest person on Earth right now."

CHAPTER EIGHTEEN

THE SOUTHERN ARC

Those searching for Flight MH370 now had an almost impossible task, though further analysis of the data had narrowed the search area to approximately the size of Australia. China and Kazakhstan were taking the lead in the search of the northern arc, where China was deploying 21 satellites, while Indonesia and Australia were taking charge in the south.

The Australians were focusing on an area 1,850 miles (2,977km) southwest of Perth.

"This search will be difficult… a needle in a haystack remains a good analogy," said John Young, emergency response general manager of the Australian Maritime Safety Authority. "It will take at least a few weeks to search the area thoroughly."

The planes they were using to look for wreckage or other debris scanned the surface using infrared technology, but they were not equipped to search underwater.

Captain Stuart Bellingham of the Australian Defence Force

Group said: "We are not looking underwater at all and we don't have the capability to pick up black boxes or underwater electronic beacons."

There is little radar coverage over the southern Indian Ocean, making it harder to narrow down the search there, and the average depth of the ocean is more than two miles (3.2km).

Malaysia's acting transport minister Hishammuddin Hussein said: "This is an enormous search area. And it is something that Malaysia cannot possibly search on its own. All efforts are being used now to reduce the search area – looking at satellite data; seeking assistance from other friends who have satellite capability; asking if they have looked at radar data to re-look at them; finally, the use of assets whether in air or at sea."

Later, China sent ships to the Indian Ocean to search 86,000 square miles (222,739 sq km) of sea.

Meanwhile, the aviation expert at the University of South Wales, Martin Evans, continued to maintain that terrorism was one of the most plausible explanations for the disappearance of Flight MH370.

"There's a supposition that the last radio transmission from the co-pilot was non-standard and, therefore, may have been made under duress," he said. Hijacking was easy – "All they have to do is trick the crew into opening the door and they have access to the cockpit."

Meanwhile, the Internet was filling up with conspiracy theories. User of the website *Reddit* "Dark_Spectre" posted an unusual theory on the website's conspiracy boards, drawing attention to the employees of Texas-based Freescale Semiconductor who had been on the flight. He said: "So we have the American IBM Technical Storage Executive for Malaysia, a man working in mass storage aggregation for the company implicated by the Snowden papers for providing their services to assist the National Security Agency in surveilling the Chinese... and now this bunch of US chip guys working for a global leader in embedded processing solutions (embedded smart phone tech and defense contracting) all together... on a plane... And disappeared. Coincidence?"

Dark_Spectre implies US intelligence shot down the plane because the experts working for them were about to be "interrogated" by the Chinese.

No less bizarre were the wildest imaginings of singer Courtney Love, who claimed she had found the missing jet. She posted an image and coordinates on her Facebook page to guide searchers to the spot. Love added red arrows in Microsoft Paint, pointing to the areas of ocean, and wrote "oil" and "plane" for clarification.

On Twitter, alien abduction was popular. Stevie Borys wrote: "After watching the news for countless hours there is only one logical explanation to the missing Malaysian flight. Aliens."

Suddenly there was possibly a more prosaic clue. On 20 March 2014, it was reported that the Australians had dispatched four military search planes to try to determine whether two large objects bobbing about in a remote part of the Indian Ocean 1,550 miles (2,494km) southwest of Perth were debris from the missing Malaysia Airlines flight. One of the objects spotted on satellite imagery was 82ft (25m) long – close to the size of the aircraft's wing – and the other one was smaller, around 15ft (5m). A Norwegian ship was diverted to the area.

Selamat Omar, father of missing passenger Mohd Khairul, said: "If it turns out that it is truly MH370 then we will accept that fate. But we do not yet know for sure whether this is indeed MH370 or something else. We are still waiting for further notice."

Others were not heartened. "No information has been provided," said a family member. "I think the news from Australia is a bit more reliable, because the satellite image was provided by America. We are in a bad mood."

In Beijing the mood in the Lido Hotel remained sombre. "The waiting has been terrible, but the result will be worse," said one relative, who gave her name as Zhou. "We have waited for 13 days, we would rather wait more than have a conclusion."

For some that conclusion had already been reached. Candles had been lit, dozens knelt down and sobbed. At the back of the room where they had clustered for 13 days, a huge board had been erected for families to write messages and prayers.

"My little Doudou, I bought the Tiffany ring you wanted," wrote the fiancé of one. "When you come back, please wear it and marry me."

Paul Lin, a psychologist who had been supporting the families, said: "The hardest thing for the relatives is the long-term uncertainty. It tortures them. After the first five to six days, some of the relatives started to accept it, but some of them still hold out hope."

The situation was taking its toll. "Some are suicidal – they are having to be looked after 24 hours a day," he continued. He explained that the loss was felt particularly intensely in China because of their one-child policy implemented in 1979 amid fears of a population explosion. Parents who had a son or daughter on Flight MH370 face a heartbreaking future. Traditionally in China when the children grow up, they take care of their elderly parents. Many faced a bleak future and some felt they now had nothing to carry on living for.

Lin and other volunteers were trying to prepare the families for the outburst of emotion inevitable if the sighting of wreckage was confirmed. He had spent many days with a five-year-old boy whose father was on the plane. "This little boy took hold of my hand this morning," he said, his eyes filled with tears. "He turned to me and said, 'Is it OK if – for now – I call you daddy?'"

Some relatives still held out hope. Captain Bimal Sharma, whose sister Chandrika was on board Flight MH370, said: "I want to believe she is still alive and will be home for her birthday on 30 March." That was still 10 days away. His feelings, he said, oscillated between "hope and then despair, and then hope and then despair".

He also paid tribute to his sister: "She was a post-graduate in social work," he said. "She did her Masters in social work from a very reputed institute in India called Tata Institute of Social Sciences. She was the general secretary of the body which looks after the needs of fish workers. I've got e-mails from all over the world – what a wonderful person she was. From all over the world… From South Africa… From Brazil…"

She was travelling on Flight MH370 on her way to a conference in Mongolia, a United Nations' meeting on food and agriculture. Captain Sharma and his sister were very close. They had spoken on Friday, 7 March before she boarded the plane from India to Kuala Lumpur.

He told the BBC: "I don't want to believe this because the aircraft was going from Kuala Lumpur to Beijing. There are too many questions. How is the aircraft now in the south Indian Ocean? How has it reached there? I was a captain at sea – I used to sail ships. I have been through that area several times. This area has got a concentration of garbage. Garbage means plastic and wood, and due to the currents and various other reasons, the winds, this area has got a lot of floating garbage, which I have been through and seen myself. So if they have identified it via satellite they have still not confirmed anything. I don't know… I don't want to believe it as yet."

Sharma did not believe that a plane could fly for seven hours without being detected by radar. "This is the unbelievable thing for me," he said. "I don't believe because there are so many radars that are scanning all over. For seven hours there is nothing? I am from a similar industry, the Merchant Navy. We also do radar scanning. For an aeroplane to go off radar, it is not believable. There is something more to it."

Missing passenger Rod Burrows' brother Greg said: "We get our hopes up for an answer and then we got nothing again. It's been up and down, up and down, up and down."

But he still held out some faint hope. "If they found the wreckage of the plane then that would be finalized because there's no hope," he said. "But while you've got hope, you've got worries too. Because if they're alive, are they being treated well, or what's happening?"

John Young, manager of Australian Maritime Safety Authority's emergency response division, said: "The objects are relatively indistinct on the imagery. I don't profess to be an expert in assessing the imagery, but those who are experts indicate they are credible sightings. The indication to me is of objects that are a reasonable size, moving up and down over the surface. Further images are expected. Ships and aircraft are searching for any signs of the missing plane. I must emphasize these objects may be difficult to locate and may not be related to the search."

However, visibility in the area was poor and he warned that the objects could also be seaborne debris along a key shipping route where containers periodically fall off cargo vessels. Satellite images "do not always turn out to be related to the search even if they look good, so we will hold our views on that until they are sighted close-up," he said. Nevertheless, he added: "This is a lead, it's probably the best lead we have right now... We may get a sighting, we may not. We may get it tomorrow, we may not. But we will continue to do this until we locate those objects or we are convinced that we cannot find them. I would advise that AMSA is doing its level best to find anyone that may have survived."

Australian Prime Minister Tony Abbott told Parliament in Canberra: "New and credible information has come to light in relation to the search for Malaysia Airlines Flight MH370 in the southern Indian Ocean. Following specialist analysis of this satellite imagery, two possible objects related to the search have been identified. I can inform the House that a Royal Australian Air Force Orion has been diverted to attempt to locate the objects."

But he warned: "We must keep in mind the task of locating these objects will be extremely difficult and it may turn out that they are not related to the search for Flight MH370."

A Royal Australian Air Force Orion was diverted to the search zone in the Southern Indian Ocean and three other planes, including one from New Zealand and one from the United States, are due to carry out a more intensive follow-up search. An Australian Hercules would drop marker buoys in the area to help provide information on where the debris may have drifted to.

However, the weather quickly closed in and the search had to be called off. Even when the weather was good, the area they were searching is one of the most inhospitable places on the planet. Given to swirling currents and high seas, it is far from land and much of the sea floor there had yet to be mapped.

Alain Bouillard, who led the search for Air France Flight AF447, said: "This disappearance is still a great mystery, and will lead to an inquiry and a search that is far, far harder than that we had looking for Air France 447. Firstly we had many more clues. We knew that the Air France plane had a problem, thanks to 24 ACARS messages sent over four minutes; we knew its precise location four minutes before impact, which allowed us to reduce our search zone to only 40 nautical miles [46 miles or 75km]. That is nothing compared to the surface area of today's search."

Even if the debris that had been spotted was part of Flight MH370, this would do little to narrow down the search area.

"Objects that have drifted for two weeks will have travelled a long way in that time," he explained. "If you have currents at four knots, that mean four nautical miles per hour [4.6 mph or 7.4 km/h] and a considerable distance in 14 days."

The debris could already be 60 miles (96.5km) from where they were seen on the satellite imagery, which itself was four hours' flying time from western Australia. And that was only the beginning of the problem.

"After you have identified and examined some debris, you can piece together how the plane broke up. Was it in the air, was it during a sea landing, or did it hit the ocean intact? From that you can build up a scenario," he said.

Mr Bouillard said reaching the wreck was not the hardest task facing search teams, even using a towed pinger locator that detects the sonic signal given off by the black box.

"We found the AF447 at around 12,000ft [3,658m]," he said. "The Phoenix Towed Pinger Locator can go down to around 6,000m [19,700ft]. The first question is: where was the point of impact? We can only send out serious means once we have defined a much smaller search area."

The search for Air France's main wreck and black boxes took two years, even though the most up-to-date equipment was deployed to find them. These included underwater drones with sonars that can sweep large areas of the seabed to locate objects; a deep-towed sonar; two remotely operated vehicles and three autonomous underwater vehicles. In the end they ignored complex equations that predicted the likely location of the wreck and simply scoured the zone systematically. Once they had located a large object on the sea floor, they sent down remote vehicles equipped with high definition cameras. Finally, the black boxes were found.

"It was a euphoric moment," he admitted.

As for the search for MH370, Mr Bouillard said: "There are three main questions you must ask in an inquiry: what happened, how did it happen and why did it happen? We have still made no progress on what happened. It will be a highly complex, colossal task and a result is anything but guaranteed."

Nevertheless searchers were heartened by the latest sighting. "It is where we were expecting it to be," said one. "If you assume the plane remained at a constant height and speed, given its fuel load, it takes you down to the southern part of the southern corridor."

Once the weather lifted, four planes flew over the area and spotted nothing. The *Höegh St Petersburg*, a Norwegian cargo vessel carrying cars from South Africa to Australia that had been diverted to take part in the search, also drew a blank.

The two Australian Orions, as well as a US Poseidon and an Orion covered an area of almost 9,000 square miles (23,309 sq km). A British coastal survey ship, HMS *Echo*, and an Australian naval vessel, HMAS *Success*, were also deployed to assist with the search. However, after an Australian Orion completed a two-hour flyover, Australia's maritime authority tweeted: "Crew unable to locate debris. Cloud & rain limited visibility. Further aircraft to continue search."

By then 29 aircraft, 18 ships and six helicopters were searching the southern corridor.

David Gallo of the Woods Hole Oceanographic Institution, who co-led the search for that AF447, said that the hunt for

MH370 need not be so protracted. "We know a lot more after Air France than we did then," he added.

Initial modelling had led searchers to at first look in the wrong place for the Air France plane. And while the hunt took nearly two years, his team spent only around 10 weeks at sea.

The cockpit voice recorder records only the last two hours of audio before a plane crash and, in the case of MH370, the plane may have flown for hours after the critical events took place.

"But there will be other clues, if the plane is treated as a crime scene. We never know what we will find," said Gallo. "There should be other things that could give a clue as to what has gone on – the cockpit itself; whatever position the pieces are in; the surface flaps and landing gear. We have the capability now of doing a very detailed forensic study of a wreck in deep water."

He was in two minds about the sighting of the debris. "In a sense we are hoping this is the plane – it means finally the mystery comes to a close, or at least halfway there," he explained. "But on the other hand, we don't because it takes away the hope some families have that someone may still be alive."

If the plane had crashed there, the searcher may just have got lucky. Charitha Pattiaratchi, professor of oceanography at the University of Western Australia, said the search area covered an ocean ridge known as Naturalist Plateau, a large sea shelf about 9,800ft (3,000m) deep. The plateau was about 150 miles (241km) wide and 250 miles (402km) long, while the area around it was close to 16,400ft (5,000m) deep. "Whichever way you go, it's deep," he said.

Nearby is the southeast India ridge, which runs from east to west and slopes down from a peak that is roughly 8,200ft (2,499m) beneath the surface to a depth of around 13,100ft (3,993m). By deep-sea survey standards, the terrain is relatively straightforward and research submarines would be able to operate without too much difficulty.

Otherwise the prognosis for the search was poor. "Those satellite images had to be gone over by hand," said Simon Boxall of the National Oceanography Centre in Southampton. "That takes a lot of experts a lot of time. But the issue is that there are very strong currents where the flotsam was located. The Antarctic circumpolar current runs at around one mile an hour [1.6 km/h], which may not sound a lot but in ocean terms is very fast. In four days, those objects could have travelled 100 miles [161km]."

And that was in calm weather conditions. In March, the Antarctic region is fast approaching autumn. Australian air force pilots out on the search mission said rough seas and high winds added up to "extremely bad" weather conditions. These are the legendary Roaring Forties.

Lying between 40 and 50 degrees latitude south, the search area lay in one of the most treacherous seas on Earth. Unlike in the northern hemisphere, there is little land that reaches far enough below the Equator. This allows fierce westerly winds and currents to circulate the globe unimpeded. The deep ocean currents break off into eddies, further hampering any search.

As winter approaches, frequent storms also bring poor visibility, lots of rain or snow, great sea swells and waves up to 33ft (10m) high are quite normal. Even radar is of little help because of the rough seas. Using infrared does not help either because floating objects soon cool to the same temperature as the water.

Objects in the water would break up in heavy seas. Fragments could quickly spread over an area covering tens of square miles, with semi-submerged material travelling at a different rate than objects floating on the surface because ocean currents can be stronger than wave-induced currents. Other debris would simply sink.

"What keeps something afloat, a wing or part of the fuselage, say, is air trapped inside it," explained Boxall. "Particularly in bad weather and sea conditions, the chances of that air escaping are really quite high."

Even if flotsam were collected by surface ship guided from the air, there would still be the task of locating the aircraft's remains on the ocean floor. Whatever was found on the surface would be a very long way from wherever the plane crashed. That too, due to ocean currents, would be some distance from whatever was on the ocean floor.

"Once a piece of the debris is found – if it did impact on the water – then you've got to backtrack that debris to try to find the 'X marks the spot' where the plane actually hit the water, because that would be the centre of the haystack," said Gallo. "And in that haystack, you're trying to find bits of that needle – in fact, in the case of the flight data recorders, you're looking for a tiny little bit of that needle."

Once experts have worked out the point of impact – a process in itself fraught with potential errors and miscalculations – accident investigators would send down autonomous underwater vehicles (AUVs) fitted with sonar to scan the sea floor or with high-resolution cameras to compile a detailed picture of the area. It could take up to a month to transport these submersibles to the area. Their job would be to find the plane's tail section where the black box containing the digital flight data is located. The hunt was time-sensitive because, while the box's data can still be recovered years after a crash, its electronic locator, or pinger, stops sending out signals after about a month. The flight data recorder registers information for the last 25 hours. However, the plane's cockpit voice recorder records for two hours, then resets itself and records over the top of the previous two hours' recording.

Although they are called "black boxes" they are usually orange so that they show up among the wreckage. They can withstand an impact of 310 mph (499 km/h) and temperatures of up to 2,000°F (1,093°C) for an hour. If the plane is underwater, the boxes send out a sonar signal that can be detected up to 15 miles (24km) away. If on land they transmit a satellite signal, but when the batteries die the signals will stop.

Two recent air crashes over water illustrate the daunting task facing the investigators. With TWA Flight 800, which exploded in mid-air soon after taking off from New York's John F Kennedy International Airport on 17 July 1996, reconstructing exactly what happened was vital to disprove conspiracy theories, one of which was terrorists may have fired a rocket at the plane. The explosion had scattered in thousands of fragments of wreckage over some 75 square miles (194 sq km) of the Atlantic Ocean floor. It took the US Navy and other divers more than 1,600 hours to find and collect the debris. Strewn along the flight path they first found a wing section, then the nose, the rest of the wings and the aircraft's tail and engines. After painstakingly reconstructing all the wreckage that they had retrieved, they found no evidence that the plane had been hit by anything from the outside. In a report issued three years after the crash, accident investigators concluded that the Boeing 747 broke into pieces off Long Island following an explosion in a fuel tank caused by an electrical short circuit.

With Air France Flight 447, there was an even more complex investigation. Although the Brazilian Navy found and removed the first major wreckage and two bodies from the sea within five days, it took four searches and nearly two years to find the rest of the wreckage of the Airbus A330. The crash site was four days' sailing from the nearest port and more than 10,000ft (3,048m) beneath the surface of the Atlantic. The voice and flight data recorders were not recovered until May 2011 and the report blaming pilot error was not published until July 2012.

AF447 was found by trawling the ocean floor. That requires reasonable conditions – you never get reasonable conditions in the Roaring Forties. Any deepwater search would need to be done in good weather. It would have to be conducted in summer. Then, the southern hemisphere was heading into winter.

Although satellite pictures picked up what appeared to be debris on the ocean surface, the coverage in this region is not continuous and is highly unlikely to have recorded the moment when the aircraft may have crashed into the sea, if that was what happened.

David Gallo said: "AF447 had a good Last Known Position [LKP], which provided search teams with an approximate location to focus a search for debris. We were able to back-track the floating debris over five days or more than a week to estimate where in that circle the plane impacted."

In the case of MH370, though, there has been no LKP. It could be anywhere along two arcs from the aircraft's last fixed radar position off the coast of the Malaysian island of Penang. Nevertheless, Gallo remained optimistic.

"It's important to be sure all the truth has come forward," he insisted. "Anything could become an important bit of evidence or a clue to finding the aircraft. If there is a will to find the plane, the plane will be found. There are many teams trying very hard to find that aircraft."

Soon the search was blessed with more moderate seas, with

waves 4.5 to 7.5ft (1.4 to 2.3m) high and winds of 6 to 12 knots (7 to 14 mph or 11 to 22 km/h). It seemed that conditions for the search were going to be favourable after all.

CHAPTER NINETEEN

LAST WORDS

On 21 March 2014 the full transcript of the communication between Flight MH370, identified as MAS 370, and the air traffic controllers on 8 March was released. It began with the conversation with "ATC Delivery" when Flight MH370 already had 227 passengers on board and requested permission to leave Kuala Lumpur International:

> 12:25:53 MH370: "Delivery MH370 Good
> Morning."
> 12:26:02 ATC: "MAS 370. Standby and Malaysia
> Six
>   is cleared to Frankfurt via AGOSA Alpha
>   Departure six thousand feet squawk two one
>   zero six."
> 12:26:19 ATC: "MAS 370 request level."
> 12:26:21 MH370: "MAS 370 we are ready
> requesting

flight level three five zero to Beijing."
12:26:39 ATC: "MAS 370 is cleared to Beijing via

   PIBOS A Departure Six Thousand Feet squawk

   two one five seven."
12:26:45 MH370: "Beijing PIBOS A Six Thousand

   Squawk two one five seven, MAS 370. Thank You."
12:26:53 ATC: "MAS 370 Welcome over to ground."
12:26:55 MH370: "Good Day."

Next comes the two-way with Kuala Lumpur ground control, which directs the plane as it is taxiing and making its final preparations for takeoff:

12:27:27 MH370: "Ground MAS 370. Good morning
   Charlie One. Requesting push and start."
12:27:34 ATC: "MAS 370 Lumpur Ground. Morning.

   Push back and start approved. Runway 32.
   Right exit via Sierra 4."
12:27:40 MH370: "Push back and start approved.

   32. Right exit via Sierra 4. POB 239 Mike Romeo

   Oscar."
12:27:45 ATC: "Copied."
12:32:13 MH370: "MAS 377 request taxi."

12:32:26 ATC: "MAS 37 (garbled) standard
route.
   Hold short Bravo."
12:32:30 MH370: "Ground, MAS 370. You are
   unreadable. Say again."
12:32:38 ATC: "MAS 370 taxi to holding point
Alfa
   11. Runway 32. Right via standard route.
Hold
   short of Bravo."
12:32:42 MH370: "Alfa 11. Standard route. Hold
   short Bravo. MAS 370."
12:35:53 ATC: "MAS 370 Tower."
12:36:19 ATC: "(garbled) Tower (garbled)."
12:36:30 MH370: "1188 MAS 370. Thank you."

Ground control then hands over to the tower, which controls the
takeoff by sight:

12:36:30 MH370: "Tower MAS 370. Morning."
12:36:38 ATC: "MAS 370 good morning. Lumpur
   Tower. Holding point (garbled) 10 32 Right."
12:36:50 MH370: "Alfa 10 MAS 370."
12:38:43 ATC: "370 line up 32 Right Alfa 10."

The plane is given permission to take its runway starting position
from the runway's "32 Right A10" entry point before beginning
its takeoff.

12:38:52 MH370: "Line up 32 Right Alfa 10 MAS
   370."

12:40:38 ATC: "370 32 Right Cleared for
takeoff.
  Good night."
12:40:43 MH370: "32 Right Cleared for takeoff
  MAS370. Thank you. Bye."

MH370 confirms that it is in position. The runway is ready and
air traffic control gives it to takeoff; MH370 copies that. Cockpit
acknowledges clearance to take off and bids farewell to the ground
tower before making contact with the next air traffic controller,
Kuala Lumpur Approach, who has MH370 on radar:

12:42:05: "MH370. Departure Malaysian Three
  Seven Zero."

MH370 confirms it is airborne.

12:42:10 ATC: "Malaysian Three Seven Zero.
Selamat pagi 'Good morning' in Malay.
Identified. Climb flight level one eight zero
cancel SID turn right direct to IGARI."

The plane is instructed to climb to an altitude of 18,000ft
(5,486m). Its routing is confirmed and it is instructed to turn
toward IGARI, a navigational waypoint above the South China
Sea, almost halfway between Malaysia and Vietnam.

12:42:48 MH370: "Okay, level one eight zero,
direct
  IGARI. Malaysian one err Three Seven Zero."

Cockpit acknowledges its clearance to ascend, confirms its route and altitude of 18,000ft.

> 12:42:52 ATC: "Malaysian Three Seven Zero contact Lumpur Radar One Three Two Six good night."
> 12:42:61 MH370: "Night One Three Two Six Malaysian Three Seven Zero."

Finally, MH370 is handed to the area air traffic controller Lumpur Control, which controls its onward flight into Vietnamese airspace:

> 12:46:51 MH370: "Lumpur Control Malaysian Three
>   Seven Zero."
> 12:46:51 ATC: "Malaysian Three Seven Zero Lumpur
>   Radar. Good Morning. Climb flight level two five zero."

After MH370 makes contact with the next air traffic controller, it is given permission to climb to 25,000ft (7,620m).

> 12:46:54 MH370: "Morning. Level two five zero Malaysian Three Seven Zero."

MH370 then acknowledges that it is climbing to 25,000ft.

> 12:50:06 ATC: "Malaysian Three Seven Zero climb
>   flight level three five zero."

It is then given permission to climb to its cruising altitude of 35,000ft (10,668m).

> 12:50:09 MH370: "Flight level three five zero
>   Malaysian Three Seven Zero."

MH370 acknowledges that it climbing to 35,000ft.

> 01:01:14 MH370: "Malaysian Three Seven Zero
>   maintaining level three five zero."
> 01:01:19 ATC: "Malaysian Three Seven Zero."

MH370 tells air traffic control that it has reached 35,000ft and air traffic control acknowledges the call.

> 01:07:55 MAS370: "Malaysian...Three Seven
> Zero
>   maintaining level three five zero."

This is not necessary as air traffic control already know that MH370 has reached its cruising altitude, but it is not especially unusual.

> 01:08:00 ATC: "Malaysian Three Seven Zero."
>   01:19:24 ATC: "Malaysian Three Seven Zero
>   contact Ho Chi Minh 120 decimal 9. Good
> Night."
> 01:19:29 MH370: "Good Night Malaysian Three
>   Seven Zero."

Dead men talking… Curiously, it was now revealed that whoever on Flight MH370 signed off that night, they did not use the casual "All right, good night" that had at first aroused suspicion, but the more formal "Good Night Malaysian Three Seven Zero."

The plane's co-pilot, First Officer Hamid, used some occasionally relaxed language, but otherwise followed standard procedure as he contacted air traffic controllers about the plane's movements as it taxied on the runway, then took off and eventually cruised at an altitude of 35,000ft.

The 27-year-old co-pilot carefully repeated each of the controller's calls back to them. The controllers were not required to reply and sometimes responded by saying "MAS 370" – a short response that takes up less air time.

"The communication until the plane went to the changeover [to Vietnam] sounds totally normal," said former British Airways pilot Stephen Buzdygan. "That kind of banter – I've done it hundreds of times. It is perfectly normal."

After reading the transcript, former Qantas pilot Adam Susz said the messages in the crucial minutes before the plane disappeared were all perfectly routine. "It sounds totally normal," he said.

There was no hint that the speaker was under duress. It is assumed that it is Hamid talking, as the co-pilot would routinely have conducted most of the radio communication.

Analysts said Hamid's communication was standard fare. The only thing at all unusual was his repetition of the plane's cruising altitude at 1.07 am. But the call –"Malaysian…Three Seven Zero maintaining level three five zero [35,000 feet]" – was not suspicious and there was no indication that he was trying to convey alarm or distress.

"It could be as simple as the pilot forgetting," said former BA pilot Steve Landells. "He might be reconfirming he was at 350 [35,000ft]."

Flightglobal's David Learmount noted that Hamid's messages departed at times from formal wording, but this was not sinister. "It is a bit sloppy," he admitted. "It is not the busiest time of the day; neither the pilot nor air traffic control are busy."

While the world's press picked over the transcript, search planes from Australia spent 10 hours scouring the area where the two pieces of floating debris had been seen, but could find nothing.

"Something that was floating on the sea that long ago may no longer be floating," said Warren Truss, Australia's deputy prime minister. "It's also certain that any debris or other material would have moved a significant distance over that time, potentially hundreds of kilometres."

Nevertheless Malaysia began contacting the handful of nations with deep sea detection equipment for help in what may be a long search for the aircraft's black box, which may be anywhere within an area of 9,000 square miles (23,310 sq km) in waters up to 13,000ft (3,962m) deep, with strong currents.

Still the search continued. John Young of AMSA's Emergency Response division said: "We want to find these objects because they might be the best lead to where we might find people to be rescued."

This gave a faint whiff of hope, but Nan Jinyan, whose brother-in-law, Yan Ling, was a passenger on MH370, remained stoical. He told Associated Press: "I'm psychologically prepared for the worst, and I know the chances of them coming back alive are extremely small."

Other relatives huddled together in groups, clinging to each other for support in the dimly lit corridors of the Lido Hotel.

Twenty-seven-year-old Wang Le sat quietly in a corner, clutching his fiancée's hand. He had a picture of his mother, Zhang Chi, who was on the plane. "She is a good mum," he said. "We can talk about everything."

He showed a reporter the last few text messages his mum had sent him minutes before the plane took off. "Can we meet up when I get back?" she wrote.

Wang worked for a Chinese social media website. He was going to get married the next month, but had put his wedding plans on hold as he now had to concentrate on looking after his grief-stricken father. "Every evening I have dinner with my father," he said. "He talks about my mum, and sometimes he cries. He tells stories about her I've not heard before."

Wang did not care about all the theories surrounding the plane's fate. "I just want to know what happened to Mum," he said.

Hiding her sobbing eyes behind sunglasses, a woman talked of her son Lin Annan. A student in his twenties, he was returning home to Beijing on the missing plane. She could not stop going over in her mind what she wanted to say to him. "There's something I really want to say to my son," she sobbed. "I love you. All of us love you."

Asked whether the idea that someone hijacked the plane made her angry, she said: "We raised our child to be someone useful to our family, to society, and the world. I think we shouldn't react with hatred or revenge."

Chen Changming, a softly spoken man in his forties, looked pale and exhausted: his brother was on the plane. Compounding his grief, when his elderly father heard the news, he died of a heart attack. Chen had to arrange his father's funeral while trying to come to terms with the fact that his brother may never return home, alive or dead. Nevertheless he turned up for the daily press conference in the hotel's ballroom. "When I go in that ballroom I have a glimmer of hope," he said. "When I leave, I have nothing."

Some of the relatives had already started the grieving process and were working out how they would tell their children or grandchildren. Others, like Wen Wancheng, were still demanding answers. The group's unofficial spokesman, he was from Shandong province in the east of China. His son was on the plane and he was convinced that information was being withheld from the families.

"Even taxis have GPS," he said. "They can be found if they are lost or stolen. How could the plane not be found? It's a joke!"

Confusion at the press conferences and discrepancies in the statements issued by the Malaysian authorities added to his frustration.

"They've been avoiding their responsibilities and talking nonsense," he added. "There are a lot of contradictory answers to our questions; that makes us very angry. I'm angry that the Malaysians don't tell the truth – they lie to the whole world. I'm totally frustrated about this. Where is my son? I'm over 60 years old and retired in China. Now this huge thing has happened and my beloved son is missing. I have to deal with the situation because all of our family is depending on my child coming back. All I want is to enjoy the rest of my life. But how can I? How can my family handle this? We can't. If it is bad news I just want to know quickly. I want to let my son know we love him. Every day I get hope and then lose it."

In Malaysia, Jacquita Gonzales, wife of the MH370's chief steward Patrick, was more phlegmatic. "If it's in the ocean, it brings us closure," she said. "But at the back of our mind we hope."

She was still praying that the jet was hijacked. "You know, they say it's a hijacking," she said. "You know that it's somewhere, then there's hope that he's still alive and he will come back to us. But if it's in the ocean, it's final, you know."

Jacquita said Patrick's two-year-old grandson, Rafael, still thought his beloved grandfather was at work. The family keep a candle burning in Patrick's bedroom, "so his soul can find its way home," said Jacquita.

Far away over the south Indian Ocean, conditions were improving. After returning to Pearce Royal Australian Air Force base from one sortie on 21 March, Flight Lieutenant Russ Adams said: "We've got a lot of hope. We got out there and had really good weather. Compared to yesterday the visibility was great, more than 10km [6 miles] visibility. There are more aircraft out there, still searching, and with any luck we'll find something shortly."

However, they were looking in what Australian Prime Minister Tony Abbott warned was "about the most inaccessible spot that you can imagine on the face of the earth".

"But if there is anything down there, we will find it," he added. "We owe it to the families of those people to do no less. It is a very large team effort, with the international community providing technical support and information, and we're all grateful for that."

The search area was so remote it took aircraft from Australia four hours to fly there and four hours back, leaving them only enough fuel to search for two hours. Usually, searchers scanned the area with radar. Then, if they discovered anything, they would go in for a closer look. But this method was not working.

"Noting that we got no radar detections yesterday, we have re-planned the search to be visual," said John Young of the Australian Maritime Safety Authority. "So, aircraft are flying relatively low, very highly skilled and trained observers looking out of the aircraft windows and looking to see objects."

Even so they found nothing more interesting than a wooden crate and some smaller objects. But the current was running at 3ft (0.9m) a second in the area, so a floating object could travel 100 miles (161km) in two days.

Again a shortage of any concrete news led the daily press conference in Beijing to erupt with anger. The police had to restrain the families as they rushed at officials, shouting: "You can't leave here! We want to know what the reality is," and "Give us back our loved ones!"

"We can't bear it any longer," one woman said.

And the question of money had come up again. "They're offering us compensation," the woman added, "but we've lost our entire families. This is China – they can't just tell us to come or go as they please. We're going to wait here. If they don't come, we're not leaving."

"The Malaysian government is deceiving us. They don't dare to face us," said another relative. "The Malaysian government are the biggest murderers."

Wang Zheng, whose mother and father are among the missing, said: "Biggest of all is the emotional turmoil I've been going through. We feel they're hiding something from us. I can't eat, I can't sleep – I've been dreaming of my parents every day."

The 30-year-old computer engineer added: "We're exhausted. Why did the plane fly so far away? Are the people still alive? Is this new piece of information reliable? This is how I feel – I will stay here until they give me an answer. I am not leaving until I know for certain where my parents are."

The families released a media statement saying they believed they were being "strung along, kept in the dark and lied to by the Malaysian government". It went on: "This kind of conduct neglects the lives of all the passengers, shows contempt for all their families, and even more, tramples on the dignity of Chinese people and the Chinese government."

Nan Jinyan, a 29-year-old engineer who was awaiting news of her missing sister-in-law, said she was increasingly frustrated with the airline's vague and often contradictory information regarding the missing plane.

"If they can't offer something firm, they ought to just shut up," she said. "I'm psychologically prepared for the worst and I know the chances of them coming back alive are extremely small. I never imagined a disaster like this would befall our family, but life has to continue."

In another bitter blow, in Kuala Lumpur the families were being asked to leave the hotel to make room for the Ferrari Formula One motor-racing team in preparation for the Malaysian Grand Prix. Formula One boss Bernie Ecclestone said the F1 booking was made long before Flight MH370 disappeared.

"I feel terribly, terribly sorry for these people but it is up to the hotel," said Mr Ecclestone. "What would happen if you told somebody that they no longer had a booking? You would get sued, I'd imagine. If you have a booking at a hotel, what are you supposed to do?"

Barbara Crolow, who had lost her son, and Bernd Gans, who had lost a daughter, wrote in an open letter that the relatives should also demand financial aid from the Malaysian government. Floyd Wisner, a US lawyer who represented the families of Flight AF447, said that when a plane belonging to the Indonesian airline Adam Air disappeared in 2007, he secured a deal with the insurers before any trace of it was found. "The families may seek compensation even before any wreckage or bodies are found," he said.

Adam Air Flight KI574 was flying from Surabaya to Manado in Indonesia on 1 January 2007, when the Boeing 737-400 disappeared off air traffic control screens. It was flying at 35,000ft (10,668km). The pilot had reported crosswinds of more than 70 knots (80 mph or 130 km/h) over the Makassar Strait, but no distress calls were heard. Initially there were reports that it had crashed in a mountainous region on the island of Sulawesi and there were 12 survivors but a search and rescue team drew a blank.

There were search teams on the ground, in the air and at sea, with both surface ships and submarines joining in the hunt but efforts were hampered by bad weather. Over the following weeks, debris was collected which proved to come from Flight KI574. USNS *Mary Sears*, an oceanographic survey ship, located the black boxes at a depth of around 6,600ft (2,011m). A row ensued as to who would pay for them to be recovered. Seven months later, they were brought up.

An air-crash investigation concluded the flight deck crew became embroiled in troubleshooting the aircraft's perennially faulty inertial reference systems. The autopilot became disengaged. Before they could correct it, the plane banked and dived. It reached a speed of 490 knots (564 mph), over the aircraft's maximum rated speed for a dive of 400 knots (460 mph). When they tried to pull up, the plane broke apart.

On 21 February 2007, just 51 days after the loss of KI574, another Adam Air Boeing 737-300 on Flight 176 broke its back on landing, with cracks around the middle of the passenger cabin. Adam Air's fleet of six 737s was immediately grounded. The following year, another Adam Air Boeing 737-

400 on Flight 292 skidded off the runway when landing at Batam. Again no one was killed, but amid serious concerns about Adam Air's maintenance standards, Indonesia revoked its Air Operator Certificate and the company was no longer allowed to fly.

CHAPTER TWENTY

HOPE AGAINST HOPE

Some relatives of those on board Flight MH370 continue to cling on to a final straw of hope. Liu Guiqiu, whose son Li Le was on the flight, said she had travelled from China to Kuala Lumpur as she wanted "to be the first to see my son and greet him when he returns". Weeping, she said she had not told her young granddaughter that her father was missing.

"We have a rule that no one in the family is allowed to cry or mention this issue in front of her," Mrs Liu said in an interview on Chinese TV. "She wouldn't be able to cope with this news about her father. I really just want my son to come home and to be safe. My heart is broken. My son is definitely going to be all right."

Mrs Liu offered her gratitude to the countries "trying to find our families".

"I can't understand why there hasn't been any news about my son at all. I'm going to be crazy," she said.

She had also been caught up in the fracas on 19 March that was broadcast on TV around the world. "I was surrounded by reporters," she recalled. "There was a policeman who I initially thought was about to grab me. I said, 'What are you doing? Help!' Then they put me aside… I just want to see my son return."

Patricia Coakley, who lives near Whitby, North Yorkshire, in Britain, knows only too well how she feels. Her husband, 61-year-old engineer Arthur Coakley, was one of 228 people killed on Air France Flight AF447. She only had to wait five days until the debris was found, though searchers took longer to find her husband.

"I was convinced he would be found," she told *The Independent on Sunday*. "The only thing we lived on was hope."

Mrs Coakley is of the view that the search for Flight MH370 must continue until it is found. "Otherwise, the people with [loved ones] on board will never, never rest," she said. "It will just be an ongoing nightmare for them. They have to find it. They said at the time that looking for Art's plane was like looking for a needle in a haystack. This is even worse. There's all this speculation but nobody can prove it. I know exactly what they are going through."

Mr Coakley's body was found, but 74 others were never recovered.

The leaders of Malaysia's leading faiths – Muslim, Buddhist, Christian and Hindu – were still praying that the passengers will be found alive.

"Last Friday we held a special service for MH370. Many people kneeled to pray. Some cried," said Ebeneezer, a priest at Kuala Lumpur's Sri Subang Lutheran Church. "It's our sincere prayer that they are alive. Nothing is difficult for the Lord."

At the Buddhist Maha Vihara Malaysia temple in the Brickfields area, the head monk, Datuk Kirinde Dhammaratana, said no one could be sure they were dead – "Until the confirmation, I hope we will get some good news."

Dato' Woo Ser Chai, president of the association that runs Thean Hou Temple in Kuala Lumpur, built on a hill in the Chinese-Buddhist tradition, said if there was no body, a prayer could be said, asking that the person's spirit be permitted to go to heaven. Believers could also pray in front of a photo of their loved one.

"So far, even though it is more than 10 days, there is still hope," he added. "Even though the hope is very slim, a miracle might happen."

While the search area was gradually being narrowed down, investigators were still trying to discover why the plane found its way to the south Indian Ocean in the first place. By then they had largely ruled out the possibility that Flight MH370 might have suffered a fire that knocked out all communication systems and killed the pilots. They were equally doubtful that a hijacker among the passengers could have seized control of the aircraft. After studying the transcripts between air traffic control and the co-pilot, it seemed any would-be hijacker would have had only a two-minute window of opportunity. It would have to be done between the sign-off at 1.19 am and 1.21 am when the plane's transponder was switched off. Again, the question had to be asked: were the pilots to blame?

A source close to the investigation said: "We're still on the notion of a deliberate act, but who it was is unknown and for what reason is unknown. The finger of suspicion is pointing towards the pilots. The pilots were only seriously investigated after the view emerged that someone on board did something deliberate rather than it being an accident."

After two weeks' inquiries, the source said that "the most plausible" explanation was that the pilots, either in concert or alone, locked themselves in the cockpit and hijacked the flight. However, police have found no evidence of a plot cooked up by the pilots or signs that either man had psychological problems.

Meanwhile, the suspicion surrounding the flight crew was taking its toll on their families. Twenty-seven-year-old Aishah Shah, daughter of pilot Zaharie Ahmad Shah, told a friend: "This is torturing my family. He is a nice man and a loving father."

Foreign intelligence agencies had completed a second round of vetting of each of the passengers, including two Iranians travelling on false passports, and had cleared them all. Only a Russian passenger, who is not believed to be suspect, apparently remained to be fully vetted, because the authorities in Moscow have been preoccupied with the crisis in Crimea. However, the Ukraine had managed to find time to vet its two passengers.

Another puzzle was why Flight MH370 took such a winding path before heading south – westwards across Malaysia, northwest up the Malacca Straits before turning southwards over open water. The aircraft seems to have been deliberately skirting Indonesian airspace; it took a route that Malaysia Airlines does not fly and neither pilot had flown in that area. However, Captain Shah might have been practising landings on five runways across the Indian Ocean on his flight simulator.

The police then moved in to seize the bank statements, credit card bills, mortgage documents and other personal financial records of all 12 crew members as part of a widening inquiry into the disappearance of the Malaysia Airlines passenger jet. Investigators have also obtained all the cell and home phone records of the crew, as well as details of their computer use and Internet habits. They were searching for evidence that any of the crew might have been subject to psychological or financial pressure.

The families of the two cockpit crew were segregated from the 10 families of the cabin crew. They had been sequestered in a golf resort hotel and told to avoid all contact with the media.

Shah's wife, Faisah, and his three children were asked about the living arrangements of the family, who owned two properties in Kuala Lumpur. A police source said they had "domestic issues".

The police also questioned Hamid's fiancée Nadirah Ramli about their relationship. Friends said the shattered bride-to-be feared she might never be able to enter a cockpit again.

"I need time off to work out if I want to carry on flying – before deciding if this is a job I can carry on doing," she declared.

She and her fiancé's family tried to console one another at a Kuala Lumpur hotel.

"What happened with Fariq is haunting Nadira," a friend said.

More friends came forward to vouch for Captain Shah. Nasir Osman, who had known him since school days, said he doubted the pilot had been involved in any wrongful act.

"To me he had everything in this life," he said. "He's a professional."

But others were beginning to have their doubts. A source close to the investigation said: "There seems to be nothing in the life of Fariq Hamid to suggest a motive for hijacking. The personal life of Zaharie Shah, however, is far more complex and is in the process of being unravelled."

Indeed Shah's marriage seems to have deteriorated to the point where he was no longer in a relationship with Faisah, despite the pair still living together with their children.

"One of the most dangerous things that can happen is the rogue captain," said John Gadzinski, a Boeing 737 captain and aviation-safety consultant. "If you get somebody who – for whatever reason – turns cancerous and starts going on their own agenda, it can be a really bad situation."

The police were also re-examining the nine passengers in the business-class compartment at the front of the plane as the trapdoor there gives access to the ACARS satellite data reporting system, which was switched off around the time Flight MH370 disappeared from radar screens, some 40 minutes into the flight.

"That is the best moment to try to get into the cockpit and take control," said a veteran crew member who has often flown with Shah.

Also of interest was flight steward Tan Size Hiang. He too had a flight simulator at home. But it was not known if he would have been capable of commandeering the plane, then flying it low to avoid detection, while taking other precautions to avoid secondary sources of detection.

On 23 March 2014, a French satellite spotted some more debris around 1,430 miles (2,301km) from Perth, again raising hopes. Fuzzy images showed objects floating some 575 miles (925km) north of the area where those spotted earlier had been seen. The images were so blurred that it could not be ascertained whether they were the same objects. In the area of the earlier sighting, searchers had given up as they could find nothing except seaweed.

By then the search in the northern corridor toward Kazakhstan was also at an end. Fresh calculations by Inmarsat and the UK's Air Accidents Investigation Branch concluded the plane flew south. Handshakes from the satellite and assumptions about the plane's speed helped Australia and the US National Transportation Safety Board to narrow down the search area to just 3 percent of the southern corridor. The calculation depended on the Doppler effect, which causes a slight shift in frequency due to the relative movement of the plane and the satellite. This type of analysis had never before been used in an investigation of this sort.

"We are talking about the application of a mathematical model with literally thousands of variables," explained an Inmarsat spokesperson at London's Old Street "Silicon Roundabout", where six rocket scientists "fly" the company's satellites. "It wasn't the technology that found the plane – it was the brains behind it."

The new method "gives the approximate direction of travel, plus or minus about 100 miles [160km], to a track line," said Chris McLaughlin, senior vice-president for external affairs at Inmarsat. "Unfortunately this is a 1990s satellite over the Indian Ocean that is not GPS-equipped. All we believe we can do is to say that we believe it is in this general location, but we cannot give you the final few feet and inches where it landed – it's not that sort of system."

Dr Simon Boxall, an oceanographer with Southampton University, observed: "They've probably crammed a year's worth of research into maybe a couple of weeks. Technologically, it's really quite astounding."

Meanwhile, Allianz Global Corporate & Specialty had paid out US$110 million (£67 million) to Malaysia Airlines for the loss of Flight MH370. The insurers have also agreed to make hardship payments to the families of the missing airliner's passengers, to cover their costs while the hunt for the plane continues. International rules stipulate a minimum payment of US$177,412 (£105,490) per passenger. If terrorism or negligence played a role, this could alter the size of the payouts. It was up to the airline to prove that it was not responsible for the accident, a difficult thing to do if the wreckage could not be found.

The hunt for the missing plane was still going on when a multi-million-dollar lawsuit was initiated in the US against Malaysia Airlines and Boeing. Representing families of the passengers, the

Chicago-based law firm Ribbeck Law Chartered International filed a petition of discovery in Cook County, Illinois, requiring the companies to produce evidence of possible flaws in the crashed Boeing 777.

"We believe that both defendants named are responsible for the disaster of Flight MH370," said Monica Kelly, the firm's head of global aviation litigation.

The company said it was acting on behalf of Januari Siregar, who lost his son Firman in the crash, but gave no details of the damages sought beyond describing the litigation as a "multimillion-dollar process". They expected to represent more than half of the families of the missing.

Ribbeck Law Chartered International believe a mechanical fault caused either a fire in the cockpit or a loss in cabin pressure that rendered both pilots unconscious.

"That plane was actually a ghost plane for several hours, until it ran out of fuel," Monica Kelly said.

Meanwhile, the US Seventh Fleet was already bringing in a state-of-the-art towed pinger locator. This could detect the sonar "ping" given off by the black boxes down to a depth of about 20,000ft (6,096m), said Commander Chris Budde, an operations officer. "This movement is simply a prudent effort to pre-position equipment and trained personnel closer to the search area so that if debris is found we will be able to respond as quickly as possible since the battery life of the black box's pinger is limited."

"The time for the battery life [of the pinger] is potentially only a month," said Jason Middleton, aviation professor at the University of New South Wales in Sydney. "If debris was found, it would be terrible not to have anything on site and waste time [getting a ping detector to the region]. I think they're planning ahead and getting it ready."

On 24 March 2014, after 17 days of searching, the Malaysian Prime Minister Najib Razak announced to 50 family members that there was now no doubt that Flight MH370 had plunged into the south Indian Ocean.

"This is a remote location, far from any possible landing sites," he said. "It is therefore with deep sadness and regret that I must inform you that according to this new data Flight MH370 ended in the southern Indian Ocean."

Speaking of the families of the missing passengers, he said: "For them the past few weeks have been heart-breaking. I know this news must be harder still."

On hearing the Prime Minister's statement, one woman fell to her knees, crying: "My son! My son!"

Another relative screamed: "It's not possible!"

Some of them had already received the announcement by text message in English by Malaysia Airlines, saying simply: "We have to assume beyond all reasonable doubt that MH370 has been lost and none of those on board survived."

Selamat Omar said: "We accept the news of the tragedy. It is fate."

Maira Nari tweeted: "God loves you more daddy… God loves them more."

She added: "I don't know what to say, what to think. I feel so lost, so blank. I'm just so tired. Goodnight, daddy. Sigh … *hugs*."

In Beijing's Lido Hotel, medical teams carried one elderly man out of the conference room on a stretcher, his face covered by a jacket. Minutes later, a middle-aged woman was taken out on another stretcher, her face ashen and her expressionless eyes staring off into the distance. Most of the relatives refused to speak to reporters and some of them even lashed out in anger.

Security guards restrained a man with close-cropped hair as he kicked a TV cameraman and shouted: "Don't film. I'll beat you to death!"

Police officers had to keep order.

"This is a blow to us, and it is beyond description," said Nan Jinyan, whose brother-in-law Yan Ling was on the flight.

One relative yelled: "We've been waiting for 17 days. You simply tell us this! Where is the proof? It's wrong to announce the information like this!"

One woman, blinded by tears, emerged from the ballroom to a list of family members she had just been told had perished on the plane.

"My only son… My daughter-in-law… My little grandson…" she sobbed. "All destroyed, all gone!"

Wang Zhen, whose parents were missing, excused himself, saying: "Can we talk later?"

"I'm devastated, devastated, devastated!" wailed one elderly woman.

Another refused to believe the Malaysian Prime Minister's announcement. "The information they released is wrong! Those governments just keep lying to us!" she screamed. "do they have children? Their children must be dead!"

Some sat silently – the men smoking, the women pale with grief. One group stood quietly, away from the cameras, weeping. A grieving Chinese woman said: "This was the wrong way to release this information. It's all so black."

Two men hurled themselves in rage at the media throng.

"Murderers! Murderers!" one man screamed as he was dragged away by the police.

The families' feelings were chillingly summed up in a statement on the Malaysia Airlines MH370 Family Committee website, which said: "Malaysia Airlines, the government of Malaysia, and the military forces of Malaysia have concealed, delayed and hidden the truth from the relatives and the people of the world. This despicable act aimed to fool the relatives of the 154 Chinese passengers has devastated us physically and mentally, while misleading and delaying the rescue operation, wasting a lot of manpower, material resources and leading to the loss of precious rescue time. If the 154 of our loved ones have lost their lives, then Malaysia Airlines, the government of Malaysia and the military are really the executioners. We will do everything possible to pursue these three, to hold them responsible for their unforgivable crime."

Later, wearing white T-shirts bearing the words "Let's Pray for MH370", relatives and their supporters marched on the Malaysian Embassy, chanting: "Tell the truth! Return our relatives!"

The police laid on four buses to ferry them to the Embassy and it seems the protest had official sanction. But the relatives grew impatient and made their way on foot as the police closed some of Beijing's busiest roads and diverted traffic.

They unfurled banners that said: "MH370, don't let us wait too long!" and "1.3 billion people are waiting to greet the plane".

A woman named Zhang said: "We've waited for 18 days and still you make us wait. How long are we supposed to hang on?"

Although the protest was permitted by the authorities – a thing almost unknown in China – the relatives were being kept under close surveillance. Meanwhile, the Chinese government was demanding that the Malaysians hand over the Inmarsat's analysis that had led them to draw the conclusion that the plane was now at the bottom of the ocean. President Xi Jinping sent a special envoy to Kuala Lumpur to increase the pressure. Chen Kun, one of China's most famous actors and singers, with 72 million followers on China's equivalent of Twitter, called for a boycott of "all goods and travel to Malaysia".

Twenty-seven-year-old computer engineer Wang Yongang was on board Flight MH370.

"Both parents are in their fifties and Wang is their only child," said Cao Kaifu, his former headmaster at a school in Jiangsu province. "It is so sad. Wang has always been the pride of his parents – they are heartbroken."

The son of a maths teacher and a gynaecologist, Wang had been a star pupil. He scored an outstanding 695 points in his country's notoriously difficult "gaokao" university entrance exam and admission tutors from Peking University and Tsinghua both came to the school to try and enrol him. Wang chose Peking University, where he studied electronic engineering and computer science, graduating with a PhD in 2013. Employed by China's Ministry of Industry and Information Technology, he was returning from lecturing in Malaysia on Flight MH370. He was planning to marry his girlfriend later in the year.

"I can't imagine his family's grief," said Mr Cao.

And Wang was not the only only-child on Flight MH370. Among them were thought to be Ding Ying, an employee of Qatar Airways from Chongqing; Zhang Meng from Zhengzhou and Yan Peng, her husband. All three were aged 28, but in China, almost anyone born between 1980 and 1990 is likely to have been an only child. Chinese parents consider themselves "orphaned" when they lose the only child the state has permitted them to have.

Emotions were raw in Malaysia too, where the co-pilot's father, 52-year-old Abdul Hamid Mad Daud, refused to say funeral prayers for his son.

"I will not accept my son is dead until I see a body," he insisted at the mosque.

He also dismissed the suicide theory, saying, "He is a good son. He prays five times a day at the mosque when he is not flying. He is not the sort to commit suicide."

Around the world people found it difficult to come to terms with the loss of the plane, so one aviation expert outlined its last few minutes.

"The plane would not have dropped like a stone, it would have glided down for around 10 to 12 minutes after it exhausted its fuel," he explained. Descending from 35,000ft (10,668km), it would have been travelling at around 600 mph (966 km/h) by the time it reached the sea. "It would have hit the water with a massive impact – as though the plane had landed on concrete. Nobody could have survived that – there would have been a huge explosion with the wings ripped off."

Following news that all aboard Flight MH370 had been declared dead, the Malaysian music festival, Twin Towers Alive, that would have featured Christina Aguilera, Rick Astley and Craig David was cancelled and the razzmatazz surrounding the Malaysian Grand Prix was scaled down, though Nico Rosberg and his team-mate Lewis Hamilton would feature "Come Home MH370" messages on their side panels. Work also stopped on the Australian disaster movie *Deep Water*, with a plot-line that featured a plane crashing in a remote region.

Still those in the aviation industry were coming up with their own theories. Veteran pilot Eric Moody told the *Daily Mirror* that he believed that Flight MH370 was brought down deliberately. If there was a fire on board, the pilot would have wanted to land the plane straight away, he said, and not continue flying for seven hours after the last contact.

"It is all pointing to suicide by someone on board – whether that is one of the pilots or somebody else," he said. "They were flying in a controlled manner and somebody switched off the communication equipment."

Seventy-two-year-old Moody was at the controls when all four engines on the British Airways flight from London to New Zealand failed as he flew through a volcanic ash cloud over the Indian Ocean in 1982. The ash cloud was so thin that the crew noticed nothing until the passenger cabin began to fill with sulphurous smoke. Then all four engines flamed out and the crew had no idea why they had lost power.

The plane was now gliding a steep descent and they sent out a Mayday call. Due to the mountain range along the south of Java, it would have been impossible to continue gliding to a suitable landing strip and it seemed they would have to ditch in the sea – something that had never been tried in a 747. Then the oxygen masks dropped and Captain Moody had no choice but to make an announcement to the passengers.

"Good evening ladies and gentlemen," he said. "This is your captain speaking. We have a small problem. All four engines have stopped. We are all doing our damnedest to get them going again. I trust you are not in too much distress."

Convinced they were going to die, the passengers began writing notes. The plane glided for a quarter of an hour, descending from 37,000ft (11,278km) to 12,000ft (3,657km), before the engines miraculously started again. Ash sucked into the engines had melted and clogged the turbines. Eventually it solidified and broke off, allowing them to start again. The plane then headed back to Jakarta, where it landed safely, even though one of the engines had failed again. There were 248 passengers and 15 crew members on board.

Other aviation experts were coming round to Captain Moody's conclusion, reasoning that, after the last voice communication, the plane soared to 45,000ft (13,716km) – high above its maximum service ceiling of 43,100ft (13,137km) – and had kept that altitude for 23 minutes. Although the oxygen masks would have dropped automatically, they would have only supplied passengers with oxygen for 12 minutes, which was usually enough time for the pilot to bring the plane down to an altitude where the air was dense enough to breathe. After 23 minutes, the passengers – and anyone else unprepared for what was happening – would be incapacitated by hypoxia.

"This has been a deliberate act by someone on board who had to have had the detailed knowledge to do what was done," said a source close to the investigation. Afterwards the plane made several turns, showing it was still under the control of someone who knew how to fly.

Then the story of what really happened on board Flight MH370 began to crack. A fellow pilot told the *Daily Express* "on condition of anonymity" that Captain Shah may have set off on "one last joy ride" after his wife had said she was leaving him. He was "terribly upset". The *New Zealand Herald* said his "world was crumbling".

The pilot, who had known Shah for a long time, said: "He's one of the finest pilots around, and I'm no medical expert, but with all that was happening in his life he was probably in no state of mind to be flying."

He was also having problems with the woman he was seeing.

Shah's colleague said his friend was in a dark mood that he kept hidden from others, and he could have incapacitated his co-pilot Fariq Abdul Hamid in some way and kept other flight crew out of the cockpit, and it was "very possible neither passengers nor other crew knew what was happening until it was too late".

While pilot suicide had not been ruled out, all known instances had occurred within an hour of takeoff. Shah's youngest son, 26-year-old Ahmad Seith, insisted his father was not responsible.

"I know my father better," he said. "We may not be as close as he travels so much but I understand him. Now, we are just waiting for the right confirmation for the wreckage or bodies. I will believe it when I see the proof in front of my eyes."

However, Shah's wife Faisah revealed that her husband had stopped speaking to her weeks before the fatal flight. He had spent hours alone in his room, where he had built a flight simulator.

"He just retreated into a shell," she said.

The couple were on the brink of a divorce after nearly 30 years of marriage.

Shah's daughter Aishah also admitted in the last days before Flight MH370 disappeared, he "was not the father I knew". In her last conversation with him, she almost did not recognize him.

"He seemed disturbed and lost in a world of his own," she admitted. "He wasn't his usual self – he was distant and cranky." However, she insisted: "I don't believe he would ever intentionally endanger the lives of his crew and passengers."

Despite his evident distress, suicide seems unlikely. Either he would have had to overpower his younger, fitter co-pilot, or Hamid would have had to leave the cockpit just as the plane left Malaysian airspace. No one who knew Captain Shah thought that he would have been so callously indifferent to the lives of the passengers and his fellow crew, or to the happiness of their families. If he had wanted to kill himself, why would he have chosen this method? After killing or disabling the passengers and crew, he would then have had to fly on, on his own, for seven hours before crashing horribly into the sea, leaving no suicide note, no message and no trace. Plainly it is a possibility, though, and Malaysia Airlines have since introduced a new regulation that a third member of the crew must be in the cockpit when one of the pilots takes a lavatory break.

CHAPTER TWENTY-ONE

MORE MYSTERIES

By 26 March 2014, it was clear to everyone that Flight MH370 had crashed in the south Indian Ocean. Eighteen days had passed and there was no prospect of finding any survivors clinging to the wing. The Malaysian newspaper *The Star* devoted 10 pages to the tragedy. It carried the letters "RIP" on the front page and, on the back, the simple statement: "No farewell words were spoken, no time to say goodbye, you were gone before we knew it, and only God knows why." The *New Straits Times* put a Boeing 777 on its front page, with the headline "Goodnight, MH370", while Ahmad Shah, the Sultan of Pahang – the third largest state in Malaysia – said that flags should be flown at half-mast for three days as a mark of respect. There were fears that the crash would harm the Malaysian economy, though the whole world seemed to share its grief.

But there were still numerous mysteries surrounding the loss of Flight MH370. One of them was the partial handshake at 8.19

Malaysian time. Electronics analyst Thomas Withington told the *Daily Telegraph*: "It sounds like the aircraft began to squawk a message and for some reason this was curtailed. It could be because the aircraft was at a catastrophic phase of its flight – that something was causing it to crash – or there could be some atmospheric disturbance."

Then there were other possibilities.

"Was a crew member trying to send a message?" Withington continued. "Was the aircraft trying to send a message? Was there a malfunction? Those questions can only be answered if the cockpit voice recorders and flight data recorder are recovered."

Or did the plane turn upside down just as it hit the water? Inmarsat's Chris McLaughlin said: "The partial handshake would be the plane running out of fuel and faltering for a moment, so the system went off network and then briefly powered up and had communication with the network. The plane looked for a final communication before it went off – and that was it."

With the engine's faltering, they would have tried to communicate their condition to Rolls-Royce, via Inmarsat, but did not have time to get the message off before the plane crashed into the sea.

According to Stephen Buzdygan, a former British Airways pilot who flew Boeing 777s, the plane may have rolled onto its back because the engines would have shut down asymmetrically.

"Without fuel, assuming the crew were unconscious and no one was flying the plane, it would glide," he explained. "Engines have separate fuel supply, so the chances are it won't go in with the wings level. With no autopilot correction, it would slowly turn on its back and go down at an angle and the wings would be ripped off."

Though Inmarsat's neat piece of mathematics had narrowed

down the search area considerably, no one really had a clear idea where the plane might be. Mark Binskin, the vice-chief of Australia's Defence Force, said: "We're not trying to find a needle in a haystack; we're still trying to define where the haystack is."

Underwater geologist Dr Robin Beaman, from James Cook University in Queensland, Australia, said: "It's very unfortunate if that debris has landed on the active crest area, it will make life more challenging. It's rugged, it's covered in faults, gullies and ridges."

David Ferreira, an oceanographer at the University of Reading, said little was known about the detailed topography of the seabed where the plane was believed to have crashed.

"We know much more about the surface of the moon than we do about the ocean floor in that part of the Indian Ocean," he declared.

Furthermore, the search was being hampered by poor weather that was closing in.

Kerry Sieh, director of the Earth Observatory of Singapore, said: "I worry that people carrying out the rescue mission are going to get into trouble. This is a really rough piece of ocean, which is going to be a terrific issue."

After searchers had drawn a blank with the debris so far spotted in the sea, the search area was moved some 600 miles (966km) to the north, which was now correspondent to their best estimate on where Flight MH370 was likely to have come down. It seems from further analysis of the Inmarsat data that the plane was travelling faster than was first thought and had run out of fuel sooner. Then more debris was spotted there – by a New Zealand air force pilot.

By then Wang Zhen, whose parents were aboard the missing plane, said he was becoming exasperated.

"There is nothing I can do but to wait, and wait," he said in Beijing. "I'm also furious, but what is the use of getting furious?"

Sarah Bajc, still waiting for word of her fiancé, said: "I've stopped listening to the news – it's too heartbreaking. There are so many false leads and then they change their minds all the time. They are covering something up and I'm sure we will find out in the future. There is the trauma of maybe he's dead, maybe he's not. Maybe he's still alive and we need to find him, maybe he died within the first hour of the flight and we don't know. There's absolutely no way to reconcile that in my heart."

The new search area was in calmer waters and closer to land, but it was still the size of Poland.

"It would be an incredibly challenging place in which to work," said Dr Gallo, from the Woods Hole Oceanographic Institution in Massachusetts. Called Broken Ridge, "it is a plateau that gets as shallow as 600 metres [1,968ft] but as deep as 5,600 metres [18,372ft] and there is one scarp that runs along the south side that is immense. It will be a real challenge to try to get in there with a vehicle and pick up bits of aircraft."

"We will continue hoping until there is absolute evidence that they are all gone," said Chng Khai Cheik, a Malaysian whose 33-year-old sister, Mei Ling, was on Flight MH370. Eliz Wong Yun Yi, whose father, Wong Sai Sang, was also on the flight, said: "After so many days, still no plane. We will not believe what they say until the plane wreckage is found."

Wing Commander Rob Shearer, New Zealand's most senior Orion pilot who spotted the pieces of debris, said: "Because there were so many of them, it all pointed to a bit of a debris field, but nothing conclusive linking them to what we are looking for."

A large blue panel, he said, "looks promising". But images would need to be analyzed to confirm if it came from the lost

Boeing 777. The Orion dropped a tracker beacon and a flare over it so they could take higher-resolution photographs. Meanwhile, ships closed in on the area. Because of the raging currents in that region, the newly sighted debris could even have been the same pieces that had been spotted before.

Boeing had supplied the crew with a list of items from the downed Malaysian aircraft most likely to be floating. These include wing sections containing empty fuel tanks, lighter parts built of composite materials, seat cushions and wooden cargo pallets. However, cargo pallets often fall off container ships too.

A Chinese military Ilyushin IL-76 also spotted debris in the area, but Australian officials warned that a lot of flotsam and jetsam had been hauled from the southern oceans. None of it came from Flight MH370. Yet again, the sea debris proved to be garbage.

A group of Chinese relatives of the missing passengers flew into Kuala Lumpur to hold a protest on 30 March. They held up banners that said: "We want evidence, truth, dignity" in Chinese and "Hand us the murderer. Tell us the truth. Give us our relatives back" in English.

The search was now a race against time. Every commercial black box is fitted with a low-frequency underwater locator beacon that is activated as soon as it comes in contact with water and emits a continuous pinging noise from a depth of up to 2.5 miles (4km). Usually it has a battery life of about 30 days, though factors such as depth and temperature of the water and crash-impact damage can reduce the battery life. By 1 April 2014 the deadline was drawing dangerously near.

Some black boxes have not been recovered from aircraft wreckage, although that does not mean they never will be. For example, on New Year's Day 1985, an Eastern Airlines Boeing 727 on Flight 980 from Asunción, Paraguay, to La Paz, Bolivia, struck Bolivia's second-highest mountain, Mount Illimani, at an altitude of 19,600ft (5,974m). All 19 passengers and 10 crew were killed. Nearly 20 years later, in 2006, a climber, Roberto Gómez, discovered part of the aircraft's fuselage, along with photographs, children's clothing and what seemed to be crocodile hides from the cargo hold at the crash site. He was able to do so only because the Andean mountain's glacier was melting. It is thought that the bodies and the black box will, one day, emerge from the ice.

British nuclear submarine HMS *Tireless* was sent to join the search, along with a private plane provided by *Hobbit* director Peter Jackson. Hollywood director James Cameron, who made *Titanic* and *The Abyss*, and a five-mile (8km) dive in the Mariana Trench in 2012, also offered his help. Australian Defence Vessel *Ocean Shield* was fitted with a US Navy TPL-25 towed pinger locator, plus a Bluefin-21 Autonomous Underwater Vehicle was also on station. Its job was to pinpoint signals from the transponder, or pinger, attached to the missing aircraft's black box recorder in what was already being billed as the most difficult search ever. This was compounded by the fact that no wreckage had been found to give the searchers a clue where to look. Also, while the drones that pick up the sonar signal have a range of 20,000ft (6,096m), the sea there was 19,000ft (5,791m) deep, so the device would have to be almost right above the black box to detect it. And, as the batteries ran down, the signal from the pinger would weaken.

Then suddenly, with two days of battery time left, the Chinese announced that they had picked up the sonar pulse from the black box. The search ship *Haixun 01* towing a pinger locator first picked up a signal on Friday, 4 April in remote waters off western Australia. It was transmitting on a frequency of 37.5 kHz, matching that emitted by the flight recorder on the missing Malaysia Airlines' plane. After monitoring the signal for 15 minutes intermittently, members of the crew alerted authorities in Perth. The ship picked up the same signal again the following day, this time for 90 seconds some 1.2 miles (1.9km) from the location of the first pulse. It was around 55 miles (88.5km) from where the latest debris had been seen. The sea at that point was some 15,000ft (4,572m) – almost 3 miles (21km) – deep and the sea floor is criss-crossed with submarine mountain ranges, with peaks rising 8,000ft (2,438m) from the seabed.

Two other Chinese naval ships with detection equipment, *Jinggangshan* and *Kunlunshan*, were sent so they could triangulate and fix the position of the black box precisely but former US National Transportation Safety Board member John Goglia warned the hunt was far from over. "There is an awful lot of noise in the ocean," he said. "One ship, one ping doesn't make a success story."

By that time the search operation involved 10 military jets, four civilian planes, 11 ships and a British nuclear submarine, all searching 84,000 square miles (217,559 sq km) of the Indian Ocean, about 1,000 miles (1,609km) northwest of Australia.

By then, however, it was hard to excite any of the waiting relatives. Jack Song, whose sister was on the plane, told CNN: "I don't believe it. There's no piece of debris, so how can you find the black box? So you can just wait for more news tomorrow. Maybe it will be another mistake."

Jiang Hui, another passenger's relative, said in a text message: "There is no confirmation, and we are all waiting patiently."

Sixty-three-year-old Chen Zesheng, whose cousin was on the plane, said his family was treating the latest developments with caution. "We are sort of getting used to this kind of new finding now," he admitted.

Selamat Omar, whose aviation engineer son was a passenger, said he did not believe the report. "I will wait for more concrete information," he insisted.

But air safety investigator Phil Giles said: "That's not going to be a whale or a porpoise, or a squid or anything like that – it's got to be a mechanical device. If that is kosher, then it's probably coming from a pinger on a black box. I would think that it's very unlikely that somebody has dumped another black box down there less than a month ago in the Indian Ocean. The chances are pretty good that it's from MH370."

There are many clicks, buzzes and other sounds in the ocean from animals, but the frequency of 37.5 kHz was chosen specifically so that it would not sound like anything else in the sea.

Flightglobal's David Learmount was sceptical as there was no wreckage nearby. However, if the plane had "belly-flopped", the impact would have been less severe, meaning larger, heavier pieces would have survived.

"We don't know how this one hit the water," he said. "If it was an intentional effort to kill themselves and everybody else – and we have no proof but that's the Malaysian government's best guess – I doubt they would have attempted to belly-flop it. They might have put the aircraft into a very much higher-speed impact with the water, so the pieces would be smaller and much harder to see."

But Woods Hole's David Gallo was optimistic. "We have found the haystack," he declared. "Now all we have to do is find the needle."

Then on 6 April, the Australian ship *Ocean Shield* also picked up a signal – but in a different area. Search co-ordinator Australian Air Chief Marshal Angus Houston described the pings as "an important and encouraging lead". But he too urged caution.

"What we've got here are fleeting, acoustic events," he said. "That's all we've got. It's not a continuous transmission. If you get close to the device, we should be receiving it for a longer period of time than just a fleeting encounter. The job now is to determine the significance of that event. It does not confirm or deny the presence of the aircraft locator on the bottom of the ocean. We are dealing with very deep water; we are dealing with an environment where sometimes you can get false indications. There are lots of noises in the ocean and sometimes the acoustic equipment can rebound, echo if you like."

Meanwhile, thousands of people, including relatives of those on board the flight, attended a prayer service for the missing in Kuala Lumpur. Malaysian MP Liow Tiong Lai, who organized the event, said: "This is not a prayer for the dead because we have not found bodies. This is a prayer for blessings and that the plane will be found."

However, the sounds picked up by *Ocean Shield* were more promising than at first thought. The ship had picked up two separate signals late Saturday night and early Sunday morning within a remote patch of the Indian Ocean, far off the west Australian coast that search crews had been criss-crossing for weeks. The first signal lasted two hours and 20 minutes before it was lost; the ship then turned around and picked up a signal again – this time recording two distinct "pinger returns" that lasted 13 minutes, Houston said. Each leg took eight hours.

"Significantly, this would be consistent with transmissions from both the flight data recorder and the cockpit voice recorder," Houston continued. "Clearly this is the most promising lead in the search so far. We've got a visual indication on a screen and an audible signal, and the audible signal sounds to me just like an emergency locator beacon."

Again, he urged caution. "I would want more confirmation before we say this is it," he insisted. "Without wreckage, we can't say it's definitely here. We've got to go down and have a look. It's like playing hot and cold when you're searching for something and someone's telling you you're getting warmer and warmer and warmer. When you're right on top of it, you get a good return."

The sea depth there was 14,750ft (4,496m), near the limit of an underwater search vehicle's capability.

Geoff Dell, discipline leader of accident investigation at Central Queensland University in Australia, says it would be "coincidental in the extreme" for the sounds to have come from anything other than an aircraft's black box.

"If they have got a legitimate signal, and it's not from one of the other vessels or something, you would have to say they are within a bull's roar," he said. "There's still a chance that it's a spurious signal that's coming from somewhere else and they are chasing a ghost, but it certainly is encouraging that they've found something to suggest they are in the right spot."

Experts were already dismissing the signal picked up by the Chinese who, they said, merely dangled a hydrophone over the side of a small boat. To detect a black box that way was technically possible but extremely unlikely. The equipment aboard the British and Australian ships was dragged slowly behind each vessel over long distances and was considered far more sophisticated.

Then the sea went quiet as search ships tried to relocate the elusive ping of the black boxes. The following day, they heard nothing. Already the hunt for Flight MH370 had cost hundreds of millions of dollars and it has now become the most expensive search for a downed plane in history.

Meanwhile, in Beijing, relatives of the missing held a tearful vigil marking one month since the aircraft was lost. Family members placed candles in the shape of a heart surrounding a plane on the carpeted floor of the Lido hotel.

"We've been waiting and holding on here for already 31 days," said Steve Wang, one of the relatives. "Don't cry anymore. Don't hurt anymore. Don't despair. Don't feel lost."

But it did no good. Sitting in a circle around the candles, some were audibly wailing while others remained silent, pressing their palms together in gestures of prayer.

Maira Nari, daughter of chief steward Andrew Nari, refused to give up. She tweeted: "Today's the day. Exactly one month the Flight MH370 went missing. We are still hoping. Come home, dad. We're here waiting for you."

Izzat Nazli, the nephew of leading steward Wan Swaid Wan Ismail, said he found it hard to believe that the plane's flight may have ended in the southern Indian Ocean, and thought it was hijacked to another place. "MH370 has left us for a month, I am still hoping for their safe return. Never lose hope. Uncle Swaid, we love you," he tweeted.

Dr Mohd Ghouse Noor, a schoolmate of Captain Shah, said: "His sisters still believe that miracles do happen. We are not giving up hope until we are definite that the wreckage has been found, or bodies recovered." He served as moderator for the Facebook group, Friends of Captain Zaharie MH370 (FOCZ).

Mohamad Sahril Shaari, a cousin of passenger Muhammad Razahan Zamani, prays that solid evidence will emerge soon. "If the plane is no more, we want proof," he said. "If it really ended in the Indian Ocean, there must be debris, at least one piece. Only then will we believe one hundred percent."

Farah Faisal, friend and classmate of engineer Suhaili Mustafa, a passenger, said she was deeply missed by her friends and family. "She was really sweet and kind, and we all miss her," said Farah.

She also paid tribute to Suhaili on her blog, saying: "Su, like I told you on your birthday: I love you always. I am a better person for having known you. You are the kindest person I know, you never had a bad thing to say about anyone".

Seventy-six-year-old Ibrahim Abdul Razak held a special prayer meeting in the hope that his 33-year-old son Mohamad Sofuan Ibrahim and the other 238 people on board the missing aircraft would be found, safe and well. "I just hope that if he is still alive, he will be able to come back home soon," he said. "We are missing him badly... all of us do."

Sofuan had boarded the flight on 8 March to report for duty at the Malaysian International Trade and Industry office in Beijing. Around 100 family members and neighbours attended the prayer meeting and sought divine assistance in the missing aircraft's search and rescue mission.

Still nursing doubts that her fiancé Philip Wood was dead, Sarah Bajc flew from Beijing to Kuala Lumpur, where she became convinced that the Malaysian military had known when the missing 777 was flying across their airspace. She told CNN: "The jet had actually been accompanied by fighter planes, there are some witnesses to that. I am sure that the military in Malaysia knew that plane was there and has tracked that plane in some way. Now whether they were in control of it or not, I don't know. Many people are saying that the United States is involved but the general thinking across the families here and even non-families believe this was a military operation of some sort."

She believed that the plane was intact on the ground somewhere and her boyfriend Philip Wood was still alive. There had been, as yet, no evidence that MH370 had crashed. The focus of this conspiracy theory turned again to the US military base on Diego Garcia when freelance journalist Jim Stone claimed to have received a blank photograph from Wood's iPhone 5, whose metadata showed from GPS co-ordinates that it was taken not far from the airbase there. Stone said that a voice-activated text that came with it read: "I have been held hostage by unknown military personal after my flight was hijacked (blindfolded). I work for IBM and I have managed to hide my cell phone in my ass during the hijack. I have been separated from the rest of the passengers and I am in a cell. My name is Philip Wood. I think I have been drugged as well and cannot think clearly."

Diego Garcia was within range of Flight MH370: it has a runway long enough for a Boeing 777 to land and was one of the landing strips on Captain Shah's flight simulator. It was also reported that all leave there was cancelled.

Meanwhile, MTV Lebanon reported: "Russian Intelligence confirmed to Russian daily *Moskovsky Komsomolets* that unidentified perpetrators had hijacked the plane, which now lays in Afghanistan near Kandahar and the Pakistani borders. The passengers are said to be living in shacks and huts and starving, while around 20 Chinese experts have been locked in a warehouse in Pakistan for possible negotiations with the United States or China. Said sources further added that 'Hitch' is the name of the hijacker who gave instructions to the pilots so as to steer it off course."

Over in Britain, *The Sun* also carried the story. It said that an anonymous source in Russia's FSB secret service had told a Russian newspaper: "All the passengers are alive, they have been divided into seven groups and are living in mud huts with almost no food."

The report said around 20 Asian "specialists" among the 239 passengers and crew had been captured and smuggled to a "bunker" in Pakistan.

After three days of silence, on Tuesday, 8 April *Ocean Shield* picked up more sonar signals, one lasting five minutes 32 seconds, another around seven minutes. The strength of the signal had decreased since Saturday, nevertheless it was said to be "stable, distinct and clear". The Royal Australian Air Force then moved in to drop 84 sonar buoys, each of which would lower a hydrophone on a cable to a depth of up to 1,000ft (304m) below the surface, sending their results back via floating transmitters. The floating matt of ears should help get a better fix on the source of the ping.

"What we're picking up is a great lead," Air Chief Marshal Houston said. "I'm now optimistic that we will find the aircraft or what is left of the aircraft in the not-too-distant future. But we haven't found it yet."

An oil slick was found 3.5 miles (6km) downwind of where the pings were detected. HMS *Echo* moved in on the area where *Haixun 01* made the first sonar contact to provide acoustic background checks, while other ships and planes continued the search for floating wreckage, based on the latest estimates of current and wind-driven drift.

Still the family members clung on, supporting one another through the ordeal. "If we go back to our homes now it will be extremely painful," said Steve Wang. "We have to face a bigger pain of facing uncertainty, the unknown future. This is the most difficult to cope with."

One family lit candles on a heart-shaped cake to mark what would have been the twenty-first birthday of passenger Feng Dong, who had been working in construction in Singapore for the past year and was flying home to China via Kuala Lumpur. Feng's mother wept as she blew out the candles.

On 10 April 2014 an Australian P3 Orion picked up signals during Thursday's search from the sonar buoys. They picked up two more pings, some 6 miles (10km) apart. These were around 16 miles (26km) from where the first pings were picked up by *Ocean Shield*.

Then the sea went silent again. It was now thought that the batteries in the black boxes were dead so the Australians decided to deploy an autonomous drone known as Bluefin-21. The 16-ft (5m) long mini submarine would make a sonar map of the sea floor in the search for the wreckage of Flight MH370. Each Bluefin-21 mission was to have lasted 24 hours, with the unmanned sub spending 16 hours on the sea floor, where it travelled at just 4.5 knots (5 mph or 8 km/h). Four hours were taken in diving and resurfacing, and it would take another four hours to download the data.

However, when it was first deployed on 14 April, its seafloor search was cut short when it exceeded its operating limit of 15,000ft (4,572m). A built-in automatic safety feature returned it to the surface after just six hours. The search would continue, but there were now grave doubts that the black boxes would ever be found.

Even if they were found, there was the question of who should have custody to be decided. Normally it is up to the country of origin of the downed plane to handle the investigation, but Malaysia had asked Australia to lead the search in the southern ocean and, while pings were still sounding, the Malaysian Attorney-General Tan Sri Abdul Patail flew to the UK to discuss the matter of custody with the International Civil Aviation Organization (ICAO). He also dismissed the idea that the co-pilot had made a telephone call as the plane flew low over Penang, which was now being officially discounted.

And would the black boxes clear up the mystery of Flight MH370 anyway? Probably not as there would be no recording of the crucial events in the cockpit while the plane was diverted over the South China Sea, some seven hours before it crashed into the ocean.

Key to the mystery of Flight MH370 is that none of the theories fits all of the facts – unless you look at its disappearance from another angle. What do we actually know about Flight MH370? On 8 March 2014 it took off from Kuala Lumpur International Airport at 00.41, local time. Air traffic control received a last message from the plane at 01.19 and the transponder went off at 01.21. Around that time, New Zealand oil worker Mike McKay saw a burning plane and, later, debris was spotted in the South China Sea. The plane caught on radar over the Straits of Malacca could have been any plane; it could not be identified as Flight MH370 as it did not have its transponder on.

Earlier, there had been a joint Thai-US military exercise in South China Sea. China had been invited to participate for the first time, along with personnel from Singapore, Japan, South Korea, Indonesia and Malaysia. The drill was to involve mock warfare on land, in water and in the air, and would include live-fire exercises.

Say a participant accidentally shot down Flight MH370. Such things do happen. The cruiser USS *Vincennes* shot down Iran Air Flight 655 over the Persian Gulf in 1988. No one wants another Lockerbie, so those involved would have every reason to keep quiet about it. Indeed, through anonymous and contradictory sources, they might release misinformation, leading people to search in entirely the wrong place – a place where the environment is so hostile that it is unlikely that anything would ever be found. After all, no wreckage has been found in the south Indian Ocean, which in itself is suspicious. And if a black box was found, who was to say that it was from Flight MH370? Another black box could have been dropped in the sea 1,000 miles from Perth while the search was going on in the South China Sea. In these circumstances, with the amount of baseless speculation abroad, it is best to be sceptical.

This makes a great conspiracy theory. After all if the US had shot the plane down, they would hardly own up to it. But there is one big problem here. To maintain the cover-up America, China and Vietnam would all have to sing from the same hymn sheet. What are the chances of that happening?

Now I am not saying that's what happened but if a black box is found, who is to say that it is from Flight MH370? Another black box could have been dropped in the sea 1,000 miles from Perth while the search was going on in the South China Sea. In these circumstances, with the amount of disinformation abroad, it is best to be sceptical.

Meanwhile Michael Hoebel, a 60-year-old pilot in New York, claimed to have found a satellite image on the Internet showing the plane in one piece in the Gulf of Thailand, just about where it was when it made its last contact with air traffic control on 8 March. Then Australian exploration company GeoResonance said they had found what they believed to be the wreckage of a commercial airliner in the north of the Bay of Bengal, 3,000 miles (5,000km) from the current search area. It appeared there between 5 and 10 March when satellite scans were made. Using recently demilitarized Soviet technology from Sevastopol National University of Nuclear Energy in the Crimea, they said they found aluminium, titanium, copper, steel alloys and other materials found in a Boeing 777. The site was at the corner of another of Sanderson's Vile Vortices. The mystery continues.

CHAPTER TWENTY-TWO

LIGHTNING STRIKES TWICE

Four months after Flight MH370 went missing, the conspiracy theories went into overdrive when a second Malaysian plane disappeared from the radar screens. But when Flight MH17 from Amsterdam to Kuala Lumpur vanished from the skies over Ukraine on 17 July, it was only too clear what had happened to it. It had been shot down. All 298 people on board were killed.

The Russians immediately blamed the Ukrainian government. The incident had taken place in their airspace and it had been shot down, they maintained, by an air-to-air missile from a Ukrainian Air Force fighter.

The rest of the world blamed pro-Russian insurgents using a Buk surface-to-air missile fired from territory they controlled. They were known to have a Buk system, either captured from the Ukrainian government or supplied by the Russians. The BBC even reported that the Russians themselves were operating a Buk missile launcher in the area at the time.

One eyewitness saw the missile-launcher roll off a low-loader at Snezhnoye, around ten miles from the crash site, at around 13.30 local time (10.30 GMT), just three hours before the plane was downed.

"We just saw it being offloaded and when the Buk started its engine the exhaust smoke filled the whole town square," he said.

The eyewitness told the BBC that he thought the crew were Russian soldiers.

"[They were] Well-disciplined, unlike the rebels, and not wearing the standard Ukrainian camouflage uniform sported by government and rebel troops alike," he reported. "They had pure Russian accents. They say the letter 'g' differently to us."

Most people speak Russian in eastern Ukraine, but the Buk crew did not speak with the local intonation. A second eyewitness added that an officer in a military jeep escorting the Buk launcher spoke with a distinct Muscovite accent. The crew were thought to be part of the Kremlin's "Ghost Army" – thousands of Russian soldiers who have been reportedly infiltrated into Ukraine to tip the military balance heavily in the rebels' favour. Despite the Kremlin's denials, video had surfaced showing a mechanized battalion column of Russian tanks and military hardware.

Flight MH17 had taken off from Amsterdam's Schipol Airport at 12.31 local time (10.31 GMT) and was due to land at Kuala Lumpur International Airport at 6.10 (22.10 GMT). The flight had two captains, fifty-year-old Wan Amran Wan Hussin and Eugene Choo Jin Leong, forty-five, and two co-pilots, Ahmad Hakimi Hanapi, twenty-nine, and Muhd Firdaus Abdul Rahim, twenty-seven. The crew of fifteen were all Malaysian. Among them was forty-one-year-old flight steward Sanjid Singh Sandhu, whose wife Tan Bee Gok was a stewardess who had been due to fly on MH370, but swapped shifts at the last moment. Sanjid had also swapped shifts, tragically, in an effort to get home earlier to her.

About two thirds of the passengers – 193 – were Dutch. There were forty-three Malaysians, twelve Indonesians, twenty-seven Australians and ten British people. There were also four Germans, four Belgians, three Filipinos, one Canadian and one New Zealander on board.

One Australian family suffered a double blow. Kaylene Mann's stepdaughter Maree Rizk and her husband Albert were returning home to Melbourne from a four-week European holiday on MH17, while Kaylene's brother Rod Burrows and sister-in-law Mary Burrows were on Flight 370 when it vanished in March. However, Dutch cycling star Maarten De Jonge, who rode with Malaysia's Terengganu Cycling Team, was doubly lucky. He had switched from MH17 to take a later flight and save money, and he had also been booked on MH370, but had changed flights to avoid a lengthy stopover.

At least twenty family groups were on board the aircraft, and eighty of the passengers were under the age of eighteen. Six passengers were delegates on their way to the Twentieth International AIDS Conference in Melbourne. This included Joep Lange, a former president of the International AIDS Society, which organized the conference. Also on board were Dutch Senator Willem Witteveen, Australian author Liam Davison, and Malaysian actress Shuba Jay.

The fates of the two Malaysian flights were inexorably linked. While the world was engrossed in the mystery of Flight MH370, Russian forces stealthily annexed the land of Crimea. It had been part of Ukraine since 1954, and remained Ukrainian territory when the republic became independent in 1991, though Russia paid to use naval bases there as a home port for its Black Sea Fleet.

When pro-EU protestors in the Ukrainian capital of Kiev ousted the pro-Russia president, Russian flags appeared in Crimea, where the majority of people were ethnically Russian. On 27 February Russian special forces moved in with their insignia hidden. These were known as "little green men". A new pro-Russian prime minister was installed. A controversial referendum was held on 16 March. This agreed that Crimea should become part of Russia and Russian President Vladimir Putin formally annexed it on the eighteenth.

Meanwhile pro-Russia separatists in eastern Ukraine began to make similar demands and a low key civil war broke out, pitting Ukrainian government forces against Russian-backed rebels. In the Donetsk region where MH17 was shot down, pro-Russian activists seized control of the regional government building, declaring the "Donetsk People's Republic" on 7 April, and asking for Russian intervention.

In the wake of the 2014 Crimean crisis, a few airlines had already started avoiding Eastern Ukrainian airspace. In early March, Korean Air, Asiana Airlines and British Airways stopped overflying the area. In April, the International Civil Aviation Organization warned governments that there was a risk to commercial passenger flights over Ukraine. The American Federal Aviation Administration issued restrictions on flights over Crimea, to the south of MH17's route, and advised airlines flying over some other parts of Ukraine to "exercise extreme caution". However, this warning did not extend to the region where MH17 was downed and some airlines continued overflying eastern Ukraine. About nine hundred flights flew over the Donetsk region in the seven days before MH17 was lost, some fifty-five on that very day.

On 14 June, a Ukrainian Air Force Ilyushin Il-76 aircraft was shot down on its approach to Luhansk International Airport, killing all forty-nine people on board. Together Donetsk and Lunhansk were known as Donbass, and this was where the anti-government fighting raged. Two weeks later the insurgents got hold of the Buk missile launcher.

Then on 14 July, a Ukrainian Air Force An-26 transport plane flying at 21,000 feet (6,400 metres) was shot down. The insurgents reportedly claimed via social media that a Buk missile launcher had been used to bring down the aircraft. American officials later said evidence suggested that the aeroplane had been shot down using a Buk on Russian territory.

Two days later, a Sukhoi S-25 close air support aircraft was shot down. The Ukrainian government said that it was brought down by a Russian fighter. Russia dismissed this as "absurd". A second Su-25 was hit by a portable surface-to-air missile, but that pilot was uninjured and managed to land his plane safely. Meanwhile rebels in eastern Ukraine claimed they had shot down the two jets. The Ukrainian government in Kiev then warned European countries, including the Netherlands, of the dangers of flying over eastern Ukraine.

Already the air lanes below 26,000 feet (7,900 metres) over the Donetsk Oblast had been closed by the Ukrainian government and on 14 July, those below 32,000 feet (9,800 metres) were closed. On 17 July, it was thought that another An-26 Transport was scheduled to bring in Ukrainian paratroopers, and that according to Russian expert Vadim Lukashevich, the separatists "might have been waiting just for them". MH17 was now a disaster waiting to happen.

With air lanes below 32,000 feet closed, the plane entered Ukrainian airspace at flight level 330, which is 33,000 feet or 10,060 metres. It planned to climb to flight level 350 at around

Dnipropetrovsk, but another aircraft had climbed to occupy that air lane. At 16.00 local time (13.00 GMT), MH17 asked Dnipropetrovsk Air Control whether it could divert twenty miles to the north, because of the weather conditions. This was approved, but it was not allowed to climb to 34,000 feet, as that air lane was also occupied.

At 16.19 local time (13.19 GMT) Dnipropetrovsk Air Control noticed that the flight was 3.6 nautical miles (6.7 kilometres) north of the centre line of the approved path, and instructed MH17 to return to the track. At the same time, Dnipropetrovsk Air Control contacted Russian Air Control in Rostov-on-Don Air Control by telephone, requesting clearance to transfer the flight to Russian air control. After obtaining the permission, Dnipropetrovsk Air Control tried to contact MH17 at 16.20 (13.30 GMT) for the handover. After MH17 did not respond to several calls, Dnipropetrovsk Air Control contacted Rostov-on-Don Air Control again to check if they could see MH17 on their radar. Rostov-on-Don Air Control confirmed that the plane had disappeared, though two other commercial airlines – Singapore Airlines SQ351, a Boeing 777 en route from Copenhagen to Singapore, and Air India Flight 113, a Boeing 787 en route from Delhi to Birmingham – were clearly visible. The Air India plane was just sixteen miles away from where MH17 should have been.

According to the Dutch air investigation team, MH17 broke up in mid-air after being hit by "numerous objects" that "pierced the plane at high velocity" from outside the cabin and above the level of the cockpit floor. There was "no evidence of technical or human error", it added. Fragments of a suspected Russian missile were found at the crash site. The missile had detonated before it hit the plane and the resulting shrapnel had ripped the airframe to pieces. The Dutch Safety Board concluded that the warhead of a surface-to-air missile fired from a Buk launcher exploded above and to the left of the cockpit, less than one metre away. Preformed pieces of metal shrapnel pierced the skin of the aircraft, killing the crew on the flight deck. The cockpit and the business-class section broke off. It was estimated that the remaining passengers would have lost consciousness within nine seconds due to the sudden decompression of the aircraft and the lack of oxygen at 33,000 feet. During that time they would not have known what was happening. However, the crash report stated: "It cannot be ruled out that some occupants remained conscious for some time during the one to one-and-a-half minutes for which the crash lasted."

When the shattered sections of the aeroplane hit the ground, the middle part of the passenger cabin was consumed in an intense fire, ensuring that no one survived. Immediately afterwards, a post appeared on the VKontakte social media profile attributed to Russian Colonel Igor Girkin, leader of the Donbass separatists, claiming responsibility for shooting down an An-26. But after it became clear that it was a civilian aircraft that had been shot down, the separatists denied any involvement, and the post was taken down.

The wreckage of MH17 was spread over 13 square miles (34 square kilometres), though some parts of the plane were found five miles (eight kilometres) from the main debris site. Pieces of broken fuselage and engine parts were mixed with bodies, luggage and passports. Some of the wreckage fell close to houses. Dozens of bodies fell into crop fields, and some descended into houses. They had landed in a combat zone and it was weeks before air-crash investigators were allowed in to examine them.

This allowed the conspiracy theorists free rein. They drew attention to the seeming coincidence that the two planes were both Boeing 777-200ERs – the "Extended Range" version. Their registration numbers were similar – M9-MRO on Flight MH370 and M9-MRD on Flight MH17. M9-MRO was new and had never been repainted. The flag on its side lay parallel to the line of the windows. This was not the case on M9-MRD. What's more M9-MRO had been modified. The rearrangement of the interior meant that the window next to the second door on the right-hand side had been blocked. This had not been done on M9-MRD, but the first pictures of the wreckage of the plane showed the window blocked. Later pictures that appeared on Reuters, the conspiracy theorists claimed, had been Photoshopped to show the extra window.

It was also claimed that the time signatures on videos concerning the shootdown show they were created before MH17 went down. Various websites presented evidence suggesting that Flight MH17 had in fact been cancelled, while the passports collected from the crash site appeared to be pristine. Some had been clipped or hole-punched, indicating they had been cancelled and could not have been used on the flight. It was also said that the US had satellite imagery showing Ukrainian troops shooting down the plane.

Award-winning former Associated Press reporter Robert Parry was quoted as saying: "What I've been told by one source, who has provided accurate information on similar matters in the past, is that U.S. intelligence agencies do have detailed satellite images of the likely missile battery that launched the fateful missile, but the battery appears to have been under the control of Ukrainian government troops dressed in what look like Ukrainian uniforms."

The pro-rebel website *Russkaya Vesna* quoted Igor Girkin as saying he was told by people at the crash site that "a significant number of the bodies weren't fresh", adding that he was told they were drained of blood and reeked of decomposition. Others said that the remains gave off a green glow in the twilight – indicating the presence of formaldehyde, a preservative used in embalming. The remains bled a colourless liquid which, again, smelt of formaldehyde.

Jason Kissner, professor of criminology at California State University, pointed out that there were too many similarities between Flight MH370 and Flight MH17 to be coincidence. Contact had been lost with both of them before they went missing. Both had made course alterations beforehand – MH17 had strayed into a warzone.

He then came up with what he called "curious tidbits", viz: "The flight 17 crash shares an anniversary with the demise of TWA 800, which AT's own Jack Cashill has compellingly argued was, in fact, brought down by a missile on July 17, 1996 and subsequently covered up by the US government. And, the maiden flight of flight 17 occurred in 1997 on the date of, you guessed it, July 17. Moreover Russia's last ruling monarch of the Romanov family Tsar Nicholas II, together with his wife Tsarina Alexandra and their five children Olga, Tatiana, Maria, Anastasia, and Alexei were executed on 17 July 1918. Subliminal message to Putin? No doubt it's another 'coincidence'."

Cashill writes for *AmericanThinker.com*, as well as *Fortune*, *The Wall Street Journal*, *The Washington Post*, *The Weekly Standard* and *WorldNetDaily*.

Others point out that, when MH370 first went missing, there was speculation that it had been hijacked and landed somewhere safe ready to be used on some future mission.

"The US military base Diego Garcia is conveniently located within flying distance of the spot where MH370 disappeared from the radar," said Alexander Light on *humansarefree.com*.

This was where Philip Wood was thought to have sent a photograph from his iPhone from.

"If the US secret services got possession of the MH-370 jet, then it was child's play for them to set it up for a false flag operation suiting their needs," Light continued. "After the story of a passenger jet having been shot down by pro-Russian separatists broke loose, Russia lost a lot of credibility and support due to the US propaganda machine."

But they had been caught out by the extra window. Why had efforts been made to falsify the picture if they had nothing to hide?

The theory runs that MH370 had been hijacked and taken to the top-secret US base on Diego Garcia to be used for a "false flag" operation. The plane, loaded with the corpses of people who had died some time before, was then flown over Ukraine when MH17 was in the vicinity. It was shot down by Ukrainian forces so that the incident could be blamed on the pro-Russian insurgents. It gets better.

According to Light: "Forbidden in the government-controlled media, is mention that a SECOND aircraft was nearly on top of Malaysian Flight 17 when it was supposedly shot down by a Ukrainian missile in separatist hands. Who was in it? Why were they there? Why won't anyone talk about it, or question the pilots? A clue may be found in the real-life Operation Northwoods – a declassified top-secret plan devised by the US military, to instigate and 'justify' a war with Cuba. Much of Northwoods involved staged 'shootdowns' of military and civilian aircraft, and faking crashes."

Rejected by President John F. Kennedy in 1962, after the Communist takeover of Cuba, the secret files on Operation Northwoods were said to have included a number of false-flag operations. In one of these, *humansarefree.com* said: "An aircraft at [a US military base] would be painted and numbered as an exact duplicate for a civilian registered aircraft. At a designated time the duplicate would be substituted for the actual civil aircraft and would be loaded with selected passengers, all boarded under carefully prepared aliases.

"The actual registered aircraft would be converted to a drone. Take-off times of the drone aircraft and the actual aircraft will be scheduled to allow a rendezvous ... From the rendezvous point the passenger-carrying aircraft will descend to minimum altitude [in order to disappear from the radar] and go directly into an auxiliary [military base] where arrangements will have been made to evacuate the passengers and return the aircraft to its original status. The drone aircraft meanwhile will continue to fly the filed flight plan.

"When over [the target area] the drone will begin transmitting on the international distress frequency a 'MAY DAY' message stating he is under attack by [the chosen enemy]. The transmission will be interrupted by destruction of the aircraft which will be triggered by radio signal ... a pre-briefed pilot would fly tail-end Charley at considerable interval between aircraft. [After giving the distress call] the pilot would then fly at extremely low altitude and land at a secure base. The aircraft would be met by the proper people, quickly stored and given a new tail number. The pilot and aircraft would then have disappeared. At precisely the same time that the aircraft was presumably shot down, a submarine or small surface craft would disburse F-101 parts, parachute, etc. Search ships and aircraft could be dispatched and parts of aircraft found.

"Once you know the plan, perhaps what is unfolding now will make more sense..."

But then it made no more sense when Metrojet Flight 9268, a Russian passenger plane, crashed over Sinai in Egypt on 31 October 2015, killing all 224 people on board. The terrorist organization ISIS claimed responsibility. The Russians eventually conceded that the plane had been brought down by a bomb after the residue of explosives was found among the wreckage. They offered a $50 million reward for information on those who had brought it down.

In an attempt to put an end to empty speculation regarding the disappearance of Flight MH370, on 3 December 2015 the Australian Transport Safety Bureau issued an update on their previous reports. It confirmed that they were searching in the right area and were now honing in on a hotspot. There was a 90 per cent chance of the plane being found in this area, their scientists said.

The new report said that the plane had been lost due to a sudden catastrophic loss of power on board. While the other systems remained disabled, power was restored to the satellite data unit, which logged on again and completed its "handshake" with Inmarsat. Shortly afterwards, the in-flight entertainment system logged on, setting up a ground connection via the satellite communications system for passengers' emails and texts. The hourly "pings" from the SDU then continued throughout the flight.

However, in the early hours of 9 March the SDU lost power again. The Auxiliary Power Unit kicked in and the SDU logged on with Inmarsat again. However, this time the in-flight entertainment system did not log on.

The ATSB boffins deduced that the right engine flamed out first. The left-hand engine, having been serviced more recently, continued running for another fifteen minutes as the plane slowly spiralled down towards the surface of the ocean. When the left engine flamed out too, power was lost and the Auxiliary Power Unit autostarted again, giving just enough power for the SDU to make its partial handshake. It hit the water soon after.

The report then gives a number of possible reasons for the initial power failure. These included equipment malfunction, the power being turned off by the pilots using the overhead switches in the cockpit, or someone gaining access to the electronics-and-equipment – or E/E – bay, pulling the circuit breakers and then resetting them.

The Daily Beast asked an expert on the 777 to evaluate these possibilities. He said that the idea that a pilot went down into the E/E bay to pull one or more circuit breakers was extremely unlikely.

"Few airline pilots would even know how to get down to the lower deck while in flight," he said. "And even if they tried, few would be familiar with the locations of avionics components, or be able to find the relevant circuit breakers to pull. That kind of information is not even contained in the typical pilot training or operating manuals."

The pilots could have tripped the overhead switches in the cockpit, but they would have been following "non-normal" procedures in response to failure messages flashing on their instrument displays, rather than attempting to harm the plane.

The expert said that the pilots could very well have been implementing "a well-defined non-normal procedure" due to a "very complex failure". Cutting the power was exactly the sort of action the pilots should have taken in circumstances beyond anything anticipated in their training – something like a severe uncontained fire on board. At the same time, they would have been trying to get onto the ground as soon as possible.

Without electricity powering the main avionics systems, the pilots would have lost control of the plane. The result would have been the so-called "zombie scenario", where the plane flew on, on autopilot, until it ran out of fuel.

The problem with this theory is that it does not explain how the plane changed course a number of times during its continued flight. The report says simply: "The specific settings input into the autopilot in the case of MH370 are unknown. Furthermore, it is also unknown what changes (if any) were made to those settings throughout the accident flight."

In other words, "case not closed". It is still wide open until the wreckage of the downed plane is found. That is going to happen shortly, experts still keep assuring the newspapers. The press, at the same time, hint that the search will probably be called off in June 2016.

CHAPTER TWENTY-THREE

SECRET FILES

The mystery of Flight MH370 endures. However, there are those on the inside who know that we are not being told the truth. The former boss of Proteus Airlines, Marc Dugain, said that the missing plane had been blown out of the sky by the US Air Force.

His theory was that the plane had been taken over remotely by hackers and flown towards the US base on Diego Garcia as a 9/11-style flying bomb. After all, a large aircraft decked out in Malaysia Airlines colours had been seen flying that way.

In an interview with *Paris Match* that ran to six pages, Dugain also claimed to have seen pictures of an empty Boeing fire extinguisher washed up on a beach on Baarah island nearby – in fact, it is at the other end of the archipelago, nearly a thousand miles to the north. The extinguisher had floated ashore, indicating that it was probably empty. This would mean that a fire on board would have triggered the release of its contents.

According to the local mayor, aviation experts had confirmed that the object was an extinguisher, but it was seized by military officers before it could make headline news.

Dugain believed that Boeing planes were particularly vulnerable to hijacking, and could have been set on fire remotely, forcing the crew to turn off its electrical devices. This would explain why MH370 had vanished from air-traffic controllers' radars.

"In 2006, Boeing patented a remote control system using a computer placed inside or outside the aircraft," Dugain told the magazine.

Diego Garcia was an important terrorist target.

"It's an extremely powerful military base. It's surprising that the Americans have lost all trace of this aircraft. Without getting into conspiracy theories, it is a possibility that the Americans stopped this plane," he said.

Other sources claimed that Britain, who have title to the island, has forced the suppression of the flight records to hide their complicity in the US policy of "extraordinary rendition".

According to Dugain, the passengers and crew could have died from asphyxiation, but the fire did not damage the exterior of the plane, allowing it to continue on autopilot until it ran out of fuel and glided down into the sea.

Dugain's views were echoed by Emirates Airlines chief Sir Tim Clark, who told German magazine *Der Spiegel* that something was amiss. He thought that someone had taken control of the plane.

"MH370 should never have been allowed to enter a non-trackable situation," he said. "The transponders are under the control of the flight deck. These are tracking devices, aircraft identifiers that work in the secondary radar regime. If you turn off that transponder in a secondary radar regime, that particular airplane disappears from the radar screen. That should never be allowed to happen. Irrespective of when the pilot decides to disable the transponder, the aircraft should be able to be tracked … At Emirates, we track every single aircraft from the ground, every component and engine of the aircraft at any point on the planet. Very often, we are able to track systemic faults before the pilots do."

He was puzzled as to how the tracking system had been disabled.

"Disabling it is no simple thing and our pilots are not trained to do so," he said. "But on flight MH370, this thing was somehow disabled, to the degree that the ground tracking capability was eliminated. We must find systems to allow ACARS to continue uninterrupted, irrespective of who is controlling the aircraft. If you have that, with the satellite constellations that we have today even in remote ocean regions, we still have monitoring capability. So you don't have to introduce additional tracking systems."

He said he was still struggling to come up with a reason why a pilot should be able to put the transponder into standby or to switch it off.

"MH370 was, in my opinion, under control, probably until the very end," Sir Tim concluded.

He was sceptical of the official line. In his opinion, secrets were being kept from the public.

"All the 'facts' of this particular incident must be challenged and examined with full transparency," he told the magazine. "We are nowhere near that. There is plenty of information out there, which we need to be far more forthright, transparent and candid about. Every single second of that flight needs to be examined up until it, theoretically, ended up in the Indian Ocean – for which they still haven't found a trace, not even a seat cushion."

According to Clark, the lack of debris in the area where the plane was supposed to have gone down is, in itself, suspicious.

"Our experience tells us that in water incidents, where the aircraft has gone down, there is always something. We have not seen a single thing that suggests categorically that this aircraft is where they say it is, apart from this so-called electronic satellite 'handshake', which I question as well," he said. "There hasn't been one overwater incident in the history of civil aviation – apart from Amelia Earhart in 1939 – that has not been at least 5 or 10 per cent trackable. But MH370 has simply disappeared. For me, that raises a degree of suspicion. I'm totally dissatisfied with what has been coming out of all of this."

While, as an airline manager, Clark did not feel that he could do anything to improve government transparency in these matters, he said: "I will continue to ask questions and make a nuisance of myself, even as others would like to bury it. We have an obligation to the passengers and crew of MH370 and their families. We have an obligation to not sweep this under the carpet, but to sort it out and do better than we have done."

Aviation expert Jeff Wise, who lent his expertise to CNN's coverage of the disappearance of MH370, was also puzzled by the lack of wreckage at the supposed crash site. As part of the Independent Group of investigators who shared their analysis, he also noticed that, no matter how you looked at the data, you could not make it line up so that all the pieces fitted neatly into the jigsaw puzzle. As a result, he concluded that some of the bedrock "facts" were not facts at all.

He noted that it was incredibly difficult to get the Malaysians to release the raw Inmarsat data. Was there something wrong with it? Reviewing it, he saw for the first forty minutes of the flight that everything had been completely normal. Then suddenly the plane went electronically dark. It had been picked up by military radar, though this only became apparent when the radar records were reviewed later. However, Wise noticed that three minutes after the plane had flown out of range of the military radar, satellite communication resumed, giving it six more handshakes over the next six hours, until it eventually disappeared completely.

The final handshake had not been completed, it was thought, because the plane had run out of fuel, cutting the power. When the emergency power system had cut in, the satcom system had fired up just long enough to reconnect before the plane crashed into the sea.

Inmarsat had found two ways to analyse the signals that it had received from the handshakes. The first was called "burst timing offset" – or BTO. This measures the time between the signal leaving the satellite and the response from the system on the plane being received back. As a result, it was possible to work out how far the plane was from the satellite.

The satellite was geostationary. That is, it was in an orbit above the equator and circled the Earth once every twenty-four hours. This meant that it should appear stationary directly over one fixed spot at zero degrees latitude. Consequently, the plane could be anywhere on an arc, travelling either north or south. Initially assuming it had travelled, Malaysian prime minister Najib Razak had appealed to the president of Kazakhstan, Nursultan Nazarbayev, formerly first secretary of the Communist Party of Kazakhstan and an ally of Vladimir Putin, to allow Malaysia to set up a search in Kazakhstan. But further analysis indicated that the plane had travelled south.

Inmarsat had only started recording BTO data after the loss of Air France Flight AF447 over the Atlantic in 2009, believing that these figures may be useful if a plane disappeared over the ocean again. However, its use in identifying where a plane happened to be located, was widely known.

The second set of data was called "burst frequency offset", or BFO. This utilizes the change in frequency or a signal, depending on the relative velocity of the sender and the receiver – just as the pitch of a siren changes as a fire-engine speeds past. The change in pitch is called the "Doppler shift".

From the BFO, it was reasoned that you could tell how fast the plane was travelling relative to the supposedly stationary satellite. However, since the satellite was old and running out of the fuel it needed to keep it precisely on post. It wobbled, adding an extra component of relative velocity to the calculations that the mathematicians had to somehow disentangle.

The experts at the Independent Group had trouble fitting the BTO and BFO data together. To make them match up, the plane would have had to have flown south, slowly along a curved path. This made no sense. An autopilot would naturally have flown the plane in a straight line at a higher speed, because this saved fuel. Jeff Wise again began to consider the possibility that the plane may have flown north.

He then discovered that it was theoretically possible to generate bogus BFO data. As the airwaves are full of radio transmissions – from aeroplanes, ground stations, TV channels, radio stations, walkie-talkies, satellite links, mobile phones and myriad other pieces of electronic equipment – communication between the plane and the satellite had to be restricted to an incredibly narrow band. Consequently, in the satcom system on the plane, circuits worked out what the Doppler shift would be, and compensated for it.

This equipment was in the "electronics-and-equipment" – or E/E – bay. In a Boeing 777, the E/E bay could be accessed through a hatch in the front of the first-class cabin. If a hijacker got in there, they could take over all the systems on the aeroplane, including the flight controls. But to do such a thing would have taken a remarkably sophisticated hijacker – probably someone who was state-sponsored.

Then Wise remembered that the satcom equipment had been turned off when the plane first left its initial flight path. It was then rebooted three minutes after it had disappeared from the military radar over the Straits of Malacca. The only way to do this was to get into the E/E bay, after which you had pull three specific circuit breakers. Even the pilots on board a 777 were not trained to do this.

You could not do this on every plane. It had to be a 777 – in the Airbus and even older Boeings, the E/E bay was not accessible. Former 777 pilot Matt Wuillemin had written a master's thesis on the vulnerability of the plane's E/E bay in 2013, and circulated it in the hope that a lock might be installed. He also noted that the system controlling the locks on the flight-deck door were also in the E/E bay, along with the cylinders that provided oxygen in the event of the cabin becoming depressurized.

The satcom unit had to be one of those made by Honeywell if false data was to be fed into it. The Airbus used a unit made by Raytheon. For the false data to have been convincing, it would have had to have been fed to an old satellite that was running low on fuel, where the mathematics would have been further complicated by the wobble. Any misdirection would have to start from a point close to the equator, where the Doppler shift was at a minimum, and point towards the middle of a vast ocean where it would difficult, if not impossible, to find the missing aircraft – so if there was no trace there would be no suspicion.

Once Wise had decided to ignore the BFO data, it became clear to him that the plane had gone north. Just as the aircraft had followed the border between Malaysia and Thailand when it crossed the Malay Peninsula, its path northwards would have fallen along other national borders and it would have been running low on fuel when it reached Kazakhstan. There are few places in central Asia with a runway long enough to land a 777. However, the last handshake – if the plane was travelling north – put it at Baikonur Cosmodrome. Leased by Russia, it had a runway nearly 15,000 feet long, built to land the Buran space plane, the Soviet Union's version of the Space Shuttle.

Not only was it long enough to land a 777, it was also the only airstrip in the world built specifically for self-landing planes. The 777 has an autolanding system. This meant that anyone who did not have any commercial flying experience – including a hijacker – could land the plane safely.

Even at Baikonur, it would have been difficult to hide a 777. The region was flat and treeless. Wise worked out that, if MH370 had landed there, the hijackers would have had just ninety minutes to conceal it before the sun came up. Then he studied satellite images of the area and noticed a huge building that had been left to rot after the Soviet space plane project had been abandoned. Six months before MH370 went missing, work began to demolish it. This continued throughout the winter, even though the temperature dropped to -26°C (-15°F). A large rectangle, coincidentally the size of a 777, was bulldozed. It had a trench along one end. Days after MH370 had gone missing, the area was covered over with rubble from the demolished building.

If the disappearance of MH370 had been a hijacking, Wise thought that he had better find some hijackers. Checking the passenger list, he found two Ukrainians and a Russian were on board. Little was about the Ukrainians, Oleh Chustrak and Serhei

Deinka, except that they were from Odessa, the former Soviet naval base, and were ethnic Russians. They were also the only two employees of an online furniture company that, curiously, only took cash. The Russian, Nikolai Brodsky, had a similarly murky background, but he was a man of action. Brodsky's hobby was scuba-diving – he was the kind of character who would fearlessly dive under the ice at Lake Baikal in mid-winter. He was sitting up front in business class, while the two Ukrainians were sitting further back in economy.

In Wise's ebook *The Plane That Wasn't There: Why We Haven't Found Malaysia Airlines Flight 370*, he proposes a "speculative scenario". Wise suggests that Brodsky came onto the plane carrying a bag of scuba gear, amongst which were three full-face masks.

According to the envisaged scenario, once the plane had taken off and climbed to cruising altitude, Brodsky waited until the flight attendants began making their way back down the cabin to take orders. Then he pulled back the carpet, opened the hatch, slipped into the E/E bay and closed the hatch behind him. Once inside, he turned off all communication from the plane, detached the aerial from the satcom system, plugged in the portable equipment he had brought with him and started uploading the false BFO data.

On the flight deck, the pilot was already feeling sleepy as the plane started to bank. Grabbing the yoke, he tried to keep the plane flying straight, but it did not respond and the aircraft began its turn to the left. The pilot and co-pilot then ran through their checklist to try to find out what had gone wrong. Nothing was working, not even the emergency frequencies that would allow them to send out a distress message. They may have figured out that something had gone wrong in the E/E bay, but by then the cockpit door was open and their way was blocked by two burly men wearing oxygen masks. Soon afterwards, the pilot and co-pilot, the rest of the crew and the passengers were unconscious.

With a new flight plan fed into the autopilot, the plane flew across the Malay Peninsular, but as there had never been a hostile incident on the Malaysian-Thai border, no one was watching out for any blip that might appear on the radar screen.

As soon as they were out of radar range, Brodsky reconnected the satcom unit ready to broadcast false data next time a handshake was made. Weeks later, when the mathematicians at Inmarsat studied the BFO data they collected, they would congratulate themselves on deducing that the plane was flying south – although, in fact, it was flying north.

When the plane reached Baikonur, the satcom gave one final stuttering half handshake, making it appear that the plane had crashed into the sea, while the 777 made a fully automatic landing on the purpose-built runway there. It was then disposed of according to the plan prepared for the purpose.

But like every theory concerning MH370, his hypothesis has one fatal flaw. Jeff Wise can offer no motive for the hijacking of the plane and the murders of 239 people. However, it could be reasoned that they were not murdered. After the hijackers were in complete control of the plane, the cabin was repressurized and the passengers were revived. Among them were twenty employees of Freescale Semiconductors, some of them electronic experts – even, it was said, experts on the latest stealth weaponry "cloaking" systems.

Back in the Soviet era, it was not unknown for Moscow to purloin Western electronic experts. During the Vietnam war, the F-111 was the very latest tactic attack aircraft. While the front-seat pilot was just a jet-jockey who flew the plane, the back-seater was a highly trained electronics officer. When an F-111 was shot down, the front-seat pilot was kept in a prison camp in Southeast Asia and, if they were lucky, returned home. The back-seaters were taken to Russia, where their brains were picked, according to a source in the NSA. Analysis of the details of returned prisoners of war shows that they never came back.

In World War II, British airmen who knew about radar, and were shot down and ended up in German prisoners-of-war camps, were later "liberated" by the Red Army, and ended up in Soviet factories developing radar equipment. With regard to this kind of activity, Russia has form.

In my investigations of the fate of American prisoners of war in the Vietnam war for the book *The Bamboo Cage* and British prisoners of war in World War II for *The Iron Cage*, I found that, due to Cold-War politics, the fates of the missing men were consigned to secret files that were only to be opened years after the event, if ever. Since the annexation of Crimea, relations between Russia and the West have grown cold again and it is not beyond the bounds of possibility that some more electronic experts have been consigned to the same dusty archives, although this time the dust is electronic and may prove even harder to brush off.